D1808324

BUILD YOUR SAILING CRUISER

BUILD YOUR SAILING CRUISER

George Taylor

WESTERN ISLES
LIBRARIES

6. 5942

623. 822

Nautical

Copyright © George Taylor 1980

First published in Great Britain 1980 by
NAUTICAL PUBLISHING CO. LTD.
Nautical House, Lymington, Hampshire SO4 9BA

in association with
George G. Harrap and Co. Ltd., London

ISBN 0 245 53527 6

Filmset and printed by
BAS Printers Limited, Over Wallop, Hampshire

Contents

Line drawings by **Richard Everitt**

Photographs of fitting out by **A. R. E. Taylor**

Photographs of boats kindly supplied by the
respective builders.

I

Introduction

Fitting out from scratch can be a richly rewarding experience both in terms of personal satisfaction and achievement, and also financial terms. Depending upon the amount of work that you are prepared to undertake then the cost of the mouldings will average about 40–50 per cent of the total cost of the finished boat—taking hulls from 24 to 28 feet overall (7.3 to 8.5 m). Much above 30 feet (9 m) the cost of other items of gear and equipment, especially above decks, starts to escalate and the percentage devoted to hull and superstructure mouldings decreases. Nevertheless, by adopting a pragmatic approach costs can be minimized; for example there is no need to use expensive mast winches—rope and block tackles served well for years. Wooden booms and spinnaker poles cost less than aluminium extrusions—and if you use good old galvanized mild-steel in place of stainless steel confections, then you could even fabricate them yourself with the minimum equipment. Read on and I'll tell you how.

Much depends on how much money you have, what size boat you would like, how skilled you are, and when you want to get her afloat. A kit boat, whatever size, offers savings. True, you will not be saving much, certainly under 20 per cent of the finished boat price. You will however, get afloat fairly quickly and the actual skills you need for such an undertaking are not excessive. A certain amount of methodical work is called for and throughout this book you will find guidance on what you need to know.

If, like me, you start from a bare hull and superstructure, then provided certain design parameters are followed, the interior layout you decide on can be a very personal thing. The boat may be offered as a kit with seven berths—you may think that excessive and opt for five, or fewer. With a kit, or part completed boat, you will be faced with a fixed layout with little room for personal preferences. We chose to use mahogany tongue-and groove matching around the saloon. Softly gleaming under the gentle light shed by brass lamps, her interior contrasts greatly with the harsh 'plastic' approach used by her builder. In fairness, he could not afford to devote the man-hours to her interior to achieve the same looks.

If you possess the time, inclination and basic expertise, then starting well back in the fitting-out game may let you get the boat you really want—but cannot afford. Alternatively the same approach may enable you to end up owning a much larger boat for the same cash outlay. In real terms there is not much difference in the costings for a kit 24 footer (7.3 m) and a bare 28 foot sailboat. The difference in boat is considerable. If you can stretch things to a 32 footer (9.7 m) then your range is extended. But, be warned, the amount of work involved in a boat of this size is bordering on the limits for single-handed fitting out. (Examples of suitable craft will be found among the text).

If in doubt my advice would be think BIG. There is no escaping the fact that boats shrink when you add water. Add a couple of small children and a blustering day, and boats can assume near microscopic proportions.

Bigger boats offer more scope for interiors, and below-decks costs do not escalate as rapidly as you may imagine. For example the cooker with oven for a 20 footer (6.1 m) will cost the same as one for a 32 footer. The WC and engine for my 28 footer (8.5 m), her washbasins, galley pump, bilge pumps, batteries, and so forth would also suit a larger boat. Unfortunately, the same cannot be said to apply to gear above-decks; the cost of spars, sails, rigging, toggles, bottle-screws for a 32 foot boat could cost out at nearly twice that of a 28 footer. Still, there are savings to be made and a lot of fun to be had. Some might even say that embarking on a project of this size could tend to draw a family together. Cynics might say the reverse!

When your small child starts treating you as a stranger perhaps its a warning that you have been spending too much time on your boat.

One aspect of doing your own thing that I should warn you about early on is that, in my experience,

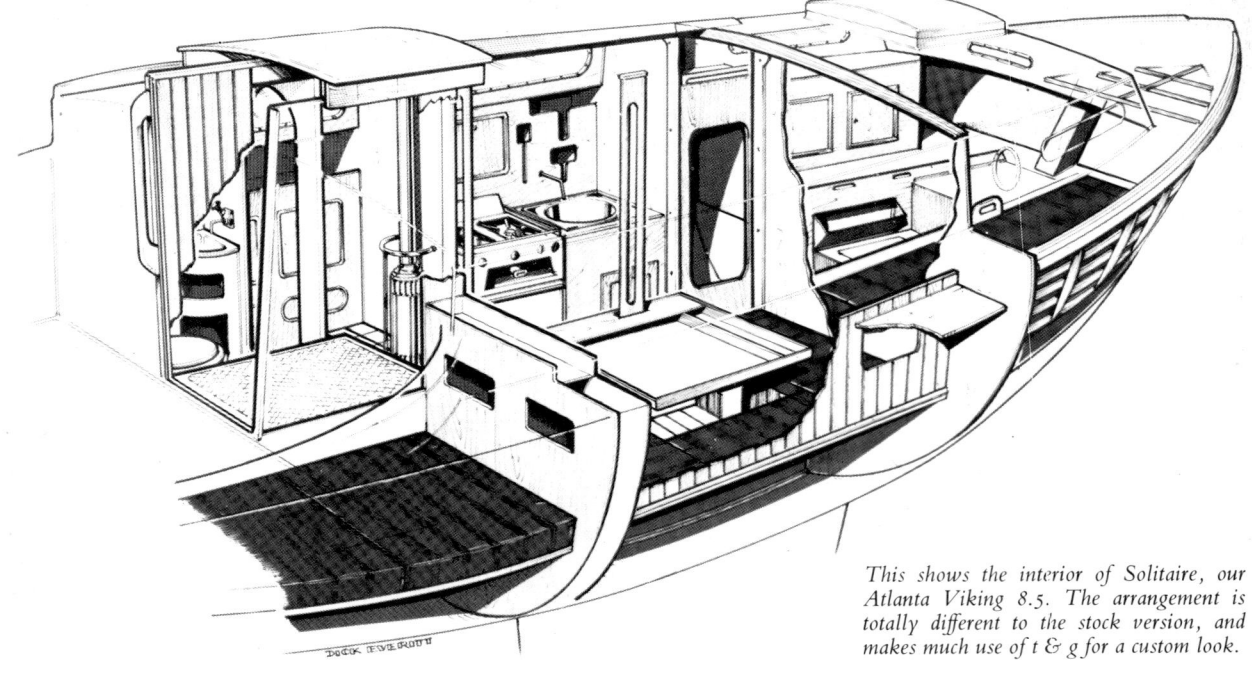

This shows the interior of Solitaire, our Atlanta Viking 8.5. The arrangement is totally different to the stock version, and makes much use of t & g for a custom look.

picking a boat is akin to choosing a wife. In other words, what might suit you may not coincide with the desires of another soul. An extreme interior, rig, or some eccentric engine conversion, may considerably diminish the resale value of the boat. Conversely, a smart well-executed interior mated to a seamanlike approach to her rig will appeal to the discerning buyer.

Fitting out a set of mouldings calls for few basic skills other than an aptitude to work with a number of different materials. If you are the average sort of 'man-about-the-house'; painter, occasional plumber and electrician, sometime plasterer and paper-hanger, then fitting out an empty hull should cause you no real problems. If you complete a kit-boat then even fewer skills are involved.

Whatever you are fitting out the actual work may tax you physically on occasions, and run your resources thin—particularly towards the end of the month. On the other hand your wife will know where to find you—'*he's out in the boat*' is a common-enough greeting to visitors.

One of the hardest aspects to come to grips with is logistics—getting the necessary materials and fittings in the right order—when they are needed! You are undertaking probably the largest single job of your life investing both money and time. It is important that the outcome is successful. At the same time there is an undoubted urge, which you should recognize, to get on

with the job and get her afloat as soon as possible. This means that to make best use of your time without cheating on your work, and ending up with a 'mess', each stage of completion must be carefully planned; chase those materials and fittings long before you actually need them to hand.

If you are in full-time employment—and you'll need to be with today's prices—then perhaps your partner might like to take on the responsibility of secretary, trouble-shooter and storeman. That is in addition to being head-cook and bottle-washer! Be warned, it is a thankless task and her only reward will be that the boat is finished that much faster and her garden can return to normality sooner. In other words she can start cutting the grass again.

Although several chapters of this book are devoted to my experiences with a boat measuring 28 feet length overall (8.5 m) they apply equally well to smaller and larger boats. As previously mentioned the cost of fitting out a kit 24 footer equates very well with starting from scratch with one measuring 28 feet along the deck. If you can scrape together just enough capital to embark on a 'finished' 28 footer then one of 30 or 32 foot might become feasible if you can tackle more of the work yourself.

Similarly, much of those same chapters apply to smaller boats. If you are going to fit out a kit you will be faced with the problems of bonding in furniture and installing below-decks equipment. Safety considerations apply across the board and so does painting.

One of the biggest mind-leaps that the newcomer to fitting-out from scratch must make is to appreciate the order in which things are done. For instance, after levelling the site and actually plumbing the boat up true, the first jobs are those of putting on the deck hardware. You might have assumed that sort of thing could be left until last. But all those cleats, stanchion-bases, pulpits, pushpits and the like will need wooden pads under them to reinforce the deck structure and spread the loads. It will be too late to start thinking about fitting pads when you have already glassed in the deckhead liner, or worse still if you find that the bulkhead by the heads compartment neatly bisects the fasteners for a stanchion socket.

The same forward-thinking extends right through the boat, and you must never bond or fasten anything in that may interfere with some subsequent operation. At the same time you should also be aware of the fact that one day you may need to get at those 'hidden' fastenings to re-bed, say, a deck fitting and so stop an annoying leak.

Careful planning can cut down on the time spent undoing perfectly good work. Careful planning also means that you should have at least three different jobs on the go at any one time.

Should you be held up on one then you do not waste time drinking coffee and moaning about it—you simply get on with something else.

This discipline, apart from being good for the soul, also means that you should be able to plan your work schedule to take into account prevailing weather conditions. By that I mean that it is no good trying to lay up resin and glass reinforcements late on a winter's afternoon with the air temperature around zero. Far better to save the electricity bill and work instead on fabricating a pulpit, stanchions, or else carve a few stout cleats and grabrails in teak. Swopping from job to job like this makes the best of your available time, leaving the long weekends free for those parts of the project which demand your continuous attention. It also stops you getting bored!

Then there is the '*hoarding instinct*', or '*the new boat box*'. This is an easily acquired state-of-mind if you are remotely interested in boats. And if you are not, why are you reading this?

It boils down to scouring your local boat-yards, chandlers, boat-and-gear auctions, jumble-sales, demolition sites and even the local tip, looking for bits and pieces which might be useful. If you start collecting soon enough you won't be panicked into buying in haste—synonymous to buying expensively.

For instance, demolition timber is often burnt on site. A word with the foreman, and a quick arrangement,

will provide all the joist and floorboards you will need to build a support cradle for a fin-keel hull—and the boarding ladder too if you decide to make one. Shop-fitters fall into a similar category—and if you find them refurbishing a local bank you've struck pay-dirt. Those lovely mahogany counters which banks install at their customer's expense, will provide all the hardwood needed to complete your interior. This scrounging is strictly 'first-come' and if you have to go home for your car and fit a roof rack the golden opportunity may pass.

Cultivate your friends. That sounds terribly mercenary, but you will be surprised how many of them—and even slight acquaintances too—will produce unexpected gifts. Headboards of old beds yield good hardwood planks for instance. Alternatively a friend may provide transport or even skilled labour. Why they do it is occasionally a mystery; perhaps they are urged on by some inner-desire to emulate you. Perhaps they secretly hope that you will take pity on them and invite them on a long cruise. If they are close neighbours then suspect that they simply want your boat out of the way—its damning property prices!

A few months of single-minded scrounging can reduce costs considerably, and so may seeking the assistance of friends and colleagues when it comes to fitting boat equipment. Everyone should be able to plumb-in a marine toilet—but could you design and fit an adequate electrical system throughout the boat, or refurbish a second-hand diesel engine? Chances are that you *know* someone who could.

At the risk of seemingly putting more carts before the proverbial—have you found out where you are going to keep your boat? Yards, moorings and marinas get ever more crowded and actual boating resources seem to be drying up in some areas. The offer of a drying mooring eminently suited to a twin keel and skeg boat may sway you away from that fin-and-spade model on your short list. True the sailing performance won't be the same—but then neither will the drain on your pocket since 'mud-moorings' will always be considerably cheaper than deepwater and marina-type berths.

Boating costs in general rise annually—just like everything else. But some component costs rise faster than the norm and an eye on the market will indicate which items may be advantageously purchased right now, and what may be left until next year. Take hulls and superstructures for example. The resins from which they are moulded are derived from the petro-chemical industry—which itself is subjected to periodic turns of the screw by OPEC oil price increases. The main ingredient of glass is, as I am sure you know—silica. There are millions of tons of sand around, but it is the other parts of the manufacturing process with their huge power demands that push up the price of glass fibre

COLVIC UFO 27
The UFO 27 is the smallest of three similar Colvic boats from the design-board of Holman & Pye; the other UFO's are 31, and 34 feet overall. Suited to club and IOR events the UFO 27 rates around 19.1 feet and is a lively performer. Any stage from bare mouldings available. Moulders are Colvic Craft Ltd, Wheaton Road Industrial Estate East, Witham, Essex.

Overall length   27 feet
Waterline length   24 feet
Beam   10 feet
Draft   5 feet
Displacement   7,500 lb
Ballast   2,240 lb
Sail area   375 square feet.

materials. Aluminium too is a high-energy material, and so are stainless steel rigging wire, diesel engines, mechanical fasteners, and the like.

All this means that you need to have an awareness of what is happening. A small percentage increase in the price of a major component will blow a hole through a careful budget.

Enough of these fiscal meanderings. Buy what you can when you can even though it may not be the order in which you will fit them.

There are numerous factors which may influence your final choice of boat, and the range from which you may choose is enormous—something like 400 boats are available in the UK alone from 15–40 feet; and those are just the sailing cruisers! Almost every builder will sell you a set of mouldings and most will be prepared (if not delighted) to do some of the fitting-out for you. For anything but the smallest boat I would recommend that

you get the hull and superstructure supplied ready joined. This is a tricky business and calls both for lots of hands who know what they are about, and also special equipment—like an overhead gantry for example. I am not saying that it is impossible to achieve a proper job— it's just very difficult.

This hull and deck join is a very important one for several reasons. Firstly, the mouldings are still 'green' in the sense that they are freshly made and not yet fully cured. This means that should you stand them around with a twist in them that twist may become permanent. Also the hull moulding by itself is rather floppy, but bond on the deck and it assumes a box-like rigidity which is helpful in resisting distortion. Mostly the join between the two major components is made by mechanical fasteners and then by bonding with reinforcing layers of resin and glass (Fig. 1). If the rubbing strake is then fitted with more through-bolts a very strong

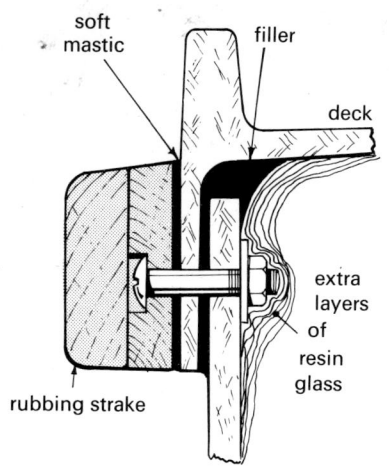

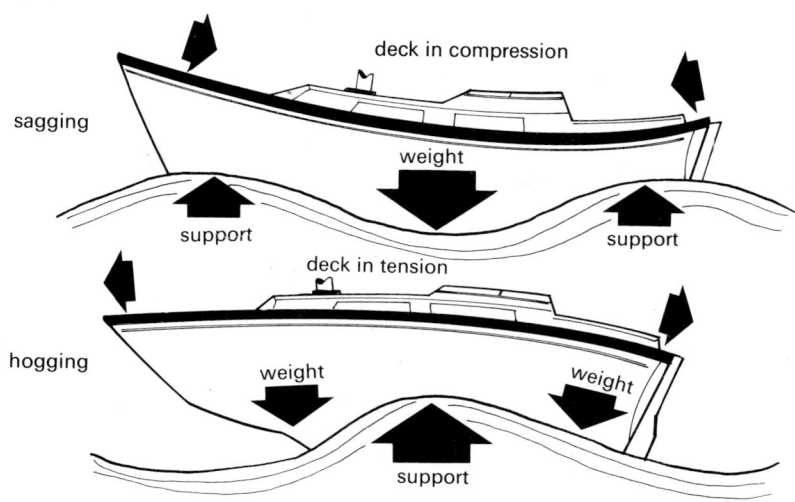

FIG. 1. The hull/deck join must be properly made if subsequent troubles are to be avoided. Several methods may be employed—this typical one, uses a combination of mechanical and chemical (resin) fastening. Note that special adhesives may also be used.

FIG. 2. When a boat passes through the water she is continuously subjected to sagging and hogging (FIG. 3.). At the same time 'wracking', or twisting, loads are imposed.

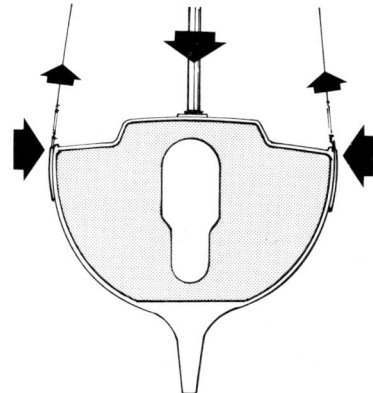

FIG. 4. At rest the loads in a boat's rigging and mast are minimal. Under sail in a strong breeze they quickly escalate and must be shared into her structure with no risk of mechanical failure.

arrangement is made. This is important when you come to using the boat, for to have spouts of water bursting in when she is heeling to a good sailing breeze is very distressing—and damp.

A good bond is also essential for structural reasons. When the boat is sailing she is sometimes only supported at either end by a pair of waves—thus the hull tends to want to sag in the middle (Fig 2). Conversely, when she is supported at the centre by water, her bow and stern sections may be clear of the water and be in a condition known as 'hogging' (Fig 3). All this means that the beam-like reinforcements made when joining hull and deck are alternately in tension and compression. The designer of course knows this and arranges the structure accordingly. But if you make a bad job of the join his skills go for nothing. Other loads such as those exerted by the mast and standing rigging also call for a strong hull/deck join.

If you have any doubts about your ability then it may be wise to have the moulders fit the main structural bulkheads too. These are important to the integrity of the boat as a whole, since the designer positioned them to absorb the high localized loads imposed by the mast and rigging (Fig 4). That apart, most hulls are wide open for you to do your own thing so far as the interior accommodation goes.

When I fitted out my own boat four years ago I had the builders fit partial bulkheads under the mast. They also installed the main companionway sliding hatch and washboards, the rudder, chainplates and rubbing strake. I then completed her interior virtually single-handed (though absolutely backed to the hilt by my wife) which is why I christened her *Solitaire*. The reasons for this yard work were thus: as stated the main bulkheads are structurally important and they are easy to fit if cut to templates and put in before the hull and deck were

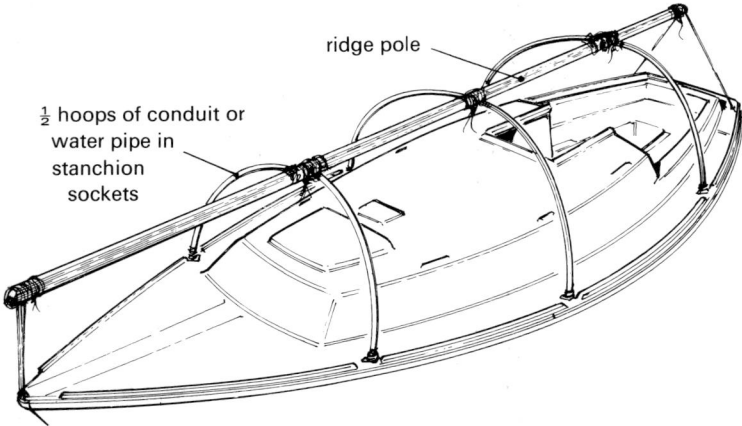

FIG. 5. *Deck fittings go on first, and may be used to help erect a shelter to protect the hull from winter rain and frosts.*

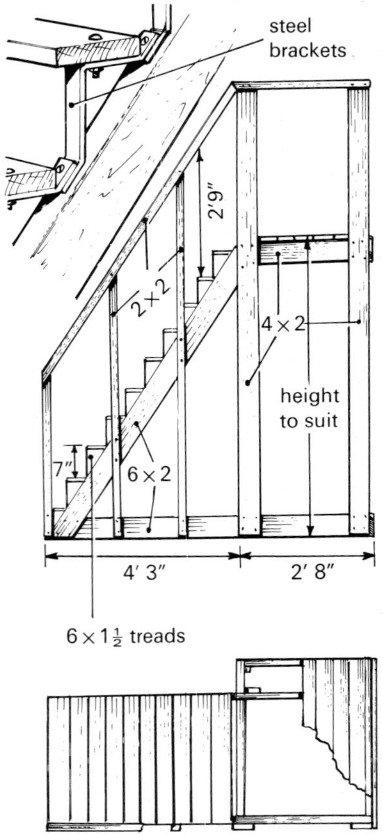

FIG. 6. *A ladder like this may seem a luxury, but the initial effort and expense will be repayed many times over. Note that the steel brackets overlap each other and share common screws.*

bonded together. Fitting the rubbing strake calls for two men working in unison and I was largely on my own. The fitted companionway allowed me to lock her up for the night and leave valuable tools and gear on board without fear of pilfering—once I had fitted the forehatch and cockpit locker lids—that is.

Solitaire is an Atlanta Viking 8.5 sailboat with a self-draining cockpit. Thus among the first jobs was to fit the cockpit drains and seacocks to prevent her cockpit resembling a bath tub. I had arranged her delivery for early spring and that gave me progressively longer—and hopefully warmer—days. This meant that I could get her interior fitted out in good weather leaving the coming winter months for welding pushpit and pulpit, stanchions etc, overhaul her engine, make a mast and booms etc, etc, etc . . .

As I have already written, a good deal of forward planning is required, and although I was making and fitting her stanchions after the interior was almost completed, I had already bonded their reinforcements under the moulded areas on deck. If the boat had been delivered in the autumn the first job would have been to

erect some form of shelter over her. By this I do not necessarily mean a proper 'house'; a quick and easy way is to fit the stanchion sockets and use them to contain the ends of half-hoops of a suitable metal pipe—electrical conduit for example. The hoops are then lashed together with a ridge-pole and covered with a near-transparent reinforced plastic sheet (Fig. 5). It may seem extravagant advice but unless you are exceptionally fortunate with your weather some form of cover is essential.

So too is a proper ladder. I made do with steps and was amazed to find that on the occasion I troubled to keep a score-sheet for trips up and down the ladder, I marked up nearly sixty in a long ten-hour day. All that climbing worked wonders for my figure—it was also very tiring. All that stepping into and out of the cockpit could have damaged the gelcoat if it had not been carefully protected. I used old lino, but old carpet or even sacking would help, for if you are not careful from the very start you will end up with a gleaming boat looking new all over—except for her decidedly second-hand cockpit. (see Fig. 6 for detailed plans to make a proper boarding ladder).

The building site

Ideally this should be as close to your home as possible. I moved house both to finance the building operation and also find the available room to do it. Not all wives are as accommodating as this. If you can get the boat in your garden then it will enable you to maximize your available time. It is no fun driving an hour to work for an hour, and then to drive home again. If your garden is too small, or your neighbours object (some local councils are not too happy either), then perhaps you may be able to rent' the corner of a field and fence it off *pro tem*. Anywhere within a 10 minute drive is ideal: the very worst is a cramped corner of a boatyard miles away.

The actual site itself need not be much larger than the boat herself—you need only a few feet of clearance all around her. I was fortunate in that my garden was half lawn, half gravel. This was superb hard-standing and in that respect I was singularly fortunate. Access to the site is important since the boat will be delivered on a trailer and you will have to get her off. Craneage is possible and need not be expensive for one lift—unless you want her lifted over the roof into a back garden. Check on insurance and get everything in writing so that you know who is responsible for her from the moment she leaves the factory to the time she sits on your site.

It is important that the hull is placed on strong wooden blocks—something like half railway sleepers is ideal. This will ease jacking-up problems when launch time comes around. The site needs to be fairly level even though you can level her up slightly on the blocks.

Naturally it is easier to level up a twin-keel and skeg craft rather than fin-keel and it helps enormously if the moulder has her waterline scribed into his moulds. If not then the waterline will be specified as being so many inches or millimetres down the stem and another dimension at the stern. Another reference at a fixed point such as the chainplates also helps setting up.

I am sure you remember that schoolboy experiment which confirmed that water in a U-tube with open ends settles exactly level. That same phenomenon may be used to check your hull against its waterline marks. Use a length of plastic hose—garden hose will need clear plastic pipes spliced on at either end to enable you to see the water levels (Fig. 7). Stakes at either end of the hull can hold the pipe vertically while you measure from these datum points to the scribed waterlines, and adjust as needed by jacks and packing pieces.

A spirit-level arranged on a trued plank which is then blocked-up equally on either side of the cabin top will set the hull up the other way (Fig. 8). Check it in two or three places and average out any errors if found. Remember that the plug from which she was made was not perfect. An alternative to the spirit level method is to use a plumb-bob dropped from the measured centreline at the deckhead to above the centreline of the hull (Fig. 8). This not so easy to apply as it seems as much shouting of orders and angles is called for since measuring is taking place inside the hull. It is worthwhile buying a good bricklayers level for it then lets you use it on the interior furniture to make certain it is fitted correctly. Just imagine sleeping with your feet higher than your brains

RIVAL 34.
Designed by Peter Brett the Rival 34 is available in part complete form and as standard has seven berths. With a longish fin keel, clean lines and uncluttered decks she is much-favoured by blue-water sailormen and has some notable passages under her keel. Her builders are Rival Yachts, Willments Ship-yard, Hazel Road, Woolston, Southampton, Hants.

Length overall   34 feet
Length waterline   24.8 feet
Beam   9.7 feet
Draft   5.8 feet, or 4.7 feet.
Displacement   10,900 lb.
Ballast   4,480 lb.
Sail area   386 square feet.

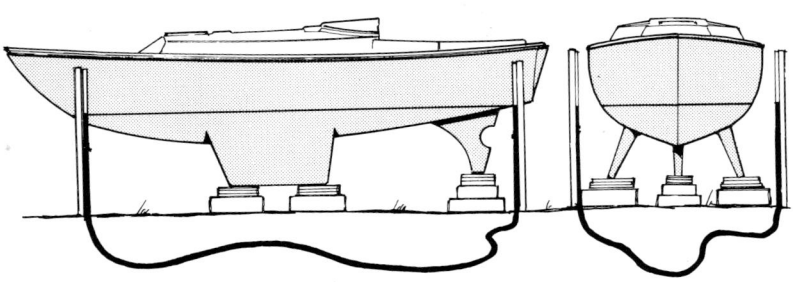

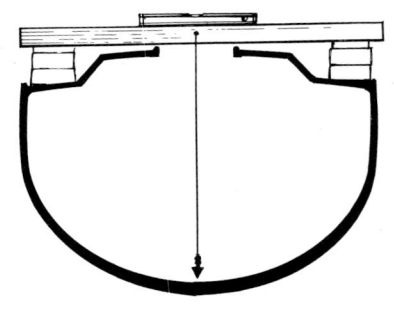

FIG. 7. *Water in an open-ended tube settles to a constant level. This may be used to set up the hull accurately to her waterlines.*

FIG. 8. *A spirit-level and plumb-bob may be used to check that the hull is level on her blocks. Periodic checks during fitting-out are recommended since she may settle.*

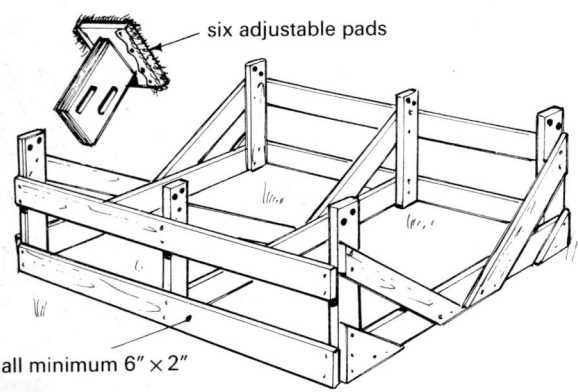

six adjustable pads

all minimum 6″ × 2″

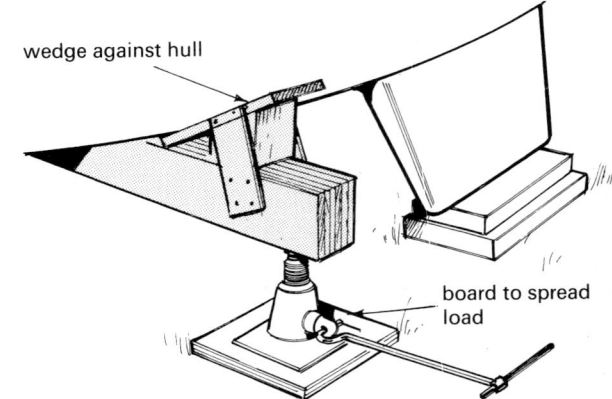

wedge against hull

board to spread load

FIG. 9. *Cradles may be made from 'demolition' timber. They need to be substantial for the boat may weigh several tons, and were she to fall over considerable damage could ensue.*

FIG. 10. *A cross-beam with chocks and pads, used in conjunction with a pair of jacks may be used to raise the hull clear of her trailer.*

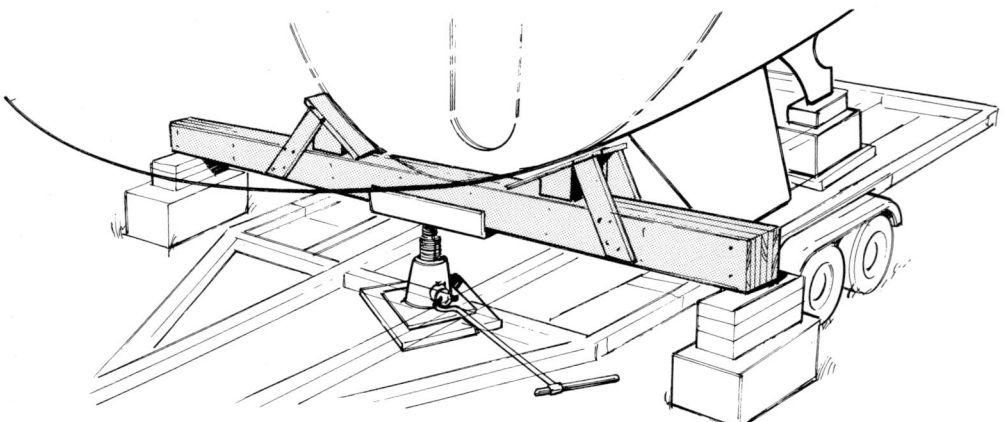

FIG. 11. *A single jack could be used, as here, to lift the hull. Note that the beam should coincide with internal bulkheads, or webs, to avoid straining the hull.*

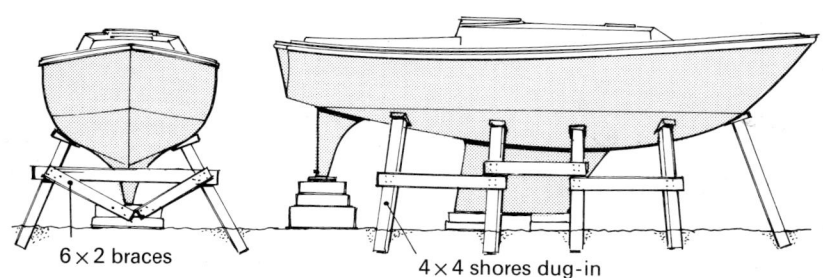

6 × 2 braces   4 × 4 shores dug-in

FIG. 12. Fin keel boats need a proper cradle—if you opt for shores make certain that they are cross-braced for security and also well dug-in. You could be onboard when she falls. . . .

PHOTO. 1. If you can hire a crane to lift the hull off its trailer then so much the better. We had to raise Solitaire up to enable the trailer to be withdrawn—and then had to lower her down on to blocks. Note the beam.

and with a list to starboard too! Having set her up plumb athwartships it will be as well to go back and check her against her waterlines again.

If you distrust both the spirit-level and the plumb-bob then the U-waterhose could be used to measure to waterlines on either side of the hull.

All this is obviously much easier with a boat that sits on the ground in three places. Fin-keel boats need a cradle and Figure 9 shows a suitable arrangement for a 29 foot motorsailer. The material used is timber— 6 × 1 inch softwood throughout—and it is doubled where the keels sits on the crossbeams.

All the parts of the frame are bolted together using half-inch coachbolts and washers and the angle braces must be positioned as high up the uprights as possible without fouling on the hull and interfering with the adjustable pads. The corner gussets need to be one-inch plywood sided 18 × 18 inches. If in doubt check with your hull supplier.

Whatever keel form the boat has you will need to get aboard her safely. Figure 6 shows access steps which you could build in preference to using normal domestic-type steps. Having used the latter I vowed to build a proper ladder next time if not for safety, then for the platform at the top which enables you to clean your shoes (or even change them) before stepping into the cockpit.

When moving your boat about with jacks you must obviously take care where you position them. The trouble is she *looks* so solid. Under the keel(s) is safe enough but even there you should use a wooden pad to prevent the jack crushing the gelcoat and possibly the rest of the laminate. If you have to jack against the hull then 'don't' is my considered opinion—the jack will damage the moulding.

I made up a beam using four pieces of 9 × 1½ inch (225 × 37 mm) softwood strongly bolted together (Figs 10 & 11). A pair of long upholstered wedges were then fitted to give a three-point touch to the hull while jacks were used at either end of the beam. The positions of the wedges coincided with that of the internally bonded bulkheads so risk of damage was minimised (Photo 1). If you can borrow toe-jacks which may be

used to lift under the keel(s) then so much the better. If not you will have to improvise. Note that mechanical jacks are best for this type of work—hydraulic units tend to be less precise when it comes to lowering. A feature that is not funny when the hull weighs two tons or more!

If you are tempted to bypass building a proper cradle—remembering all the time that you will be working in, on and around the hull then a keel-boat should have her shores cross-braced to prevent them falling away with possibly lethal results (Fig. 12). Use lots of large nails and do not forget to nail the wedges too.

One last word on the site; practise tidyness. While it may be convenient to leave rubbish around, and even under the hull, be alert to the possible fire risks involved. If you are a long way from any water you may even consider it worthwhile to have an old water tank—or an old 50 gallon oil drum full. Who knows. . . .

Planning her interior

Provided that you have the bulkhead(s) under the mast and that they are well-framed up to accept the rigging and mast loads, the rest of the interior arrangements are up to you. It helps if you can be realistic about what to use the boat for. We opted for a strictly 'weekend cottage' interior which is fine for day-sailing and the occasional overnight passage with a small crew. If you intend crossing oceans then you will need to plan her interior accordingly and your main aim should perhaps be comfort when heeled.

The main trouble with all boats is that they do not possess squared-up walls and floors like a house or caravan. Instead they curve around you in two, if not three dimensions, and generally lack space just where you need it. Thus plans drawn at deck-level seldom fit anything but deck-gear, for the hull curves increasingly inwards to the keel. This means that if you plan your sleeping arrangements at deck level with its maximum beam and length you will find that those 6 ft 6 in. (2 m) berths shrink dramatically when it comes to installing them just about level with the waterline.

If you are a draughtsman with an aptitude for visualizing volumes off lines drawings then you are fortunate—much as I was with my building site. True, it is an art which can be mastered from some of the better books on the subject—mostly out of print alas like *Yacht Design* by A. A. Symonds. One problem is that you also have to educate your wife to see things with her inner eye. This I found impossible to do, so I resorted to mocking up the interior using lengths of softwood. The same wood was ultimately to be used in the cabin furniture, so it wasn't wasted. This expedient was time-consuming, but did nevertheless have its good points.

For example we had intended to opt for a caravan type of interior with the heads up under the forehatch. This position has been tried successfully on a number of boats—and it always struck me as being a very practical solution. I obtained a set of lines drawings from Atlanta Marine, her moulders, and embarked upon a long session with pencils, scale rules and curves to design her interior. All to no avail for what was not shown on the drawings was that the moulders had inserted an athwartships beam which would be right in front of the user of our planned WC. Apart from sitting there in a crash-helmet there was nothing left but to rethink *Solitaire's* interior.

Time was pressing, the boat was in the garden and I wanted to get on, so there was no going back to the drawing board in the literal sense. So instead we knocked up 'pretend' galleys, bunks, dinette and WC compartment inside the empty hull. The only fixed reference points were the installed partial bulkheads and the anticipated engine compartment. This empirical design session offered the advantages that an experienced crew could raise valid criticisms to the proposals. Finally, the inevitable compromise was reached and the layout agreed.

Naturally, if you are a strong-minded individual then you will object to dispensing with a full-sized chart-table in preference for a cabin-heater. If you like sailing alone—fine—its your choice.

Modern interior design, boatwise that is, tends to cram as many berths into a given hull volume as possible. This means that it is common enough to find 24 footers with berths for six—although their occupants have nowhere to sit for meals, nor room to stow their gear. Starting from scratch with a realistic appraisal of your needs, rather than your desires, means that you can achieve a comfortable seamanlike layout—IF you temper enthusiasm with judgement.

It helps of course if you have owned a number of boats before embarking upon doing-it-yourself with a set of mouldings, for you will have already formulated your own ideas on what is good—or acceptable. The same will hold true if you have sailed on a range of boats of different sizes and types. Once again you will appreciate the practicalities, or otherwise, of various arrangements. But if you are starting from scratch the best advice I can offer is to steep yourself in the subject; read extensively, try to see over as many boats as possible and try to get in lots of trial-sails as a potential 'customer'. A spring-time charter holiday could help, and visits to boat shows are a must for then you can see over an enormous range of boats with the very minimum of travel. Take a notebook and rule to jot down dimension of schemes you like. A Polaroid camera is a useful tool in these circumstances. You will find that genuine boating salesmen will help, rather than hinder, and if you get rebuffed it will most likely be from a 'salesman' taken on for the duration of the show. Probably he normally sells used cars!

With a boat of around 24 feet (7.3 m) overall the choice of layouts is limited. With the main bulkheads under the mast it leaves just room for a pair of berths up in the bows. A better arrangement might be lockers for sail stowage, plus a pipe-cot which folds up out of the way when not required for sleeping. The area under the mast is generally chosen for the WC compartment. Doors can be arranged to close off the main and fore cabins and so apparently double the available volume of the heads. It may also suit you to install the WC on the port side since this will give you a comfortable seat when hove-to with right of way (in *most* circumstances, that is . . .). Perhaps a minimal advantage, but take it from me that it is impossible to use some WC's when the boat is heeled right over and pounding to windward.

FIG. 13. This is how a basic 'trotter-box' is arranged. Feet go under a useful worktop which could be a chart-table, or if deep enough, could house a sink. A ceiling of wooden slats keeps the sleeper away from an otherwise cold hull laminate—cold because the tops of berths seem to come just about on the waterline.

Note how webs glassed to the hull may also be used to help support the lockers above. If carefully arranged they could carry through the lockers to form dividers—and possibly carry on up to form bookshelf dividers, and even knees to brace the side-decks. All it takes is a little planning!

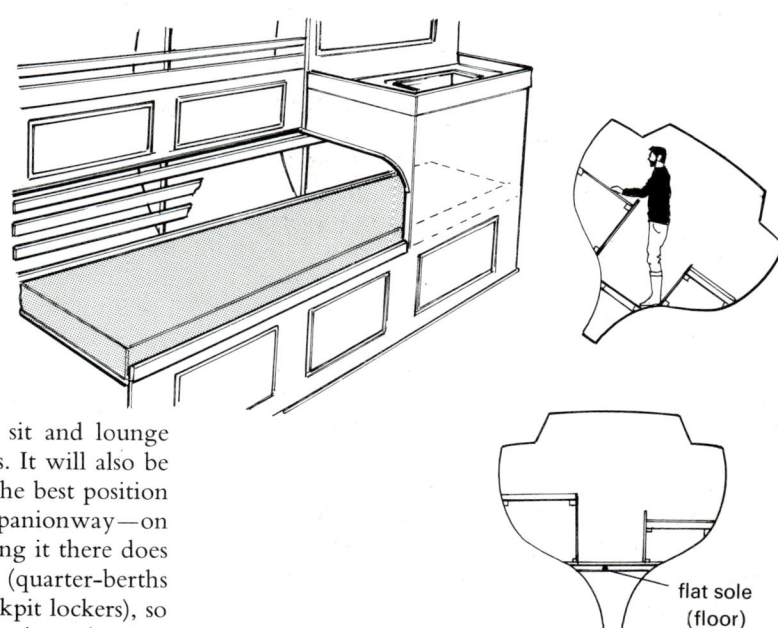

flat sole (floor)

FIG. 14. A wide, flat cabin floor, or sole, is not so advantageous as first thoughts suggest. Apart from increasing headroom, a narrower sole exposes the hull and, when heeled, provides a better floor for moving about on.

The main cabin is where you will sit and lounge during those pleasant summer evenings. It will also be where you cook, wash-up and sleep. The best position for the galley is just inside the door companionway—on the port-side (heaving-to again!). Putting it there does make it difficult to fit a quarter-berth. (quarter-berths have most of their length under the cockpit lockers), so again it's a compromise. If you are planning a 'port & starboard' layout with a pair of settee-bunks on either side of the saloon table then, unless the hull is sufficiently large and beamy to accommodate pilot-berths, the actual sleeping arrangements would number four. This may be increased by working in a double-dinette with a settee opposite. And a settee four feet long can be made to accommodate a six-footer with comfort. How this magic trick is worked will become evident when I say that the box into which his feet disappear also serves as a chart-table top, or work-top for the galley. (See Fig. 13)

One of the snags today with beamy boats is that their designers would appear to have run out of imagination and are simply fitting layouts suitable for an 8 foot (2.44 m) beam into a boat with over 9 feet (2.74 m). That means that the berths are too wide for comfortable sleeping—especially in a seaway, and if those same berths are also daytime settees then they will also be uncomfortable for lounging.

Bunks need to be around 6 feet (1.83 m) long—or perhaps a shade longer—but 6 ft 6 in (2 m) is maximum. Their widths on the otherhand should be between 24 and 28 inches (610 and 710 mm). Maximum height from the cabin sole, or floor, should be 16 inches (400 mm) and this includes the thickness of the mattress which needs to be four inches (100 mm) thick for comfort. It is desirable to have an 'air-height' over the bunk or settees of 36 inches (910 mm) for comfortable sitting, and that means that you cannot work a settee hard up against the side of the hull of an average sort of boat because of her side-decks. That is not to say that the space under the side-decks is wasted for substantial lockers may be worked in here to hold bedding, pillows and the thousand-and-one

things a well-run boat seems to need.

In fact the lockers at the back of the settees often need to be upholstered to provide a padded backrest. Alternatively a rigid lee-board may be required to reduce the sitting width down to between 18–24 inches (610–710 mm). This may be augmented if you stuff your pillows into fabric-covered 'day-bags' to make lounging a pleasure. All this care with seating arrangements may appear strange, but boating seems to be long stretches of sitting in the cockpit interspersed with long periods of sitting, or sleeping down below.

If you are planning to go 'blue-water' cruising then you need to adopt the philosophy of 'thinking heeled'. Most boats seem to travel along comfortably when heeled to an angle of 15 degrees or so. This means that your sleeping and sitting arrangements should acknowledge that fact. Take the cabin sole for example. It is a mistake to put in a flat floor giving you the maximum width of sole possible. Such a floor reduces headroom and moving about on it when you have been at sea for a long period becomes uncomfortable. However, if you allow part of the bilge to also become the sole then, because of its curve towards the keel, you will see that on either tack your feet will be presented with a near-horizontal surface (Fig. 14).

The same search for comfort when heeled extends to settees. If you cram them in too close to the side-decks then whenever you sit in them your head will lean back and find an uncomfortable corner at the cabin side against which to press. Settees need to be positioned well into the boat, and it is a great comfort if their seats are dished. This is easily achieved using slatted construction and such settees make very comfortable bunks with the addition of solid leeboards.

All this means that you will have to be honest with yourself about your plans and ambitions, and how they relate to fitting-out your empty boat. But whatever *style* you chose, *strength* is not a matter of taste. All fittings and structures need to be robust, and well bonded-in. It is wise to build as if one day the boat may be turned upside down and shaken. That is a sobering thought, but your boat as a result will be solidly workmanlike and hopefully devoid of all those boat show gimmicks that salesmen seem to admire so much.

SALTY DOG
With her wedge-type coachroof running down to the foredeck the Salty Dog is typical of many of today's cruisers. She sleeps five and has a 7.5 hp Volvo diesel engine with Sail Drive as standard. An outboard motor could be fitted. Her interior is finished out mostly in timber and she was designed by Peter Milne. Moulders are Colvic Craft Ltd, Wheaton Road Industrial Estate East, Witham, Essex. Bare mouldings and a choice of keels are available.

Length overall   26.6 feet
Length waterline . 23.3 feet
Beam   9.6 feet
Draft   4.5 feet (fin), 3 feet (twin).
Displacement   5,600 lb
Ballast   2,200 lb
Sail Area   289 square feet

2

Some thoughts on ventilation

Ventilation is important in any boat. There is nothing nice about wriggling into fusty sleeping bags—or putting on a damp shirt streaked with mildew.

The natural airflow on a boat is contrary to what you might at first imagine. Instead of flowing in at the bows and out of the companionway, the reverse is the case (Fig. 15). This means that you should make provision to assist this natural flow, for whether she is beating to windward across the Atlantic, or sitting fretting at her mooring, a good flow of air through the boat is desirable. That means that a 24 footer (7.3 m), in addition to her forehatch, would need at least two four-inch (100 mm) Dorade-type ventilators (Fig. 16) up in her fore-cabin, and preferably another pair just aft of the mast to ventilate the main-cabin. Two pairs of Dorades with their trumpet-like cowls may be arranged to give optimum ventilation without too much water entering the boat with the air—a common experience with simple mushroom style vents. There should be some provision for adjusting the airflow and in fact choking them off completely, else in anything over force 4 the amount of air entering will be excessive. You can also incorporate a 'bug' screen—although around England there is not much need for that refinement.

Finger-holes in lockers are cheaper and safer than handles which might snag on clothing. They also let air enter and circulate. If locker shelves are slatted, or kept half an inch (12 mm) away from the side of the hull, that will help to keep them aired too. What about locker shelves and bottoms, should they be angled or flat? The choice is yours when *you* fit out. Flat ones are slightly easier to build and take less material. Angled ones, tipped up at the front by about 20 degrees and fitted with fiddles four inches (100 mm) high (Fig. 17) will hold their contents secure even if their doors fly open in heavy-weather. Once again it is a question of 'thinking-heeled', and the same design features should extend to the bookshelves. Now the handiest place for bookshelves is on top of lockers under the side-decks. Instead of deep fiddles you will need a shallow lip and a fold-down

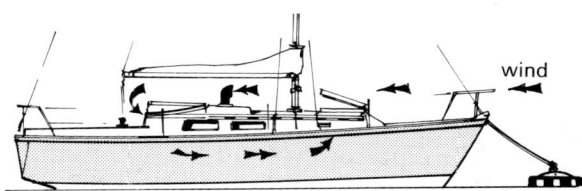

FIG. 15. *Moored-up or sailing, the air-flow is the same—from aft to forward.*

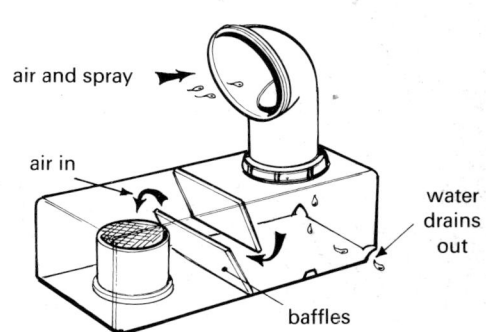

FIG. 16. *Named after a famous ocean racer, the 'Dorade' water-trap ventilator lets fresh air in and helps keep her interior 'sweet'. Some form of restrictor is advisable, or in a gale too much air will be blasted in.*

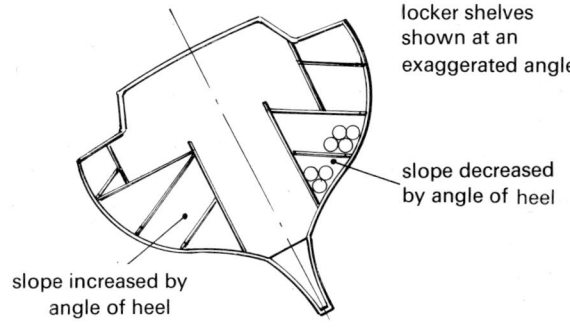

FIG. 17. *Sloped locker shelves give secure stowage even when the going gets rough. Large lockers with small doors, plus internal fiddles, have a huge advantage over boat-show 'kitchen furniture'.*

fiddle which, with brass button-on-a-plate catches, can look functionally attractive (Fig. 18). The shelves, like all the lockers, need subdividing to keep their contents in order and stop them sliding around. Bookshelves need be no more than 10 inches (250 mm) high by about nine inches (230 mm) deep. It is a help however if you reserve a space for those pilots and other thin books that have to be stowed flat.

I fitted louvred doors to *Solitaire* with two aims in mind (Photo. 2). Firstly they look attractive and starting with a pair of ready-made cupboard doors, were easy to make. The second, and perhaps more important aspect was ventilation. The WC has its own ventilator, and this in conjunction with a louvred door, keeps it well-aired and sweet. The forecabin has a pair of opening ports, a forehatch, and a louvred door separating it from the main-cabin in which there is an elegant drip-feed diesel heater. This has a variable output up to 2 kilowatts and warms the whole boat—thanks to those louvred doors. Incidently cabin heaters need to be fitted as low in the boat as possible; fit them too high and you get warm heads and iced feet. Having mentioned the forecabin on *Solitaire* let me tell you what else is in there. First there is an open-topped locker right up in the bows, followed by a chain-locker with more than enough room to take two shackles of chain. This means 180 feet of chain, for historically chain is sold in 90 foot lengths with a large link at one end to take a joining 'shackle'. Chain lockers need to be as deep in the boat as possible and if you can arrange a four or five foot (1.2–1.5 m) drop the chain will be self-stowing. By the same token a two-foot (.6 m) drop is a miserable affair which will drive you mad with frustration when it comes to weighing anchor— and a two foot drop, or less, is what you will get if the chain-locker is put as far forward as possible. Half of the chain-locker on *Solitaire* runs under the foot of a double-berth. Yes, that's right, a double-berth. The forecabin is in fact the 'master's' cabin when in port and it is a well-known fact that two people occupy less space when

sleeping together compared with what they need separately. Thus this 'double' is 3 ft 4 in (1 m) wide at the head and tapers down to a cosy 2 ft 4 in (710 mm) at its foot. Overall length is 6 ft 6 in (2 m) for I am 6 ft 2 in and when you are fitting-out you may suit yourself! (There is a full interior plan on page 10.) Under the berth are a pair of deep lockers sub-divided for comfortable stowage. There is, in addition, a hopper-locker which swings out from under the berth without taking up valuable floor-space. (See page 49 for more details). Facing the berth is a vanitory locker with cupboards and shelves, together with a hanging locker. Immediately under the forehatch and between the berth and vanitory unit is a 'boot' locker which forms a step to make exiting via the fore-hatch safe. Headroom over the berth is 3 ft 6 in (1 m) so sitting up in bed to read or drink tea is a delight.

More detailed information is given elsewhere on the actual construction, but I would like to stress again that what suits me is a personal matter—the choice is entirely yours when it comes to fitting-out from scratch.

More on interiors

Having just dealt with *Solitaire's* fore-cabin, I think that this might be a good spot to describe some of the many alternative interiors that one could fit into a 28 footer. The permutations are in fact endless; much depends upon your needs and personal preferences and I would always advocate the 'empirical' approach to interior design that I have already outlined. We were fortunate in that our 'boat box' already contained the engine, cooker, WC and other items of gear. Thus we could stand them in the hull in near approximations to their final positions and rough-in the layout around them. While this may be considered by some to be a simplistic approach, let me remind them of the habit that some manufacturers have of altering the basic dimension of their equipment ever so slightly. Thus the Mk III cooker may not fit in the space you so carefully left for the now unobtainable, Mk II cooker. Nonetheless, I don't want to imply that there is a need to rush out and buy all the equipment just to make sure that it will fit—maker's catalogues and data-sheets available from most good chandlers and marine equipment factors will give dimensions. Allow a little more clearance for luck and you will not need to rip out all that carefully fitted woodwork just to accommodate a minor dimensional change.

Once again you need to 'think-heeled', for a gimballed cooker with oven will need more volume than one fixed down rigidly. It is also a good idea to try

FIG. 18. Fold-down bookshelf fiddles are functionally attractive and easy to arrange. They look much better than elastic shockcord straps.

and visualize yourself sitting on the WC with boat heeled (Fig. 19). If the side-deck digs into your neck you might like to rearrange things. Does the position of the WC let you raise its seat and cover back through at least 130 degrees? That seems a daft question until you realise that a mere 91 degree of lift will mean that when ever-so-slightly heeled you will physically have to restrain the lid—and possibly the seat too. Then what about the actual height of the WC bowl? Your normal domestic unit bears only a passing dimensional relationship with one for marine use. You will find that for pure ergonomic reasons it will have to be raised up on a plinth. You will be aware of the need for 3 ft 6 in (1076 mm) headroom over the bowl but the lip of the bowl should be between 12 and 14 inches (300–350 mm) high. Try to visualize how you would fare if (being a male) you tried urinating while kneeling down—the safest posture when underway. Once again-think heeled.

I apologize to fastidious readers for these thoughts on what is, after all, only a basic human function. But should you get the installation all wrong the compartment could soon become unsavoury.

If you can fit a wash-basin in the WC compartment so much the better. It may be plumbed to discharge above the waterline—but you will still need to fit a seacock to its skin-fitting to prevent back-flooding when heeled. The actual water for washing hands could be either salt—pumped directly via another skin-fitting with seacock, or freshwater from the main tank. In either case I would advocate fitting a foot-operated pump to raise the water for that arrangement makes for better hygiene. (See page 85 for notes on skin-fittings and seacocks).

Incidentally, if the washbasin cannot be set high enough to drain above the waterline, let it drain into the WC, and pump it out from there.

Shelves and small cupboards, or lockers, are essen-

tially a matter of what you care to work in, but one important area concerns those seacocks. They must be positioned so that they are readily accessible at all times. Then the crew can turn them 'ON' and 'OFF' as required with the minimum of effort. This matter of 'crew drill' may save you shipping a few gallons of water which will pour out of the toilet just when you are enjoying a super sail. Of course much depends upon the height of the bowl relative to the heeled waterline, but far better safe than the other.

Seacocks are required on ALL skinfittings through the hull even though they may be well above the static waterline. That galley sink, and the WC washbasin, will start to flood the boat given the slightest chance. Also you are relying upon plastic hose and clips for integrity if you try to do without a seacock. Either of these could fail, or perhaps some badly-stowed heavy object like a kedge-anchor could shift and push the hose off its skin fitting and start a flood. Doing-it-yourself is no excuse for false economies when it comes to sea-sense—even though some 'builders' leave seacocks off there is no need for you to follow their bad example. Similarly all hose-clips should be doubled for security (Fig. 20).

Galleys need not be over-elaborate, nor need they take up much space (Photo. 3). A cooker and sink may be fitted into a very compact volume provided that the cook has enough alternative work-surfaces on which to stand hot saucepans, plates etc., without fear of them ending up in the bilge. Marine sinks as bought are too shallow for proper marine use. They are also too large

PHOTO. 2. Bulkheads under the mast must be given continuity across top and bottom if they are to realise their maximum strength. Note the 'swells' at the top of door jamb which gives a bigger 'landing'.

FIG. 19. Thinking heeled . . . gimballed cookers need to swing to at least 30 degrees and 45 would be better. Toilet seats should fold back by about the same amount.

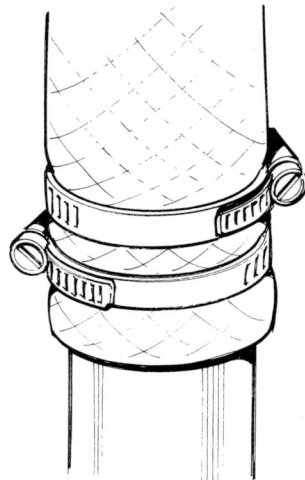

FIG. 20. Stainless steel (or galvanized) hose-clips should always be used in pairs for extra security. Pairs also give a better seal on smaller pipes where the screw portion seems to assume a large increment of the whole.

PHOTO. 3. *A galley can be worked into a surprisingly small space which need be no wider than the cooker plus sink—with a bit of room for surrounds, of course. The other 'cupboard' is in fact the wardrobe in the forepeak.*

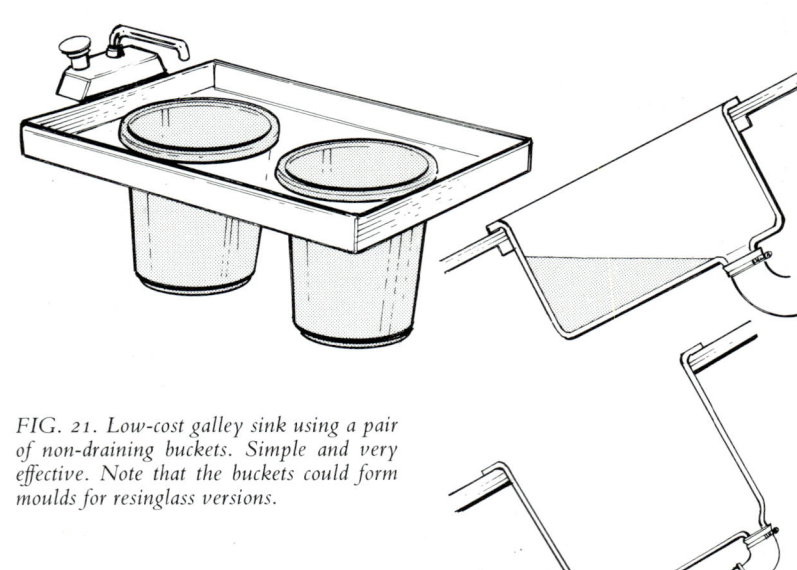

FIG. 21. *Low-cost galley sink using a pair of non-draining buckets. Simple and very effective. Note that the buckets could form moulds for resinglass versions.*

FIG. 22. *Shallow caravan-type sinks invariably have a single outlet which prevents them draining fully on one tack, or the other. Tandemised outlets beat that problem.*

FIG. 23. *Cam-blocks can be used to enable the cooker to be fixed or gimballed as required. Although hardwood could be used, Tufnol would be better.*

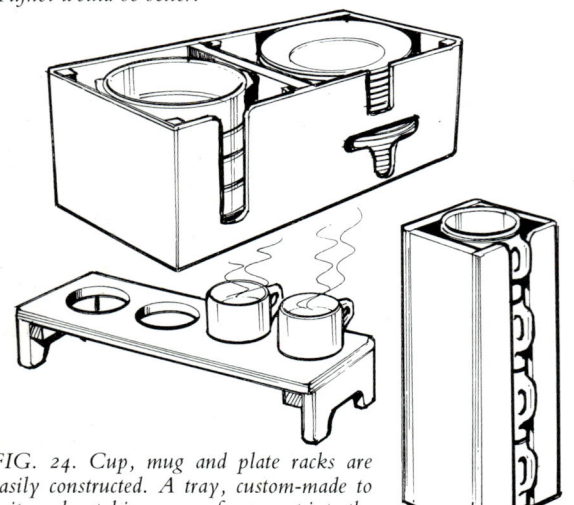

FIG. 24. *Cup, mug and plate racks are easily constructed. A tray, custom-made to suit, makes taking mugs of soup out into the cockpit safer.*

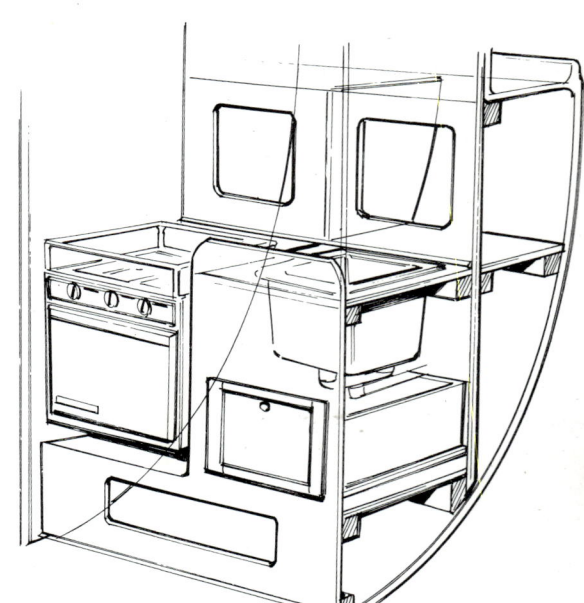

FIG. 25. *A galley between bulkheads is a safe installation and need not be over-elaborate. The drawers may have positive locks, or else catches may be arranged to give a firm closure.*

which means that they take an enormous amount of water for washing up, and being shallow they are poor depositories for un-washed crocks dirtied when sailing. A very adequate sink arrangement may be made by using two deep buckets—either round or square in section as you fancy. There is no need for drains, pipes or seacocks—you simply empty them over the side (Fig 21). (Search them for hidden teaspoons first!) The one big drawback to this otherwise eminently suitable arrangement is that plastic buckets are thermo-plastic, that is they soften when heated by a hot saucepan for instance. This may distort or damage them to a point where replacement is necessary. True, they are cheap, but a more practical solution might be to find something in stainless steel still, however you contrive it, twin-sinks are a practical idea for both blue-water and coastal-cruising (See also Fig. 22).

The cooker itself may have two or three burners, but it must have a grill, for such an implement is worth its weight in gold on a small cruiser. I would always advocate a gas cooker for I am a firm believer that they are safer than alcohol stoves and alcohol-primed paraffin stoves **PROVIDED** they are well fitted and used sensibly. But, as ever, the choice is yours. Cookers with ovens are an improvement on the simple grill but take care if you 'economize' with a cheaper caravan model. Not that there is much wrong with them that you cannot modify if you think heeled! For instance the top will be held on with two spring clips. Burner grids will be loose and located with pegs. The oven door will have no catch—just a simple spring closure. All of these things you could easily correct and the result will be a 'marine' cooker. A gimballed cooker should be located with its axis fore-and-aft, for although termed 'gimballed' they are in fact only swung. Pitching is ignored, and the available freedom takes account only of heeling angle. Swung cookers can be arranged so that they may be locked for use in port and the necessary gear is very simple—just a pair of cam-shaped brackets. When the cooker is pulled forward into the centreline of the boat it is automatically raised up to give the required clearance as (Fig. 23) shows. A swung-stove necessitates the use of a flexible connection between the cooker and the rigid copper supply-line. Flexible pipes should conform to British or equivalent standards and be armoured for safety.

A fixed cooker allows you to use copper pipe right up to the cooker connection thus eliminating a possible source of trouble. Quite satisfactory use can be got out of a non-swung cooker at sea—a pot-roast, or stew, can be made using a pressure cooker held firmly in place by custom-made clamps or steel springs.

Cooker apart, the galley needs to have adequate storage near to hand for saucepans and other utensils.

Cups, plates and bowls can all be held in special racks which may be both functional and decorative if well-made (Fig. 24).

Safety around the galley is an important consideration, for cooking at sea is not without risk. While it is easy to pour soup from a saucepan into mugs in harbour without spilling a drop, the same feat at sea is impossible. Instead the mugs should be held in a rack, and if this forms the basis of a carrying tray so much the better. It is dangerous to attempt to pour scalding liquid with one hand into a mug you are holding in the other.

A restraining strap for use when the boat is heeled is a simple-enough idea. The same straps made up firmly can also be used to prevent the cook being thrown against the cooker when on the opposite tack (Fig 14). Alternatively a special 'crash-bar' could be fitted. Similar thoughts need to be given to the role of the lockers behind the cooker. Very useful lockers and bins can be worked in under the side-decks but these are suitable only for holding stores which are not likely to be needed when actually cooking—since to reach into them means leaning across a lighted burner. . . .

A galley between bulkheads (Fig. 25) is safer than open-plan, even though the latter may look nicer. But if the cooker is adjacent to the head of a berth, or settee, think of the risk to the occupant if a pan of boiling liquid should slide off the cooker. Bulkheads will also help to restrict a possible fire which is less likely to spread rapidly through the boat. Two bulkheads also give large areas on which to fix shelves and racks. A box, or drawer is essential for keeping smaller items such as spoons and knives. Although brass cuphooks with mugs hanging on them look fun at home they have no place on a small boat where the slightest movement will cause them to clatter against each other. The need to restrict movement means that all shelves and bins need to be sub-divided to allow a good stow to be made. There are few things more irritating than the clatter of china!

Shelves should, in my opinion, not go right back against the bulkhead or hull side. If you can arrange to leave a half-inch gap then they become 'self-cleaning' in that small bits and pieces automatically get pushed off instead of being left to accumulate in the corners. It is also a good idea to have a fiddle at the front of each shelf to restrain small items, boxes of matches, egg-cups and the like.

Fiddles are also needed for all worktops around the galley and need to be at least $1\frac{1}{2}$–2 inches (37–50 mm) high; in fact 3 inches (75 mm) would not be too much. They can be arranged with gaps to let you sweep out crumbs—but I would leave them continuous around the sink to contain any spills. Fiddles may be permanently fixed, arranged on pegs for use as and when required, or hinged. Pegs seem to me to be a needless complication,

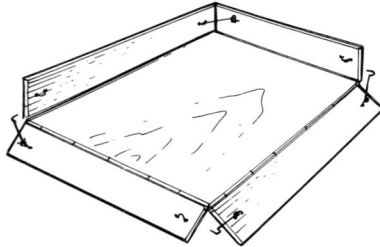

FIG. 26. *Deep fiddles are a blessing when things get rough. They need not be permanent—these sea-going ones hinge up as required.*

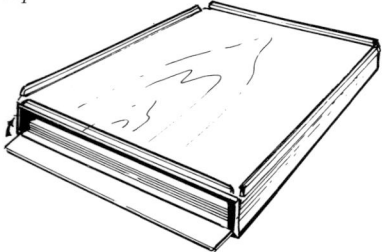

FIG. 27. *A chart 'box' may be fitted under a table. Something like 200 folded Admiralty charts may be stowed in a 2 inch (50 mm) depth.*

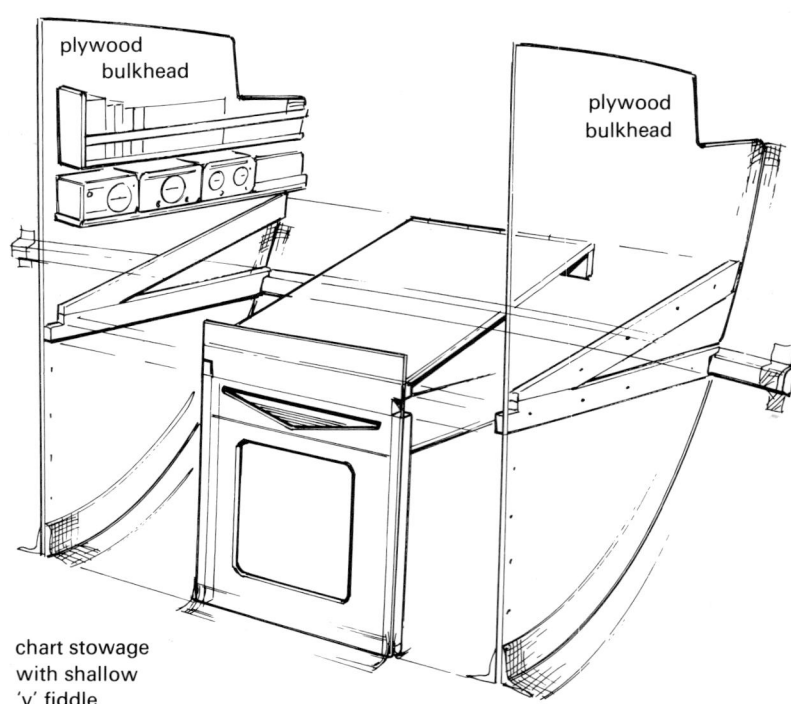

plywood bulkhead

plywood bulkhead

chart stowage with shallow 'v' fiddle

FIG. 28. *Bulkheads may be required by the navigator so that he has somewhere to fix instruments. He will also need shelves for pilots, almanacs, etc. It all depends upon the type of boating you intend doing. Note that a long, shallow-vee slot gives both security and easy-access to the charts.*

although I can see the sense of hinged fiddles around the cabin table which can be raised when needed—rather like an old-fashioned 'butler's tray'. (Fig. 26)

Cabin tables may be used to form the basis of double-berths, or 'dinettes' as the layout drawings elsewhere show. Various sliding arrangements are possible and there are also ranges of purpose-made gear available. These may be a simple clamped support-knee sliding about a vertical tube, or post, or else spring-loaded telescopic devices derived from caravan applications. Should you be unable to work a chart-table into your layout then the cabin table will have a dual-role.

The cabin-table can be made suitable for chart-work by the addition of shallow fiddles—which should be fitted anyway, and somewhere to store the charts. A lift-up lid has the merit of exposing the charts to view, but back-flap hinges are necessary to present a flat surface for working on. Alternatively one side of the table (which is now a thin box section) can have a fold-down front, or side to give access. This type of table is much easier to construct, but it does mean that you have to pull the charts out to make your selection. (Fig. 27)

The main disadvantage of using the cabin-table for chart-work is that all the other necessary bits and pieces—pilots, tide-tables etc may be some way away in a bookshelf. It is a great comfort to have them ready-to-hand and if you feel the need to be surrounded by expensive electronic navigating equipment then you will need bulkheads nearby on which to fit them.

A chart-table arranged fore-and-aft between bulkheads (Fig. 28) achieves this but it may be uncomfortable to use when the boat is heeled. An alternative is to make a desk-like structure across the boat which can be provided with a seat. If the nav' office is just inside the companionway then the bottom of the desk, or the seat, could be used to make a small wet-locker for oilies. Once again fiddles would be needed on the table, and all shelves and racks well divided to prevent their contents charging about. One large 'plus' factor that acrues from siting the nav' area just inside the companionway is that the motion of the boat thereabouts is minimal compared with say, the forecabin. Poring over a chart can be much less of an ordeal there, especially in heavy-weather.

Possible interiors are infinite—the choice is yours—and that is one of the nicest things about completing an empty hull. You can put in anything you like and not be forced into accepting the layout that the builder, with his cost-conscious accountant looking over his shoulder, stipulates. You can also pick the materials and style as well! The following accommodation plans are all based on an identical 28 foot (8.5 m) hull.

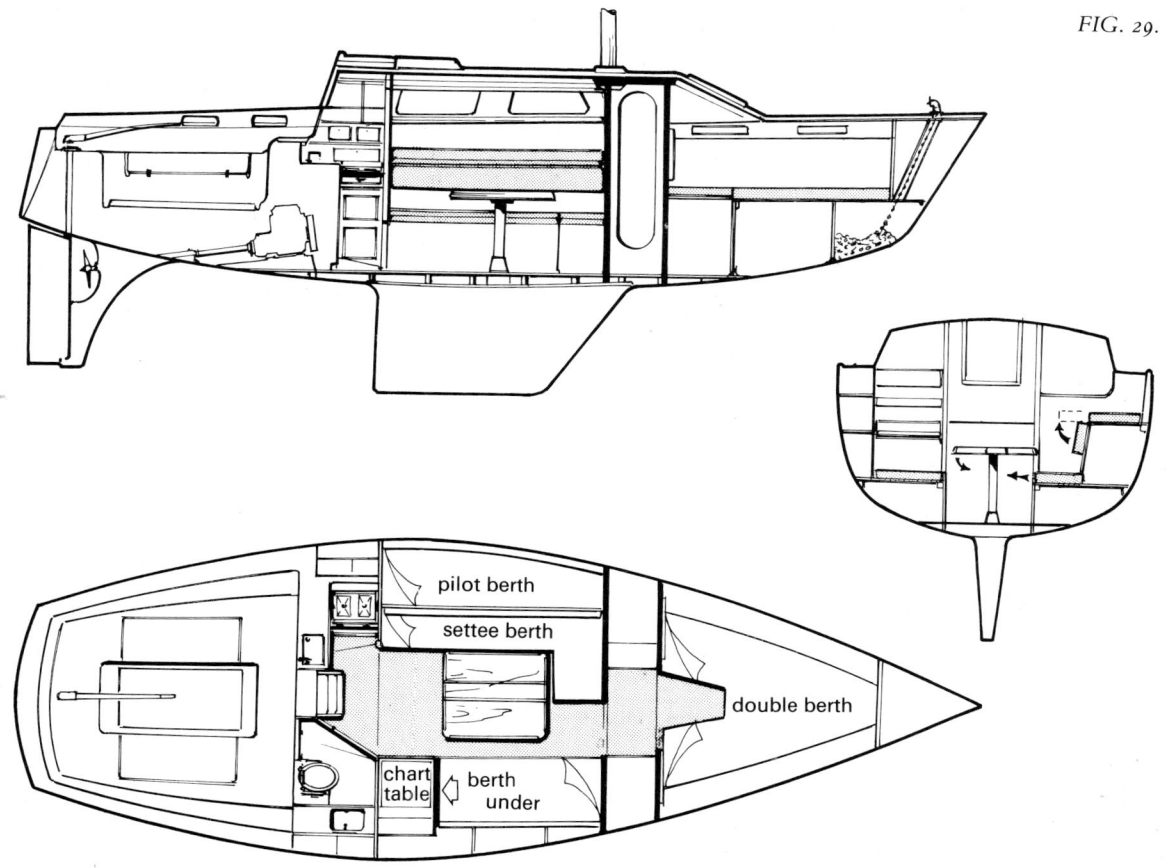

Now some working layouts

No quarter-berths are in the layout shown in figure 29. Instead a pilot-berth over the port-settee brings the sleeping quarters up to five in this typical 28 footer. A trotter-box under the chart-table extends an otherwise short berth. The WC and galley both have good headroom and the two wardrobes, or hanging lockers, with full-height bulkheads under the mast, provide a strong structure. The pair of single-berths in the fore-cabin may be converted into a double by an infill piece and an extra cushion.

While there is comfortable seating around the table it has to have folding leaves to allow easy access through the boat. Perhaps one of the settee seats could be sacrificed to give a place for a cabin heater against the main bulkhead.

Figure 30 shows how the interior starts to alter from the standard layout. The main cabin is identical, but the fore-cabin now has a double-berth. Note that what might be considered cramped at home becomes acceptable in a small boat. If a long, narrow, cabin-table

were to be introduced the port settee could be transformed into a double by lowering the table and adding a suitably-sized cushion.

When planning your interior it is best to keep the main structural bulkhead where the designer intended. Additional full-height bulkheads stiffen the boat, and if the furniture is well-bonded into the hull then the entire structure is stiffened. In fact it is a wise policy to adopt a layout which enables you to make much use of fore-and-aft and athwartships members to reinforce the original mouldings. For example side-decks, even when made with sandwich construction, will benefit from a series of 'knees'. These need not be shaped in the traditional sense; you could make use of the vertical dividers to the shelves and lockers. These must be strongly bonded to the underside of the side-decks and to the hull if they are to perform this additional role.

As you start to plan your interior you should keep in mind two important things. Firstly the structure should increase the strength of the boat and it is wise to arrange it in an even-handed manner. This means that if you adopt a system of lockers which result in ready-made

27

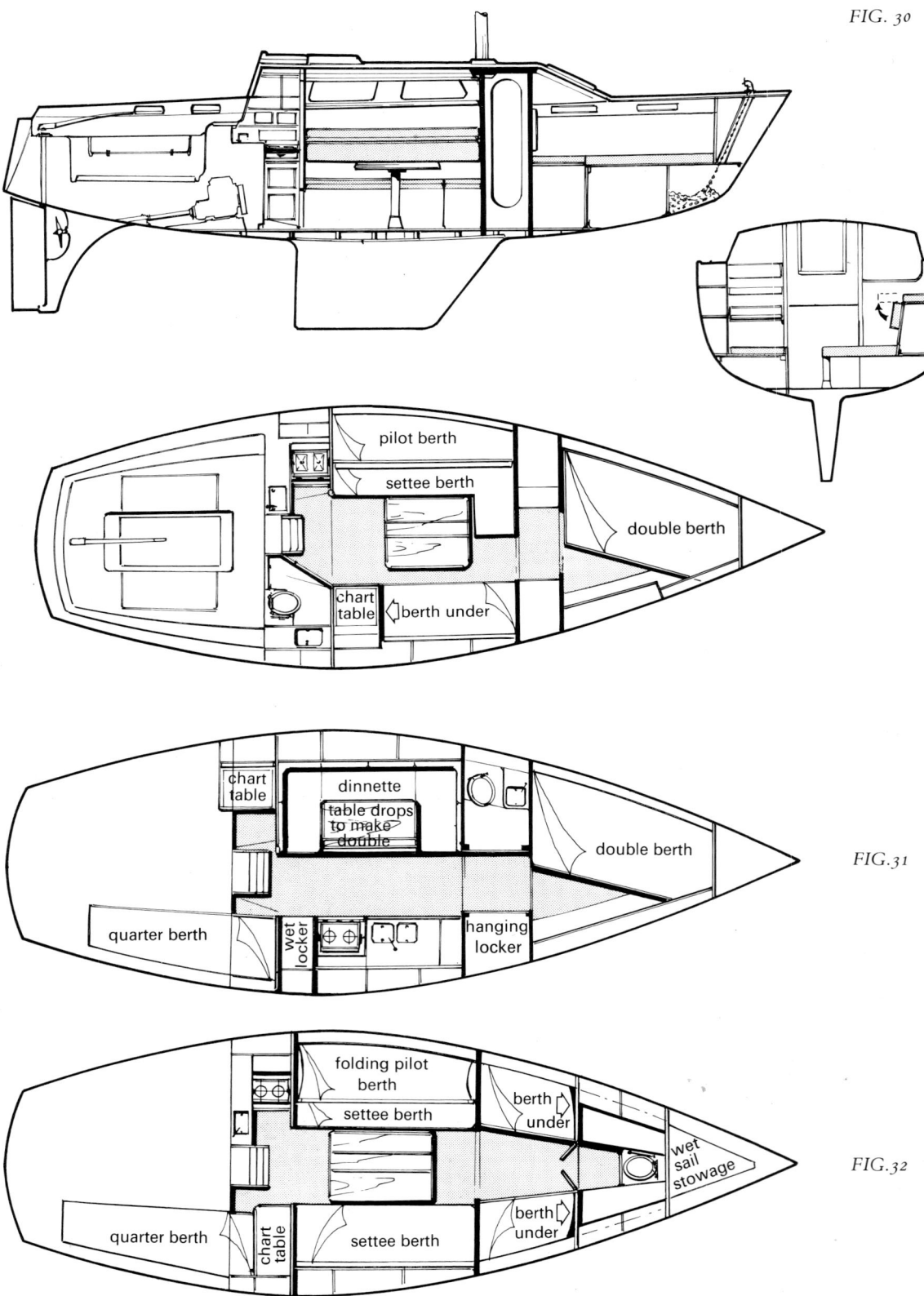

FIG. 30

pilot berth

settee berth

double berth

chart
table

berth under

FIG.31

chart
table

dinnette

table drops
to make
double

double berth

quarter berth

wet
locker

hanging
locker

FIG.32

folding pilot
berth

settee berth

berth
under

wet
sail
stowage

quarter berth

chart
table

settee berth

berth
under

knees reinforcing the side-decks along one side of the boat, you should also consider the need for similar knees opposite. Bulkheads are best arranged port and starboard in opposing pairs. But if it is impracticable to use them like this then perhaps a post could be introduced to help keep the stiffness of the structure symmetrical.

Symmetry may also be extended to weights with advantage; for example a 50 gallon water-tank on one side of the boat (230 litres) weighs some 500 lb (225 kg). Such a mass might cause the boat to go along with a permanent list unless other weights are arranged to counter-balance. These could be starter-batteries, a cooker, fuel tank, tinned-food stores etc. It is well worth keeping in mind too the way the berths are arranged or at bed-time your boat could develop a decided list one way or the other.

It is not necessary to get too involved with this aspect of fitting out, for once drawn to your attention I am sure that you will appreciate the problems that could arise.

A caravan interior (Fig. 31) with sea-going capability. The double-berth in the fore-cabin would be untenable in a seaway unless the boat is gently running before a light breeze. The WC compartment and bulkheads under the mast are ideally placed to cater for the local stresses, and the wet-locker next to the galley is a boon. Quarter-berths when not occupied can be used for keeping bedding dry if you stuff it down well out of the way.

Port and starboard settee-berths are a good starting point (Fig. 32). This layout has a folding pilot-berth over the port settee. The backrest of the settee folds up to make the pilot-berth which also needs a lee-cloth for security; it's a long way down to the cabin-sole.

The navigator sits on the head of the quarter-berth when using his chart-table. This arrangement obviously has its drawbacks, with two good settee-berths, overnight passages should cause no problems. The galley is nice and near the companionway.

The WC is under the forehatch and the two berths in the fore-cabin have trotter-boxes, the tops of which form elbow rests for anyone sitting on the WC. Sail stowage is good with access directly through the forehatch into the wet locker. Note the single main bulkhead under the mast which means it must be well framed-up and it would be wise to incorporate a deck beam and cross-web. (Fig. 33).

The arrangement of the WC and the galley in figure 34 is identical to those used in other schemes outlined here. The main difference is that the port-side settee pulls forward to form a double berth. The table must be able to fold down to achieve this. Note that there is no chart-table, although one could be worked in if a trotter-box was to be used over the starboard berth.

A single berth is fitted into the fore-cabin with the possibility of a pipe-cot over the open-topped storage bins.

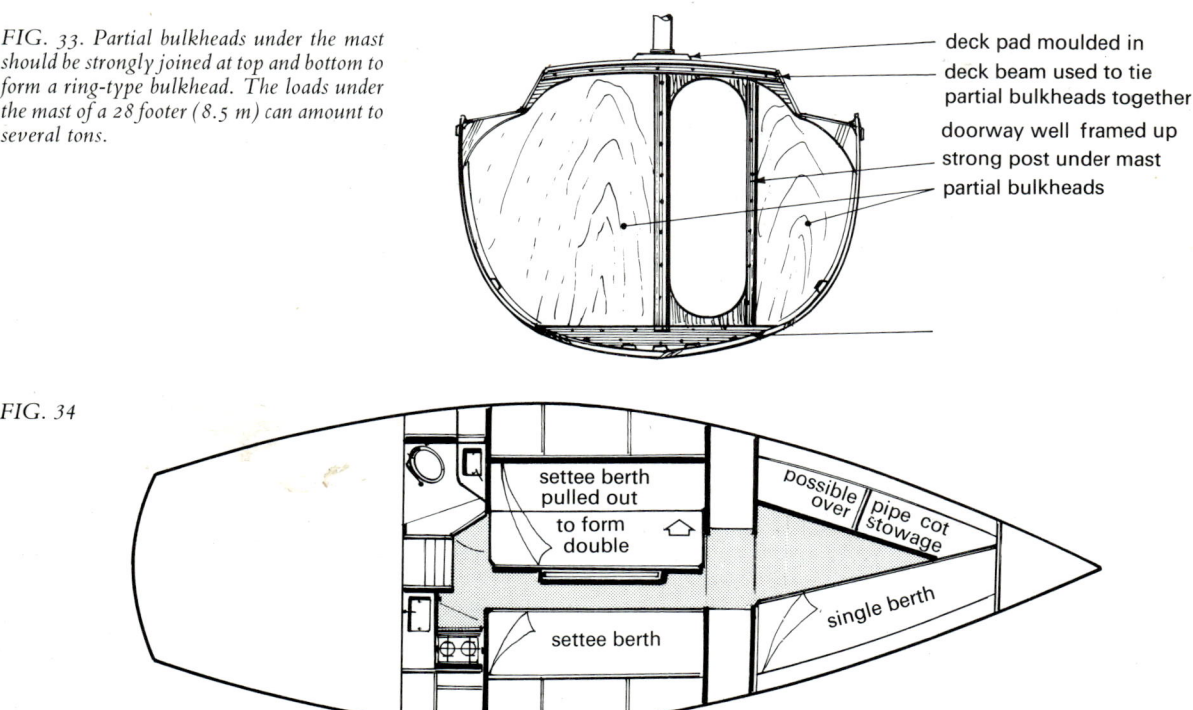

FIG. 33. Partial bulkheads under the mast should be strongly joined at top and bottom to form a ring-type bulkhead. The loads under the mast of a 28 footer (8.5 m) can amount to several tons.

deck pad moulded in
deck beam used to tie partial bulkheads together
doorway well framed up
strong post under mast
partial bulkheads

FIG. 34

settee berth pulled out
to form double
possible over pipe cot stowage
single berth
settee berth

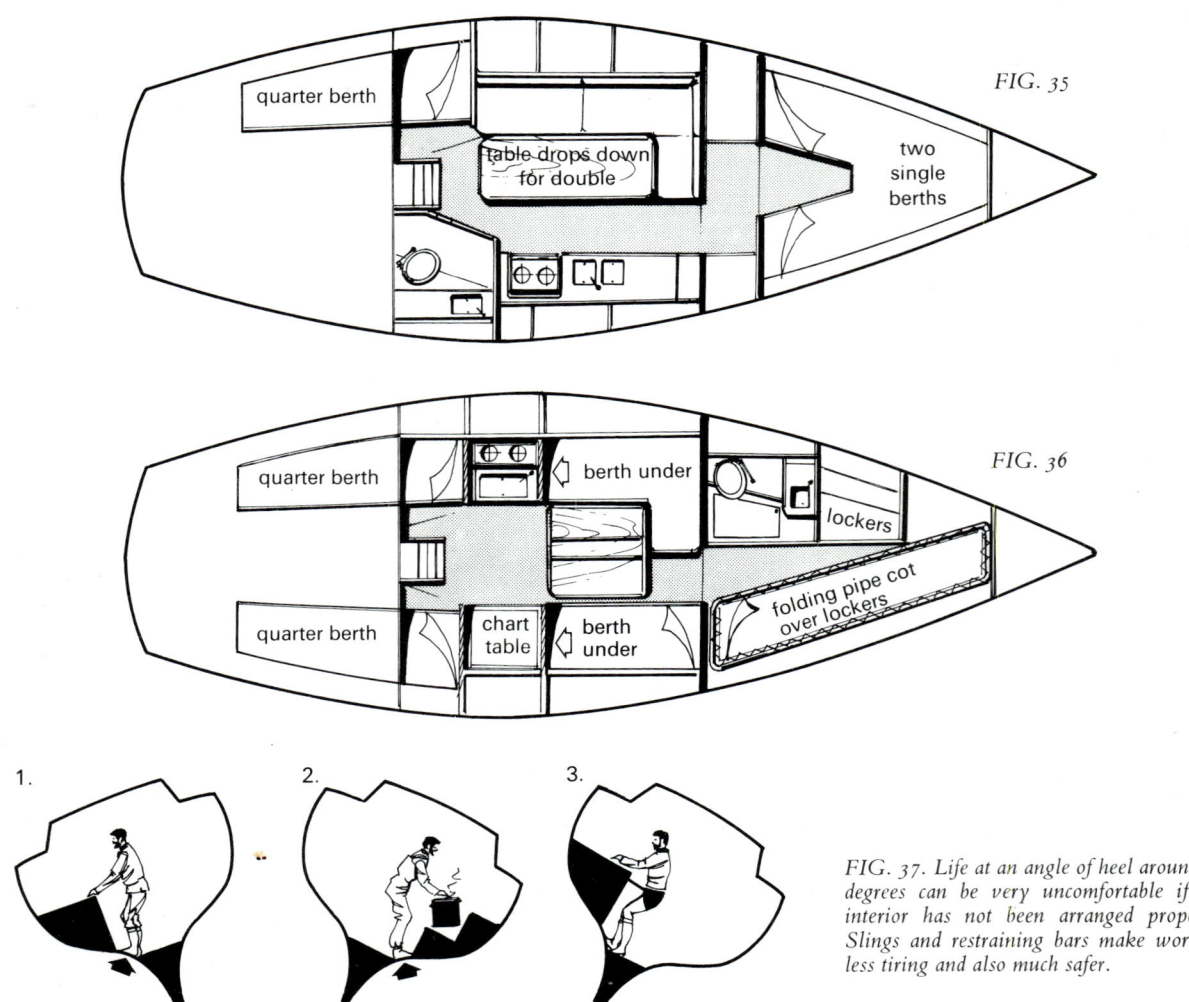

FIG. 35

quarter berth

table drops down for double

two single berths

FIG. 36

quarter berth

berth under

lockers

quarter berth

chart table

berth under

folding pipe cot over lockers

1.   2.   3.

FIG. 37. *Life at an angle of heel around 15 degrees can be very uncomfortable if the interior has not been arranged properly. Slings and restraining bars make working less tiring and also much safer.*

While it is possible to fit a WC at a slight angle to the centreline of the boat, it is not an ideal arrangement to fit it with the bowl fore-and-aft since female crew-members may have difficulty using it—especially when heeled. In figure 35 it has been fitted angled so as to make best use of available space and it is possible to perform one's ablutions while sitting down. Not so much of a luxury as a necessity if the headroom is limited as it probably will be if you put in a flat floor above the turn of the bilge.

The L-shaped berth turns into a double when the table is lowered, and the galley opposite gives large amounts of locker space underneath. Two hanging lockers and a pair of berths complete the forecabin. As with all the arrangements this one could be used 'mirrored'—or on the opposite sides.

With the layout in figure 36 the fore-cabin is used to house the WC which has its own compartment. There is ample storage space in the lockers and slatted bins could be used for the sails. A folding pipe-cot for occasional use gives another berth.

Both settees in the main-cabin make use of trotter-boxes where the feet of the occupants pass under other structures; in this case the galley and chart-table. The galley is between two partial bulkheads for safety and the twin-burner cooker could be arranged on slides to pull out over the sink when needed. Two quarter-berths are used here; although these are good passage-berths they need at least 14 inches (350 mm) over their mattresses for 'knee-height'. The ends of the port-settee could be trimmed to fit a cabin-heater against the bulkhead.

More thoughts on interiors

If you leave the cabin floor, or more correctly the 'sole', clear of the hull sides then when heeled to the normal sailing angle a nearly horizontal floor section is presented to the feet. This is a considerable safety factor for most cabins tend to get rather slippery when spray starts to fly. You can appreciate the need for something to restrain the body in the cases shown here in figure 37. The chap in (1) might be working at his charts, but in (2) he could be leaning into a burning gas-ring. (3) shows the need to have some form of 'bum-sling' to hold him against the chart-table or cooker. A purpose-made webbing and canvas affair is easy to fabricate, but its attachments need to be very strong to withstand the very high loads imposed. They should be arranged in tension—never shear! (Fig. 38).

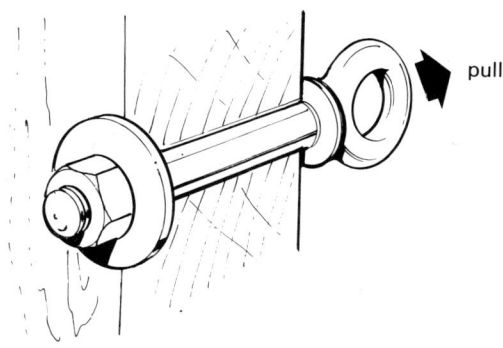

FIG. 38. Eye-bolts are intended to work in tension. They may fail under severe bending loads especially if the load is a fluctuating one— i.e. 'so many cycles to failure'.

ATLANTA FASTNET
Designed in France by Groupe Finot the Atlanta Fastnet is a fast fin keeler with room to sleep 8. She races in IOR Class IV and with almost flush decks visibility from her saloon is very limited. Originally, a Farymann 18 hp diesel was fitted, but alternative engines are possible. She makes use of extensive internal mouldings—which makes home fitting-out that much easier. Builders are Atlanta Marine, Newgate Lane, Fareham, Hants.

Length overall   33.4 feet
Length waterline   24.6 feet
Beam   11.1 feet
Draft   5.6 feet
Displacement   9,420 lb
Ballast   3,500 lb
Sail area   462 square feet

3

The materials

Polyester resin reinforced with glass fibres is known variously throughout the western world as 'fibreglass', 'glass fibre', 'glass', 'grp', or as here—'resinglass'. It was used to productionize boat-building in the 1950's, although some early boats were built in 1946, or so. It was rapidly promoted as something of a 'wonder material' and in my opinion it is still just that; though for different reasons than those which silver-tongued salesmen extolled at boat shows. Resinglass is undoubtedly a first-class material for small boat construction with minimal drawbacks. Its most important advantage, apart from bringing production prices down to a level that the man in the street can afford, is that minor repairs and alterations may be done by the average handyman. He, with not much skill, will get a perfectly sound result. If however, he was attempting to replace a damaged plank in a traditional wooden hull he would in all probability, end up in a mess.

Resinglass boats are built from the outside in; the resin and glass fibre reinforcements are applied to the mould in the order in which they are viewed from the outside of the boat (Fig. 39). Their hulls are made from one, or sometimes two-part mouldings, laid up in moulds that were themselves taken off a plug. The plug is in fact a full-sized model of the boat lovingly constructed by skilled craftsmen and faired and polished up to perfection. The degree of finish is of paramount importance for any flaw or blemish in its surface would be accurately mirrored by the mould which is taken from it. It should be appreciated that very few boats built in this way today are based on prototypes which were sailed, raced and modified before the plug was made. Tooling up for a new boat is an extremely costly venture and to keep costs down it is common for the builder to progress straight from the designer's drawing board to the pattern-shop where the plug is made. I think it sad

FIG. 39. Hulls are laid-up using a combination of tissue, chopped strand mat, woven rovings and other reinforcements bound together with polyester resin. The gel-coat resin is of paramount importance since it protects the rest of the laminate against a hostile environment.

PHOTO. 4. The start of a very expensive 'cure'. If the gel-coat blisters then it must be removed and replaced with an epoxy, or two-part polyurethane paint. Water is a surprisingly hostile environment for a resinglass laminate.

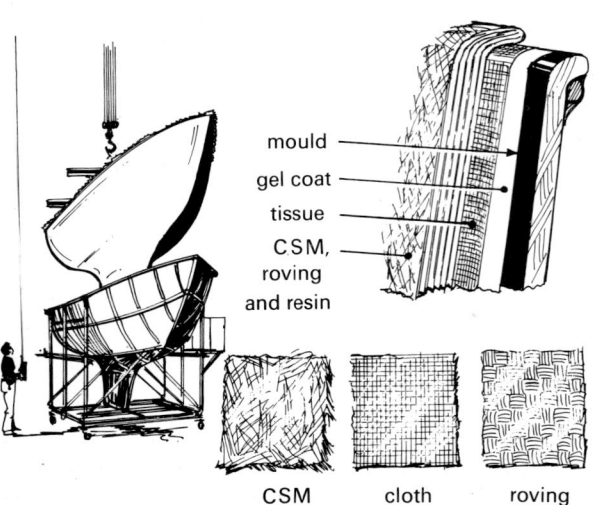

mould
gel coat
tissue
CSM, roving and resin

CSM   cloth   roving

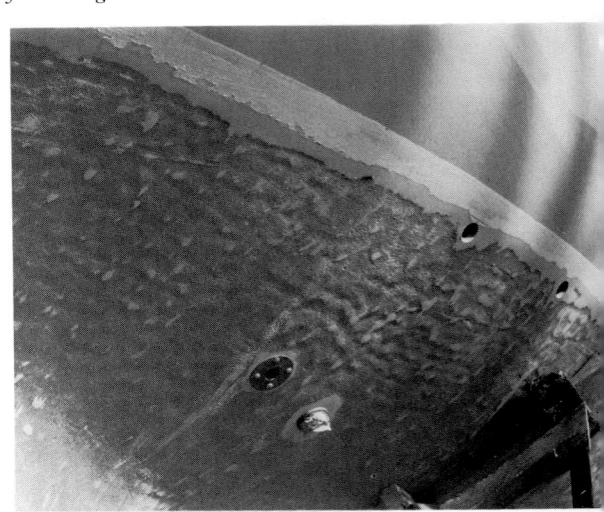

that numerous boats make their debut at international boat shows before they have even been afloat.

Once the builder has his production moulds 'craftsmanship' in its truest sense disappears as the boat is laid up. The mould is first prepared by polishing to remove any scratches, or marks, which would pick up in the finished moulding. It is then coated with wax which is allowed to dry before it is polished and then treated with a special mould-release agent—usually a polyvinyl alcohol solution (PVA). Two thin layers of gel-coat resin are then applied and this may be self-coloured, or coloured by the addition of any from a wide range of special pigments. The gel-coat layer is around 15–20 thousandths of an inch (0.5 mm) thick and must be neither too hard nor too soft, for its main function, apart from providing a decorative finish to the interior of the moulding, is to protect the underlying laminate against water take-up. Perhaps the application of the gel-coat resin is the most critical operation in the moulding sequence—and not only because the result is what the world at large sees.

If the gel-coat is wrongly formulated, extended by fillers, mis-applied, or applied under alien conditions, the resultant hull moulding may be seriously defective (Photo. 4). Some faults will show immediately: for instance should the gel-coat cure too quickly it may lift away from the mould and result in bumps and blistery bubbles. Other faults take longer to appear. If the mould temperature is too low, or the resin chilled, then the gel-coat will cure very slowly. That produces a poor surface through 'undercure', and such a surface quickly deteriorates. It may simply start 'chalking' or, more seriously, result in osmotic blistering. (See also under *Repairs*).

Moulding, or 'laying-up' should be done under closely-controlled environmental conditions. These pertain in the best moulding shops but are seldom met in old black tin sheds. International authorities around the world inspect moulding premises and will issue 'mould release' certificates for individual hulls, or series production certificates for long runs. Note that these certificates do not absolutely guarantee the boat—they are simply an indication of workmanship and materials.

Gel-coat resin is formulated to stay 'tacky' so that the next layer of polyester resin will chemically 'hitch' to it. The first layer of reinforcement is applied when the gel-coat has hardened and consists of a fine glass fibre mat called a surface tissue. This powder-bound tissue provides a resin-rich layer behind the gel-coat to improve water absorption resistance and also to prevent subsequent components of the laminate showing through the relatively thin gel-coat. One sometimes sees a hull moulding with a 'weave' in its gel-coat—more especially in dark colours such as green and blue—and

this weave is caused by a glass fibre fabric being applied too near the gel-coat layer. It is not so much a sign of bad moulding, rather that the moulder should perhaps reorganize the sequence he uses for applying the glass fibre reinforcements. ('Weave' may also develop if the moulding is prematurely removed from the mould—not to be recommended.).

Once the tissue has cured more resin is added and the laminate is built up layer by layer, using combinations of chopped strand mat (CSM) and woven rovings. While it is possible to produce satisfactory mouldings using only CSM the same is not true for woven rovings which need a layer of CSM on either side to prevent them pulling apart like the skins of an onion. The advantage to the moulder in using woven rovings is that the laminate may be made thinner and still have the high strength characteristics that the designer is seeking. There are also savings to be had in time and materials.

The polyester resins used when laying up are unsaturated and are thermosetting—they require heat to set. This is generated by a chemical reaction and the exotherm caused by the addition of a catalyst produces the heat and 'cures' the resin. The catalyst is a peroxide material which causes polymerization—an involved process which requires a depth of chemical knowledge to fully appreciate—so we'll skip it!

This need for heat during the curing process is why it is impossible to effect a cure if the ambient temperature is too low. Conversely should it be too hot a fast cure-rate is obtained. This again is bad practice since it may lock in large amounts of styrene and reduce the overall strength of the laminate. The exotherm, or internal heat build-up, means that care has to be taken not to allow too much resin to build up in any one spot. After laying up four layers of $1\frac{1}{2}$ oz (450 g/m²) CSM reinforcements work must stop until the resin has set; a bucket full of resin which has started to gel due to, say too much catalyst, may even catch fire! (See notes on *Safety*).

When the laminate is finally cured, although still 'green' in the strictest sense, it is removed from the mould. Curing takes place over quite a long period, starting off very fast where 85 per cent is attained in the first few hours and the remainder of the 'cure' continues over the next few weeks, or even months. It is recognised that good mouldings should be left in the moulding shop for at least 16 days.

Polyester shrinks slightly on curing and this means that while this feature assists the moulder in removing his finished hull from its mould it can also cause trouble for the home-completer particularly if he starts work on a very 'green' hull too soon (Fig. 40).

The inside surface of the completed moulding may be treated with a waxed resin and surface tissue to provide a non-tacky resin-rich surface. The moulder may even use

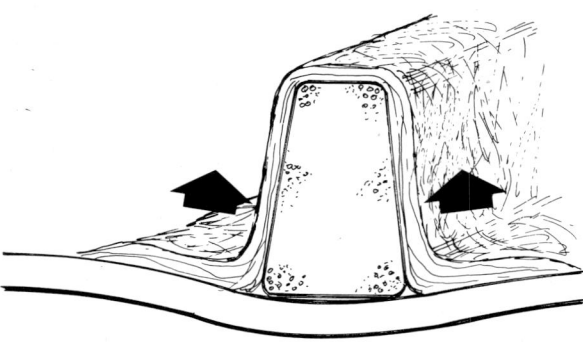

FIG. 40. If work starts too soon on a very 'green' moulding then permanent distortion may result. Polyester resin shrinks on curing and could pull the hull laminate hard up against some internal structure—web, furniture, top-hat section, etc.

a pigmented interior (waxed) gel-coat resin specially formulated to flow on leaving no brush marks. Alternatively he may just leave a tacky surface of normal laminating resin.

That very brief account of the way a hull is moulded will assist you when it is time to start work on your own hull—not that you will be laying it up, but an understanding of what was involved will help you to appreciate the reason for adopting certain practices later on. The same is true of the materials used—while you may not need all of them it is desirable to know of their existence and what they may be used for.

Polyester resins

Although usually referred to in the singular, there are nonetheless many different types of polyester resins formulated for a wide range of specific applications. Some have pigments added to make coloured gel-coats, others have enhanced heat and chemical resistance. Some are flexible, while others are intended for use in both hot and cold applications. The ones you will be concerned with are those produced for general laminating work and it is best to use those which are of good quality to British Standard, Lloyds specification or some other similar body.

It is wise to buy pre-accelerated resins which require only the addition of the catalyst for the curing process to start. While it is possible to add accelerator to pre-accelerated resins to produce a faster curing time it is not wise to do so for excessive amounts may cause the resin to cure before its maximum strength is attained.

Unwaxed laminating resin—the type to buy—sets in about half an hour, although that time may be affected by quantity, ambient temperature and the amount of catalyst added. Laminating resin stays 'tacky' on its exposed side for several days and this facility enables successive layers of resin to bond chemically to each other to produce a single laminate.

Waxed laminating resin

This is the type to use where you are seeking a superior-looking final surface. It cures non-tacky and may be sanded down to produce a fine surface. Should you be working with a waxed resin and your work flow is interrupted for more than a few hours at normal temperature (50–60°F) then the resin surface will need abrading to provide a mechanical key for the next layer of resin to cling to. Your resin supplier will be able to supply waxed resins, or a solution of wax in styrene which may be added to ordinary laminating resin by 2 percent by weight.

Gel-coat (exterior)

Suitable for rollering, brushing or spraying onto the mould surface. It comes in several types and may be pigmented (coloured) or left clear—in which case it will need painting after moulding is completed. Special types are formulated for hardness—tooling-gel for example; others are arranged for hardness combined with flexibility. Gel-coat dries tacky if left exposed to air.

Gel-coat (interior)

This is a waxed resin which may be pigmented and formulated for brushing on the inside of mouldings to provide a decorative finish. It dries hard with no tackyness. External gel-coat resin may be modified with 2 per cent wax in styrene to produce this type of resin.

Special resins

Other resins are available for such application as fuel and water tanks, and also for laminates which are heat (fire) resistant. Your supplier will recommend a specialist resin—possibly from stock.

Accelerator

Sometimes also called 'promotor' this chemical is decidely dangerous to handle being a 6 per cent cobalt naphthanate solution. It is used to speed the operation of the catalyst in curing the resin and should never be allowed to come into direct contact with it (the catalyst) for they react explosively. It is better by far to buy only pre-accelerated resins.

Catalyst (or hardener)

Once again this is a strong chemical which needs careful handling. It is usually a liquid methyl ethyl ketone peroxide (MEKP) and like all peroxides it is a powerful oxidising agent and is therefore dangerous. All splashes should be quickly washed off the skin, and should the material enter the eyes they must be washed with running freshwater for at least 15 minutes, during which time urgent medical assistance should be sought if blindness is to be avoided. Any spills of MEKP on the bench should be washed away with water. Never wipe it up with a rag or paper tissue for it will start to smoulder! Not a nice chemical to have around but it is a vital part of the chemical process and as such is indispensible. (See also notes on *Safety*).

Some laminating resins use a catalyst/accelerator system of cyclohexanone/cobalt. This is safer in that the HCH catalyst is a paste, but it is also more expensive and twice the amount of HCH is required to produce a cure. Thorough mixing with a paste-type or liquid catalyst is essential.

The amount of catalyst used is critical if the resin is to cure properly. Two-percent MEKP is about the norm—although the resin-maker may recommend from 1–4 per cent depending upon the setting time required and the ambient temperatures. Too-little catalyst may result in a poor laminate through undercure—too-much may cause rapid-gelling and poor strength.

COLVIC VICTOR 40
The largest boat from the U.K.'s largest moulders. The Victor 40 has seemingly 'acres' of sun-bathing space, and can be arranged to sleep up to 10. The 'wheelhouse' has an inside steering position and there is a bijou cabin right aft. Any stage of mouldings from hull and superstructure are available from her moulders Colvic Craft Ltd, Wheaton Road Industrial Estate East, Witham, Essex.

Overall length   40 feet
Waterline length   32.7 feet
Beam   12.5 feet
Draft   5.9 feet
Displacement   10 tons
Ballast   5 tons
Sail area   660 square feet

Pregel paste

This is a thixotropic paste containing aerosils and other materials which is used to thicken resins. The resins you will be using will have been prepared already and you should not need recourse to this material. (see also *Styrene*).

Filler powder

Usually a heavy industrial talc powder which may be mixed with laminating resin in equal parts to produce a putty. Needs the addition of the catalyst to harden and, since the resin is dispersed through the material a 4 per cent mix is about right; you are looking for a fast setting time rather than strength.

Styrene

Polyester resin contains about 35 per cent styrene monomer which is converted during the curing process into polymers. If the resin contains less than that percentage it will not cure properly and it is this feature which leaves the tacky surface on gel-coats and general laminating resin surfaces exposed to air. A waxed resin traps the styrene at the surface and so prevents loss through evaporation, thus producing a hard, dry exterior. This basic ingredient of polyester resin is not really required in bulk quantities unless you are working in unsuitable, draughty conditions through which excessive styrene loss occurs. Some 'moulders' use styrene to thin carefully-formulated resins which they then thicken up again with pregel. While this 'extends' the resin, it also weakens it, and should not be condoned.

Microballoons

These are lightweight gas-filled phenolic spheres of microscopic size. They are mixed with polyester resin to produce a useful filler material which can be used where weight is a premium. May be filed and sanded to smooth contours with minimum effort.

Vermiculite

Better-known as a loft insulating material it consists of beads of 'popped' mica which may be mixed to a dough with polyester resin to produce a cheap high-bulk filler suitable for use in skeg and hollow keel sections.

Glass fibre materials

Before embarking upon the descriptions of glass fibre materials and their uses it is worth reminding you that due to metrication we are in a state of flux so far as weights and measures are concerned.

Thus some moulders (and sellers) talk in Imperial terms of ounces per square yard for woven rovings and ounces per square foot for CSM—slightly confusing to say the least. This confusion is avoided under the metric system with one common designation of grams per square metre (gm/m^2). Note that resins are sometimes referred to in pounds weight—but you will probably be sold them in litres. All countries will sooner or later be on the metric system and these anomalies will then disappear. In any event, use only marine-grade (E glass) materials to British Standards or equivalent.

Chopped strand mat

This looks like a thin filter-pad type material made from short lengths of glass fibres held together by a binder (Fig. 39). The actual fibres are 1—2 inches (25–50 mm) long, and the binder is a bonding resin used to hold the fibres together during handling and moulding. CSM is the one low-cost general-purpose reinforcement material used by the trade today. Various thicknesses are available from 300–900 gm/m^2—approximating to 1–3 oz/ft^2. For general fitting-out work it is best to standardise on 450 gm/m^2 ($1\frac{1}{2}$ oz/ft^2) since this is a convenient weight to handle and wet out with resin. With a resin-to-glass ratio of $2\frac{1}{2}$:1 a thickness of approximately one-sixteenth of an inch is produced—or around 1.5 mm, for each layer.

CSM provides a good lay-up with especially good interlayer bonding, since its fibres interlock with those of adjacent reinforcings. It also has equal strength properties in all directions and may be moulded into fairly complicated surfaces without difficulty. It should be kept in a warm, dry place to prevent moisture take-up which will adversely affect the laminate. It needs to be protected from dirt and dust for the same reasons.

Woven rovings

These consist of a loose cloth-like material produced from bundles of continuous glass fibres (Fig. 39). Weights available are from 200–960 gm/m² and the flattened bundles of fibres are not twisted or spun as in cloth; instead they are woven in relatively large squares. Used where high tensile strength combined with flexibility is required and must always be used in combinations with CSM.

Rovings

Comprise non-woven strands of non-twisted bundles of glass fibres. Supplied on reels for use with special chopping and resin-spraying equipment and therefore not really suited to amateur use. Rovings may be used to produce mouldings with high-strength properties in one direction. Rovings are specified by the number of ends, or strands, in the bundle—60 being the most common.

Glass fibre fabric (or cloth)

Available in open-, or close-weave types (Fig. 39), the latter used in thin lay-ups where a high degree of flexibility in a good surface finish is required. Open-weave, or 'scrim', has better draping characteristics and is used where maximum strength and adhesion are needed. Both of these materials are mostly employed for sheathing applications.

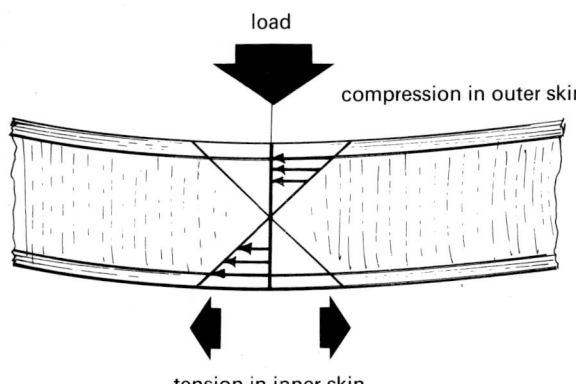

load

compression in outer skin

tension in inner skin

FIG. 41. *The principle of the sandwich deck is shown here. A suitable core material is combined with two layers of resinglass laminate to provide extra stiffness. Note how compression on one side of the sandwich is transformed to tension at the other face. For this to be satisfactory it is essential that both resinglass layers are perfectly bonded to the core material.*

Chopped strands

Supplied in tins or bags according to quantity and comprise short random lengths of glass fibres which may be mixed with pre-catalysed resin to form a gap-filling dough. The same filler may be made in small amounts by teasing scraps of CSM apart.

Surface tissue

May be used to produce a smooth finish on a CSM lay-up. Also used as a membrane to reinforce resin-rich surfaces such as gel-coats. May also be used to improve the final waxed gel-coat resin in moulded water-tanks and the like. Note that the 'hairy' side of this very thin material (300 gm/m²) is laid down into the resin while the dressed shiny side produces the smooth exterior.

Glass fibre tapes

Used extensively in 'stitch-and-glue' plywood small-boat construction. A woven material rather like a loose bandage with selvedges for strength. Available in widths from 1–6 inches (25–150 mm) wide this material is useful as a repair bandage, edging or joining strip.

Other special tapes which comprise uni-directional continuous rovings lightly woven may be used to produce high tensile frames and stiffeners when used in conjunction with CSM.

Core materials

Some boat-builders and moulders use core materials to produce a sandwich laminate which consists of layers of resinglass on either side of a layer of foamed plastic or end-grain balsa wood. Such a sandwich (Fig. 41) is lighter and stiffer than just layers of resinglass necessary to produce a comparable laminate. This combination of lightness and stiffness makes this form of construction very suitable for deck and cockpit areas where the designer is seeking to reduce weight. Sandwich construction is also used to produce one-off hulls—but these are unlikely to be available for the back-yard amateur to complete. Nonetheless foams may be useful in a number of ways and therefore cannot be entirely ignored.

Polyvinylchloride (pvc)

This is generally used as a structural hull material and you are most likely to find it under the 'Airex' brand name. Made in Switzerland, Airex comes in various densities and is an air-expanded material—no chemical blowing agents are used in the manufacturing process and thus there is no chance of resin contamination with the possibility of poor results through incompatibility. Note that PVC foam is a closed-cell material and this means that it will not absorb water since each cell consists of a separate compartment entirely isolated from its neighbour.

Polyurethane

This foamed-core material is slightly inferior to PVC in several respects, but being another closed-cell material and available in various densities, it is a practical material both for custom-building and fitting-out. It can be used in strip form to produce 'top-hat' reinforcements for moulded structures (Fig. 40). Immune to rot and water take-up and readily available, polyurethane foam is also cheaper then PVC.

In addition to pre-formed sheet material, polyurethane foam may be produced 'on site' by two-part packs. These consist of two liquids which when mixed together produce a rigid brown foam suitable for buoyancy tanks etc. Not suitable for use as a custom-boat building material since its cell structure is random in nature and its density is unpredictable too. (See also notes on *Safety*).

Polystyrene

This commonly-found insulating material is widely used by the packaging industry and is thus readily available—often for free. It is unfortunately unsuitable for marine use since the material is readily dissolved by the styrene content of polyester laminating resins. It can however be protected to some extent by painting over with a thick glue such as Cascamite which must be allowed to cure dry before the resin is applied. Minimal use—perhaps (if protected) for top-hat stringer sections.

Wood

This versatile material is found in a wide range of hulls

and superstructures as a load-bearing reinforcement. Ideally wood so used should be of a durable hardwood-type with good rot-resistance for, should it swell through water absorption, it could distort the laminate. If you use softwoods protect them with a preservative—use a non-copper-based type such as International Paints' Intertox—for copper prevents polyester resins curing properly.

One of the problems encountered in using wood structurally as a core material is that there is a large discrepancy between the elasticity of wood and the resinglass laminate. This may lead to failure of the laminate if it is severely deformed. The same characteristics apply equally to laminates incorporating metal reinforcements. Notes on using wood for fitting out are referred to later.

Balsa

A core material which is widely used by the boat-building industry both for custom-sandwich hulls and superstructures and also to produce stiff light deck panels. Sandwich lay-ups may be used for relatively large, almost flat, areas. The bond between both layers of the laminate and its core material—whatever the type—is of paramount importance if the overall strength and rigidity of the structure is to be realised. Balsa may be used in sheet form, but the most common material comprises small blocks of end-grain balsa stuck onto a light scrim. This material has a higher compressive strength than sheet balsa and can also be draped around fairly complex curves without undue difficulty. During construction the balsa should become impregnated and encapsulated with resin thus making it impervious to water take-up and possibly decay.

Other materials
Carbon fibres

An exotic reinforcement unlikely to be used in average production craft. It is a high-technology material which was developed for the aero-space industry. Although used for special one-off racers its use for the amateur is nil.

C-flex

Strictly a boat-building material and resembles rods of

resinglass with alternate bundles of glass fibre rovings combined by two layers of open-weave cloth. These 'planks' come off the roll and are self-supporting and thus may be arranged over a fairly simple framework (or 'moulds' used in the traditional boat-building sense). C-flex will accommodate compound curves without too much difficulty by arranging the rods closer together or further apart as required and once in place the material is 'hardened' by the application of a very low-shrink polyester resin. Temporary fastenings are then withdrawn and the hull is laid up with combinations of CSM and woven rovings. A large amount of filling and sanding is necessary to achieve a satisfactory finish—although just how much depends upon the initial fairness of the batten-mould and the experience of the laminators. This material is not needed for fitting out a basic moulded hull but, it could be used to custom-build a superstructure on the hull of your choice—or perhaps spurred on by the ease with which you completed your mouldings you might be tempted to go the whole-hog and build something bigger!

Paper rope

This forming-material comes in a range of sizes up to about $1\frac{1}{2}$ inches (38 mm) across, and in the larger sizes is suitable for forming ribs and other reinforcements in hulls and under decks. Although called 'rope' it is in fact a 'D' section with a wire core to enable it to be pre-bent to conform to the curve of the hull (Fig 42). It is a cheaper alternative to PVC and polyurethane foam.

Other similar materials may be used for the basis of top-hat stiffening sections. For instance paper tubes may be cut down their middle and then snipped with a series of cuts to enable them to expand, or contract, as required to fit the hull (Fig. 43). Wooden strips can be sprung against the hull and glassed in place before more CSM is added to provide a sturdy section.

Acetone

An indespensible liquid which is used for cleaning rollers, tools and brushes. Also used when preparing laminate surfaces for subsequent bonding work. It is a highly volatile material which becomes dangerous in certain circumstances. See additional notes under *Safety*.

The foregoing range of materials may seem daunting at first reading. While it is true that a certain understanding of the materials involved in modern boat-building is desirable together with what is meant by such terms as 'sandwich-construction', the basic components necessary to complete a hull are few. The following list is about all you will need unless your prowess and ambition increase to the extent where you are contemplating making your own mouldings. Laminating resin, catalyst, CSM, acetone and an 'over-the-counter' putty such as Plastic Padding, or your own mix. Not a long list is it?

Some basic tools

There are some tools which are essential when completing from scratch, and a few others which are desirable. Grouped under this heading you will also find what might be better described as utensils.

Three soft plastic buckets or similar containers. The cheapest generally seem to be the softest in formulation, and that is an advantage for when the resin left-overs cure in the bottom the best way to remove it is by beating the bucket on the outside with a stick. Alternatively one-gallon icecream containers are suitable, as are any other plastic containers which will hold 4 or 5 pounds (2 kg) of resin.

One, or two pairs of scissors. Those with long blades sold for paper-hanging are ideal.

A selection of one-, and two-inch (25/50 mm) paint

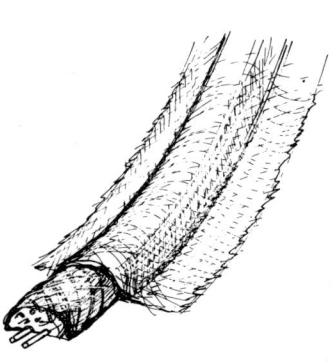

◄ *FIG. 42. Paper-rope may be used to produce internal stiffener sections. Three or four layers of $1\frac{1}{2}$ oz (450 gm/m²) CSM make a thickness of around 0.125 inches (3 mm), depending upon resin content.*

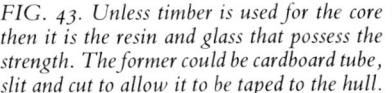

FIG. 43. Unless timber is used for the core ► *then it is the resin and glass that possess the strength. The former could be cardboard tube, slit and cut to allow it to be taped to the hull.*

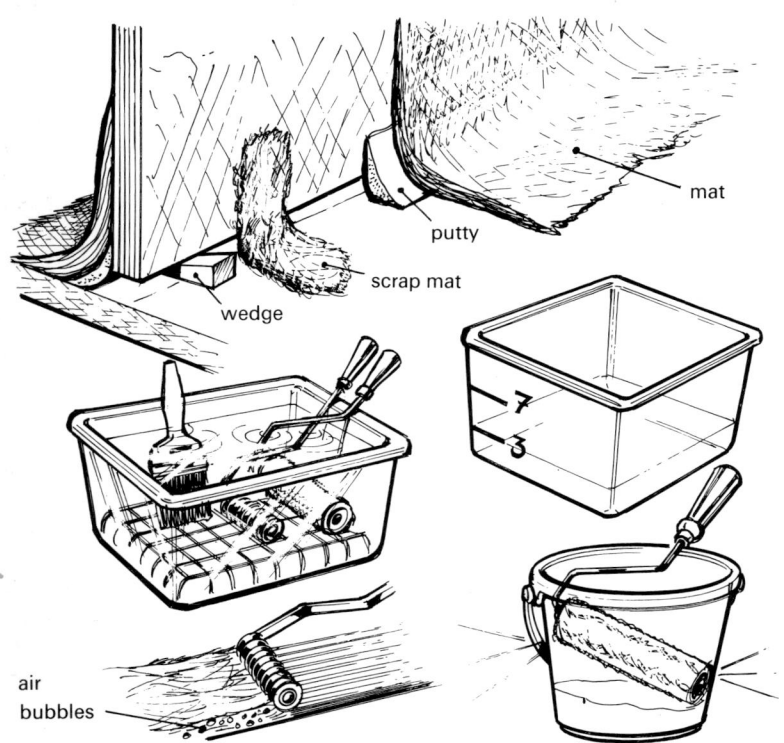

FIG. 44. *Working with resin and glass. Bulkheads and furniture should be kept clear of the hull. A resin container may be batch-marked to save weighing out resin. Buckets are OK for brushes, but not for rollers. Note that grooved-rollers are needed to consolidate a lay-up. Tools stood on a grid in the acetone 'bath' are almost self-cleaning.*

PHOTO. 5. *The resin and glass lay-up must be consolidated with rollers such as these to remove any air bubbles and also drive the fibres from one layer of glass into the next. Interlaminar bonds are hard, if not impossible, to achieve with layers of woven rovings.*

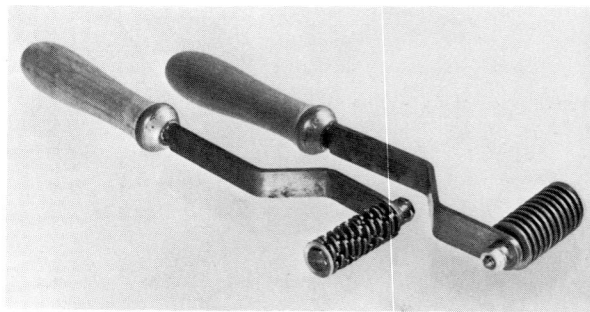

brushes preferably with non-painted handles—the paint bubbles off in the resin and makes a mess. Better still are the special white bristled laminating brushes. Six of each size well-looked after will complete a 30 footer.

Steel disc rollers—or 'parsley choppers'—used to force the air out and consolidate the laminate (Fig. 44). You will need two three-inch (75 mm) rollers. (Photo. 5).

Kitchen scales are necessary to weigh out the resin batches. However if you weigh out several increments and mark the side of your container accordingly you need then only pour in the correct amount. (Fig. 44).

A special 15 or 60 milli-litre plastic auto-dispenser for the catalyst. While a 'slurp' of catalyst will cure the resin it may also be too much, or too little, and thus affect the bucket-life of the mix. Alternatively a 2 or 10 ml syringe may be purchased from your resin supplier.

The CSM should be kept on a roller-stand with provision for cutting it. Nothing very grand is needed—the one shown in figure 45 is basically made up from a broomstick, softwood scraps and a piece of hardboard. It is well worth taking the trouble to make one.

An electric power-drill is an essential tool. Fit it with a wheel-type paddle and you can use it to stir batches of resin and thoroughly distribute the catalyst through it. Take care not to splash it about! If you are dealing with only small quantities—say under two pounds, then stirring with a flat stick will suffice.

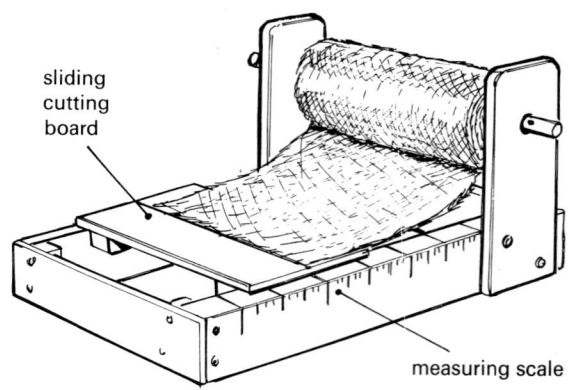

FIG. 45. *Not quite a luxury . . . more a useful tool. A cutting board for glass reinforcements may be easily fabricated from cheap materials. Protect the glass from dirt and moisture.*

A jig-saw, or as some people prefer a 'sabre-saw' is in my opinion indispensable. I got through two low-cost ones and have nothing but praise for them. Use metal-cutting blades for sawing resinglass. Special blades are available but they are expensive and unless you have large amounts of trimming to do—say around the sheer of a complete set of mouldings—the extra expense cannot be justified. Good quality blades should be selected and ordinary woodworking blades are quite adequate for most hardwoods, soft and sheet plywood.

You will also need a good selection of scrapers and putty-knives to shape resin putty to neat radii and help form generous-sized fillets as required.

A 'scratcher' (Fig 46) is essential to roughen the interior surface of the laminate locally to where you are bonding, or glassing-in. The drawing shows how to make such an implement using masonry nails and a suitable piece of hardwood. Alternatively the handle, or tang, of a file may be heated bright red, bent over and then quenched out in water. It then needs grinding up to a fairly sharp point (Fig. 47).

Other tools needed are those required for general woodworking—a couple of saws—ripping and crosscut—chisels, screwdrivers, drill bits, countersinks, sharp knife, and the hundred or so others you already (hopefully) have.

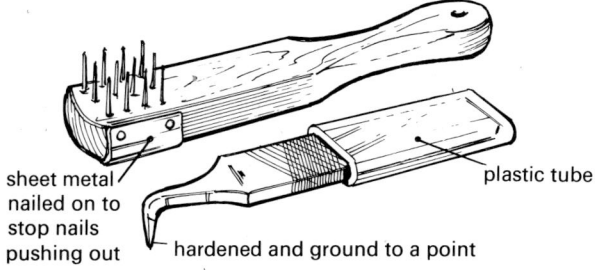

sheet metal nailed on to stop nails pushing out

plastic tube

hardened and ground to a point

FIG. 46. 'Scratchers' are needed to roughen up the hull laminate and enable new resin and glass lay-ups to 'hitch on'. Masonary nails, or an old file (FIG. 47), may be used as outlined here.

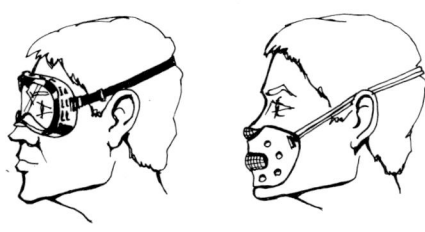

FIG. 48. Lungs and eyes need protection—hands too. Remember that you are dealing with some extremely nasty chemicals. See also notes on SAFETY.

Personal protection

Polyester resin and its associated chemicals must be treated with caution. Catalyzed resin smears on clothing are impossible to remove and so it is wise to wear coveralls, or very old clothes which may be thrown away when they become too stiff to wear. Wear a face-mask and goggles to protect your lungs and eyes when sawing and power-sanding resinglass (Fig. 48). The fine airborne filaments of glass pose a long-term health hazard. At the very best they are simply irritating—at the worst they are carcinogenic. Rub protective hand creams thoroughly between your fingers and use special resin-removing creams for cleaning yourself.

An old cap is another good idea; resin is the very devil to remove from your hair. Remedial action must be fast or its down to the barbershop!

Footwear needs to be old and scruffy. Some composite soles are attacked by resin and leave black marks wherever you step. Old deck shoes seem OK, but whatever you wear it will soon grow an extra thickness of resin and glass fibres. Plastic bags worn over your shoes will protect them but this arrangement may be unbearably hot in the summer.

Safety

THE FOLLOWING NOTES SOMETIMES REITERATE WHAT HAS ALREADY BEEN WRITTEN. I MAKE NO APOLOGY FOR YOU ARE DEALING WITH MATERIALS WHICH ARE DANGEROUS AND TOXIC, AND THUS THE NEED FOR CAUTION CANNOT BE TOO OFTEN STRESSED—EVEN THOUGH THE CHAP SELLING YOU THE MATERIALS MAY ATTEMPT TO GLOSS OVER ASPECTS OF SAFETY.

CATALYZED resin is toxic if swallowed and dangerous should splashes enter the eyes. The MEKP catalyst is a powerful oxidising agent. Wash out the eyes in continuously running water for at least 15 minutes and simultaneously SEEK URGENT MEDICAL ASSISTANCE. Do not apply oil-based eyedrops for that may worsen the situation. This washing out procedure is necessary, although even more urgently should splashes of neat catalyst enter the eyes, if blindness is to be avoided. Never wipe the eyes or lids with fingers which have recently been handling catalyst and resin. Do not wipe spills of catalyst with cloth or paper tissues since they will start to smoulder. Instead wash away with fresh water. General laminating resin will burn fiercely with choking smoke once it is well alight.

ACETONE is a dangerous material since it will burn readily and has a flash-point of -9°C (14°F). Its vapours will thus explode in contact with a naked flame and smoking must be banned from the vicinity too. The fumes will also give you a hangover, or headache. Not suitable for removing resin from skin since it will also remove the natural oils and cause dermatitis.

STYRENE fumes will explode if they too meet a naked-flame, or even the red-hot element of an electric space-heater. Prolonged breathing in high concentrations is not to be recommended since, like acetone, the fumes cause headaches and nausea. Styrene is also a respiratory irritant and may also affect the eyes—though not permanently.

PRE-ACCELERATED RESINS are the only ones which you should use since they eliminate the need to handle the cobalt accelerator. Should you open a can of resin and find a layer of purple liquid floating on its surface that could be the accelerator. Mix it thoroughly into the resin before adding the catalyst. If the cobalt accelerator and the MEKP catalyst come into contact an explosion will result!

ALL CHEMICALS should be stored out of the reach of small children. That includes the resins and any special cleaners used. Instruct all your helpers—especially the casual ones—about the possible dangers of any materials they may be handling.

CUTTING and grinding resinglass produces a severely irritating dust. Wear goggles and a dust filter-mask. Do not breathe down large amounts of filler-powder.

DO NOT LET large amounts of resin cure in buckets or paper-cups. Spread the waste resin out in a thin layer so that there is no risk of its exothermic reaction starting a fire. That may seem hard to believe at this stage but once you have experienced the heat of an over-catalysed batch of resin you will appreciate the need for caution.

SPILLS of catalyst should be washed away with water. Keep a squeezy bottle handy for just this job. Do not wipe up with rags or paper-tissues since the MEKP will start them smouldering.

NEVER PUT into your pockets rags which have been soaked in acetone—severe skin burns could result.

WHEN YOU have been handling CSM and other glass fibre materials wash first in tepid water to prevent skin irritation. A hot-wash tends to open surface pores and let microscopic pieces of glass enter and start itching.

UNLIKE epoxy resins the polyester resins used for boat-building and fitting-out do not usually cause skin-allergies provided that normal care is taken.

READ ALL maker's instructions thoroughly before using their product. If in doubt seek further information and advice.

How to pick a moulder

Not all moulders will supply hulls with certificates and in many cases you are on your own when it comes to judging 'quality'. There are however several things that you could check out before actually committing yourself to buying any particular set of mouldings, or kit.

For example ask the builder for the names and addresses of some satisfied customers. Then follow them up with letters or perhaps a visit and discuss your plans with them. Most DIY enthusiasts are only too willing to chew the fat, and many sound ideas can be gained in this way.

Some enlightened moulders actually hand out invitations to visit their factory and see how things are done. Others run a newsletter through which ideas can be swapped, and some, more established classes of boats may even have an owner's association. The more responsible the attitude of the moulders the more confident you should feel when it comes to writing out that cheque.

But should you in fact write a cheque? Perhaps in view of the large sums of money involved you should conduct your business through a legal representative who acts as stake-holder. Should the moulder object to this arrangement perhaps it might be wiser to go elsewhere.

While it may not be necessary to check up on the credit-worthiness of the company with which you may intend doing business a few discreet enquiries may be made. Most of the larger companies are members of a trade association, and many also deal with other large companies; resin suppliers for example. They may be reluctant to talk about other peoples business, but even so you may get results. There are also other possible sources; libraries keep records of court judgements for debts. It certainly does no harm to ask around, and it may even save you making an expensive mistake.

If you visit your moulder, and I strongly urge you to, then keep your eyes open for trouble. Points against him would be dirty, scruffy workplaces with slap-dash staff. So too would moulds stored in the open, drums of resin stacked up outside in the cold, and semi-finished mouldings standing in the open with water collecting in them. All the above pointers could indicate inferior mouldings: do not waste time on them.

Ask a few 'knowing' questions about his stock control—good practice is to have batches of reinforcement cut up and labelled ready for use in the mould. If the laminator goes to a roll and helps himself it could be a sign of sloppiness and indicate a potentially bad moulding. The relationship between resin and glass fibre is a closely controlled one. Too little resin (resin-starved) and the moulding is weak. The converse is also true in that a resin-rich lay-up is also a weak one. Thus stock control is important both in terms of cost and strength.

Unless a moulding is to be post-cured by keeping it at an elevated temperature for a number of hours, it should stay in its mould for several days. Premature removal will cause distortions from which the hull will never recover, it is also liable to chill the exposed gel-coat and possibly produce an inferior surface.

This means that a responsible moulder has several moulds in use at any one time. In fact much of the initial fitting out is performed while the boat is still in its mould. For example, bulkheads may be attached, and much of the furniture installed before the hull is removed from its mould and the superstructure added.

Take a look at the moulding itself. If the hull below the waterline is laid up using non-pigmented gel-coat resin—and I would always advocate this—you could visually check for air bubbles and dry patches of laminate. This may be done by shining a strong light at the moulding while viewing from the inside. Whitish patches (dry reinforcements), blotches and small flecks (air bubbles) could mean trouble. With a coloured gel-coat these are harder to detect but nonetheless it is still possible.

Look around the inside of the moulding and see how the material has been applied. All the glass mats should be inserted so as to provide overlaps which are staggered along the hull and barely noticeable. Pronounced ridges at around 3 foot (900 mm) intervals are not ideal for this means that areas of potential weakness have been built in if the laminator has failed to consolidate his lay up properly. Areas of reinforcement should overlap and it is worth while watching an operative in a moulding shop at work—does he overlap them or butt them up? That last part of the question may be a strange one but it has been done. . . .

While you are looking at the hull note how the reinforcements are stored. Are they exposed and picking up moisture and dust, or covered with plastic sheeting? Check too that any internal moulded ribs and stringers are nicely made and, especially if wood is used, that the ends are feathered to prevent a sudden change in section and hence a stress point.

Try to get a look at a hull and superstructure joined together. This is a critical operation as has already been clear. Check carefully at the transom and stem for it is in the confines of the ends that a slapdash job is often made. Working in cramped quarters with a bucket of resin is a nasty job!

More than one boat to my certain knowledge has had its foredeck start to peel upwards under the pull of the loads in its forestay!

One of the exciting operations in a moulding shop is releasing the finished moulding from its mould. Actually after a while the novelty wears off, but if you haven't seen it then you are missing something. You may also be shocked at the brute force that is sometimes employed.

Large hammers banging on the outside of the mould send unfair shock-waves into the moulding and should not be condoned—even though the moulder may assure you that it is common practice. A well-designed and prepared mould should release its moulding with the minimum of effort. Sometimes warm water is pumped in at the lowest part of the mould to break the 'vacuum'. A better arrangement is to blow air into several points to assist removal. All much gentler than that big hammer!

As the moulding comes out a few minor blemishes may be seen and these are by and large acceptable. A small amount of gel-coat resin, tape and a quick rub over will soon correct the fault. Other problems are not so easily solved.

A wrinkled looking gel-coat means that the gel-coat was undercured and attacked by the styrene in the following laminating resins. It could also result from styrene loss through undercure—perhaps not enough catalyst was used, or more probably the mould or resin was too cold.

Sometimes the gel-coat resin breaks away from the moulding in large scabs. This may be the result of a gel-coat resin which was too 'hot' or wrongly formulated so giving a fast cure. Alternatively the cause could be contamination by airborne particles, especially in the case where the resin was applied at the end of the working day and left overnight before laying-up commenced. Poor adhesion may also be caused by failure on the part of the operator to consolidate the laminate to the gel-coat.

Very occasionally one encounters 'fish-eyes'. If you try to paint over a surface which has been sprayed with a silicone polish then you will know all about 'fish-eyes'. In the case of mouldings they look like small holes, and sometimes larger cavities, in the surface of the gel-coat. Probable cause is too much release agent in the mould. More rarely it is caused by using a resin which did not flow out. In other words its viscosity was too low.

Before we leave the subject of gel-coats there is one

last area to consider. Ideally the gel-coat needs to be around 15–20 thou (0.5 mm) and applied by brush in two coats. Thickness gauges are available for checking this—ask your moulder if he has one. . . .

SEAMASTER 925
Designed for fast cruising the Seamaster 925 has a high-aspect ratio rig and large genoa. With a U-shaped dinette in her main cabin she has room for six berths and normally fits a single-cylinder Volvo diesel. Designed by Holman & Pye, builders of the 925 are Seamaster Ltd, 20 Ongar Road, Great Dunmow, Essex, Mouldings to various stages are available.

Length overall   28.25 feet
Length waterline   22.6 feet
Beam   9.9 feet
Draft   5 feet (fin).
Displacement   8,960 lb
Ballast   3,640 lb
Sail area   323 feet.

4

Some further design considerations

The stresses which occur around the mast are considerable even in a modest-sized boat. When you're beating to windward in a good blow it's no time to wonder whether the deck will depress to such an extent that the mast will bow sideways and break about its spreaders! When the boat is at rest the only loads that need to be catered for are simply the weight of the mast standing on the deck, and the additional compressive loads imposed upon it by the slight tension in the standing rigging. Once the sails are hoisted and the wind pressure heels the boat, these loads increase rapidly: they escalate even more as the boat starts pitching into a head-sea. This means that the structure needs to be capable of withstanding compressive and tensile stresses which may amount to several tons in a 28-footer. (Fig. 4).

If the mast is deck-stepped—as most are today—then a continuous bulkhead with adequate bonding to hull and decks will be strong enough to withstand the crushing loads caused by both the mast and its rigging. 'Crushing' is used deliberately, for the mast is trying to drive down through the deck and the rigging wire, although in tension, is acting at some distance from the centreline of the mast and its resultant action is to try and pinch the sides of the boat in. A ring type bulkhead under the mast is ideally suited to resisting all these forces at work in this area. Unfortunately such a continuous bulkhead is not really feasible in a modest-sized cruising boat unless she has excessive headroom for one needs to put a door through into the forecabin. The breached bulkhead then needs beefing up to replace the lost strength and this is easily done by building in stiffeners which form the door jambs and lintel. If two half-bulkheads are used then they need a substantial beam-member to join them at the top and also a stout-sectioned web across the boat to unite them at the bottom. (Fig. 33). The beam needs to be well bolted to the bulkheads and with a good fit against the underside of the deck. Knees should preferably be fitted and hitched into the cabin sides down to side-deck level.

Many designers seem to favour two pairs of half-bulkheads in this area. (Fig. 49). Placed about three feet apart and well braced with strong frameworks they form the sides of the WC compartment and also hanging space opposite. Some builders incorporate a raised plinth in the decks which accommodates a beam running fore-and-aft and sitting on two of the half, or part-bulkheads. This raised moulding also takes the base of the mast-pot or tabernacle.

If you have the mouldings supplier fit the rubbing strake then he will also have to fit the chainplates if they are of the external strap type. They may however be of the inverted U-bolt variety which type I do not personally favour for while they can be used professionally by builders who know what they are about they may conversely be abused by an amateur who fails to see the need to strengthen the hull deck area and provide adequate backing-up.

If the decks are of sandwich construction they will need special treatment. First remove the internal resinglass layer for at least six inches all round the position of the U-bolt and then take out the inner core material. The remaining laminate needs increasing in thickness by a factor of at least three with care being taken that its edges overlap the inside resinglass layer by at least 3 inches (75 mm). A plywood pad half an inch thick (12 mm) at least and covering the entire area must be fitted before the U-bolt is finally inserted. You cannot fit the U-bolt directly through the sandwich without going through this procedure or it will locally deform the deck, damage the core and eventually pull through under sailing loads. (Fig. 50).

If the deck is a single layer laminate in the area in which you intend to fit a U-bolt then unless it coincides with a special area—the toe-rail for example, it will need reinforcing with extra layers of resin and glass until it is twice as thick (Fig. 51). A pad must then be fitted to spread the load. Once again I would recommend it be at least $\frac{1}{2}$ inch (12 mm) thick plywood. Note that its periphery needs to be feathered to prevent a hard-spot which might cause the laminate to crack along an

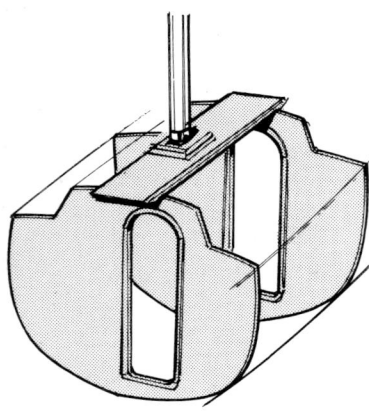

FIG. 49. A pair of bulkheads are often incorporated under the mast to form a strong 'beam' section. A w.c. compartment and wardrobe usually complete the arrangement. Note the underdeck beam which transmits compression from the mast into the bulkheads.

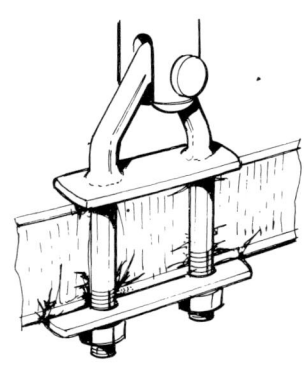

FIG. 50. A sandwich lay-up cannot accommodate high localized compression loads—while you may safely walk on one mechanical fasteners will crush the core.

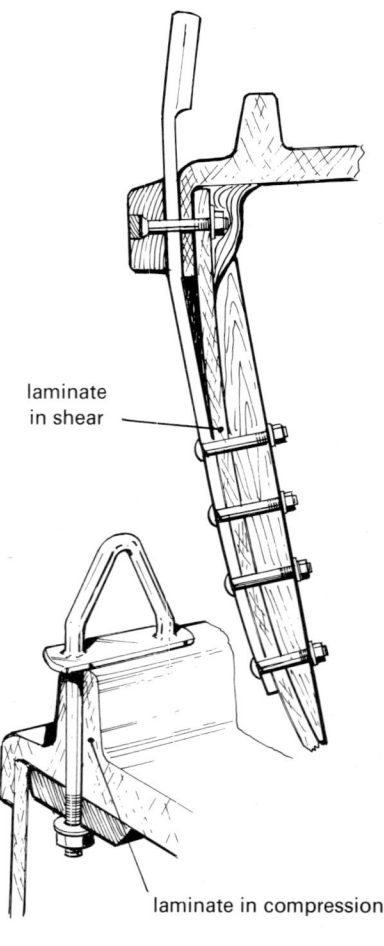

laminate in shear

laminate in compression

PHOTO. 6. We thought out the interior with sticks of 2 × 1 (50 × 25 mm), and since we had already bought such components as the toilet, and cooker, we knew just how much room to allow.

PHOTO. 7. Tongue & grooved hardwood looks nice when it's finished—but it is very time-consuming compared to sheet material. Here the locker access has been cut and the closing strips applied.

FIG. 51. Sometimes special arrangements by way of the toe-rail moulding may enable an inverted U-bolt 'chain-plate' to be used. Personally I favour the simple strap-type which may be easily fitted and through-bolted.

otherwise sharp edge. Should you attempt to bolt fittings directly through the laminate without this extra work then you run the risk of crushing the resin content of the laminate—remember that a long-handled spanner on a $\frac{1}{2}$ inch nut and bolt will produce a crushing load in excess of three tons!

Outside chainplates are the easiest (and cheapest) to fit and the metal straps used for them need to be bolted through substantial wooden pads. (Fig. 51). Alternatively special brackets may be fabricated to pick up on the chainplate fasteners and distribute the loads into some strong part of the structure—the bulkheads or special knees for example. Internal chainplates may also be fitted, passing through the deck just inside the hull laminate. They can also coincide with special arrangements—brackets and the like—well bonded to the hull. Internal chainplates need special rubber boots to keep them truely watertight and avoid drips. . . .

The inability of resinglass to resist direct crushing without damage means that you cannot bolt, or screw anything to it without taking ample precautions first. You will have gathered that bulkheads and other items need bonding-in with layers of glass fibre material and resin. They cannot be fastened with large screws passing through the hull—nor can engine beds be bolted through the hull bottom in the way they are fitted to conventionally built boats using treewood. Techniques for using mechanical fasteners are dealt with later on.

Wood for the interior

As previously outlined we designed the interior of *Solitaire* using sticks of 2 × 1 inch (50 × 25 mm) planed timber clamped roughly in place to delineate areas; the heads, galley, dinette, lockers etc (Photo. 6). This wood was not wasted for it was used to make the framework over which the cabin furniture was built. We used a mixture of plywood and tongue-and-grooved mahogany board (Photo. 7) which came via a boat-building acquaintance of long standing. The plywood came from the local timber yard. There was a temptation to opt for proper marine-grade plywood throughout but the cost difference between it and redwood-faced 'outdoor' grade plywood of the same thickness was in the order of 30 per cent. Thus we compromised and used a mixture of both types. Proper marine grade plywood in the UK is to BS 1088; outdoor grade plywood has the same type of weatherproof and boilproof glue but its inner veneers have larger gaps, and more holes and voids in them. Even so such plywood is well-suited for internal structures which are not going to be continuously soaked in water, nor going to be subjected to severe loads.

I standardized as much as possible on 9 mm plywood for bunk fronts, tops and lockers and shelves and the only trouble I met with was that 9 mm *looks* flimsy. Used as a web and prevented from buckling by a well-glued and screwed (or nailed) framework its strength is more than adequate. Its looks can be immensely improved by doubling its thickness where you see it— for instance the side of each bunk needs a fiddle to keep its mattress in place. The bunk-front may be a single layer of 9 mm plywood but the fiddle depth may be doubled using scrap offcuts. If a nice radius is worked in, along its top edge, and it is nicely swept down at the middle, the whole effect is vastly improved. (Fig. 52).

There are other ways too that will improve the visual appeal of plain plywood. Use rebated hardwood to mask the raw edge, or try thin strips of teak to conceal the edge—fasten with lots of glue and brass nails. Alternatively a solid hardwood capping piece with a rebate and bullnose could be employed. Work in a few hand-holds in the hardwood framing of a plywood bulkhead and things really start to look 'professional'. (Fig. 53).

As supplied the moulded hull should be able to absorb sailing stresses without recourse to much extra reinforcements. You will however need to fasten bunk and settee tops to longitudinal stringers glassed into the hull and if used as described on page 54 they will add considerably to the overall strength of the boat. It also makes good sense to bond the cabin furniture into the hull to provide a series of webs which also add strength. (Fig. 54). If you adopt this procedure—and you have to fix things down somehow or other—it makes each and every locker you form water-tight—or very nearly so. This has its drawbacks for should water enter a locker from above it

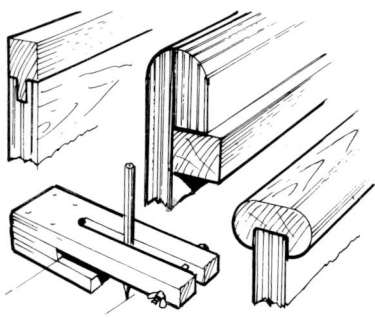

FIG. 52. Plywood furniture looks infinitely better if the thickness of visible edges is doubled up as shown here.

FIG. 53. Hardwood mouldings may be used to give a 'finished' appearance to plywood furniture. Note the marking gauge which helps line up screw holes for a neat job.

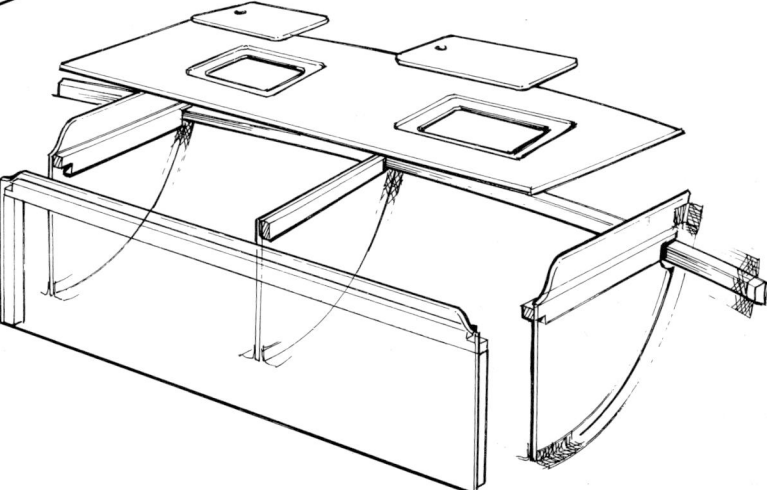

FIG. 54. All you need to make a settee berth. Glassed into the hull, such a structure helps to brace the boat.

will stay there! An alternative to bonding the actual furniture to the hull is to use instead a series of small webs to which the furniture is bolted, or screwed. The webs may be thin plywood, or even oil-tempered hardboard with 2 × 1 inch (50 × 25 mm) strips of timber fixed to their top edge. If three layers of CSM are used to glass them in then the resulting web will be a strong pick-up point. (Fig. 55).

Solitaire has a double-berth in the fore-cabin and the side of this coincides exactly with the moulded centreline of the hull. Thus a strong vertical web running from the main bulkhead and supported by other cross-webs reinforces this stressed area (Photo. 8). The cross-webs are in fact the divisions needed to make lockers under the double-berth. They are glassed to the hull and make good deep water-tight lockers. The volume under this berth is divided into three; the foremost being an extension of the chain-locker. The centre one is a general purpose locker with top access, and the third unit is a combination of the general and particular in that although it also has top-access under the mattress, it also has a pull-out 'hopper' locker for holding small items of personal gear.

Drawers are difficult to make nicely—though not impossible I hasten to add—while I reckon that anyone can make a hopper. (See also Fig. 56). You need to take into account a few factors; firstly as the hinge is at the bottom the sides cannot be rectangular like a drawer for they have to swing through an arc (Photo. 9). Now an observant reader will have gathered that the sides of most boats are not vertical, they comprise an arc too. Thus a well-proportioned hopper will fit the boat better than a drawer, and for less work. The arc through which the hopper will swing is determined by the vertical distance from the centreline of the hinge and the top of the opening which is cut in the bunk side. This means that when the hopper is closed the back of it is lower than the front which means that you need something— wooden slats—to hold its contents in place. This need becomes more acute as the boat heels. (Fig. 56).

Framing up the hopper is simple—no need for fancy joints—just lots of glue, and instead of screws I used those silicon-bronze barbed-ring nails. The piece of wood cut from the bunk front forms the back of the hopper and if it is raised an inch at the back it makes a positive stop. A new, larger piece of plywood is needed to make the front, while the sides are scrounged from that heap of offcuts you are too mean to throw away. In fact my offcuts got progressively smaller until all that was left were a few crumbs and a couple of pieces suitable to make backing pads with.

There is no need to fit a handle to the hopper—a neat hand hole is safer and cheaper. Similarly there is no real need to fit a catch for the loaded hopper is self-closing

since its centre of gravity is working well behind the hinge. This hopper on *Solitaire* worked so well I built another against the hull under the vanitory unit (Photo. 10).

Nearly all the cutting I performed was made with a jigsaw. Woodworking is not my *forte*, but this tool with its facility for cutting square or at angles, greatly improved my expertise.

Fine-toothed blades are best for cutting plywood, especially across the grain of the top laminate where a coarse-blade would raise a series of splinters. While on the subject of jigsaws, or sabre-saws as some people call them, remember that you are dealing with dusty-materials and that the cooling air intakes may quickly become blocked and the saw overheated. A periodic clean will extend the tool's life considerably, more so if you oil it as directed from time to time.

All the joints I used while fitting out were simple, and I really do mean SIMPLE. The halving joint is prominent in my repertoire and where I need to join two horizontals and a vertical I go for a 'notching-plus-a-halving' (stopped) joint. I have even been known to get carried away with enthusiasm and make a 'mitred-halving-joint' But it really seems to be over-elaborate, and anyway no one sees them for they are hidden behind the plywood facing. (Fig. 57).

Long-notched (or stopped) scarfs defeat me, as do comb joints and stopped-dovetails. I can plane strips of plywood to form a scarf, but it is much quicker to use a butt-strap. A decent butt joint on plywood needs to run for about 4 inches (100 mm) on either side and lots of glue and clenched nails make a very strong job.

Although one needs to countersink holes on the reverse side of plywood panels to ensure a good clean glue-line the obverse side does not need touching. Instead the head of a countersunk screw will pull the top veneer down sufficiently for the head to finish flush. In fact if you attempt to countersink plywood on the 'good' face chances are you will rip some of the ply surface out and make a ragged-looking job. (Fig. 58).

I used a water-mixed urea formaldehyde glue for all the internal furniture and although this type of adhesive is not strictly 'waterproof' it is good enough to be used for applications where the glue-line is not going to be totally immersed in water for very long periods. Of course the range of glues available to day is enormous and I'm sure you will find one that suits you. To achieve a good bond with any glue it is necessary to prepare the faying surfaces. They need abrading to remove the polish that the manufacturing process endows them with—be they planed or plywood. Coarse grit 'sand-paper' is just the job, or you could use something like a serated scraper—Skarsten market one world-wide.

All the furniture was cut a little 'shy' of the hull to

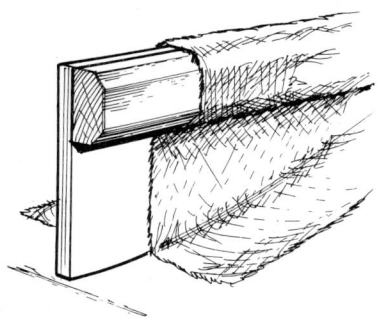

FIG. 55. *This type of web may be bonded into the hull and used to attach furniture with screws. Such an arrangement enables those items to be removed for replacement or re-finishing at home.*

PHOTO. 9. *A hopper under the forepeak berth is easier to make than a drawer and can also be opened while the user is standing very close to it. In fact a deep drawer would have been impossible to arrange is this particular situation.*

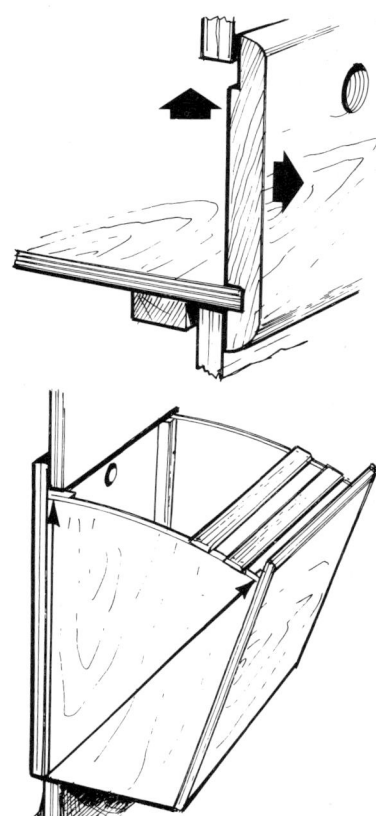

FIG. 56. *How to give a drawer a positive closure—if you arrange the necessary clearance. Also shown is the 'hopper' which offers the advantage of needing no 'foot space' even if fitted very low down in the boat. A drawer would be almost impossible to use in such a position.*

PHOTO. 8. *Vertical dividers such as this one under the forepeak double-berth serve a dual function. They divide up the volume into usable parts and also brace the hull and berth-top. This one is 'hung' on to the structure and has been cut clear of the hull to avoid a hard-spot.*

PHOTO. 10. *When closed there is about one inch (25 mm) of air space between the back of this hopper and the hull. The 'boot locker' also makes the first step up through the forehatch.*

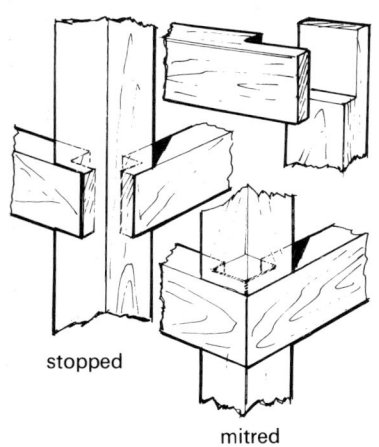

stopped

mitred

FIG. 57. *Halving joints—very simple to make and entirely adequate when clad with the rest of the furniture.*

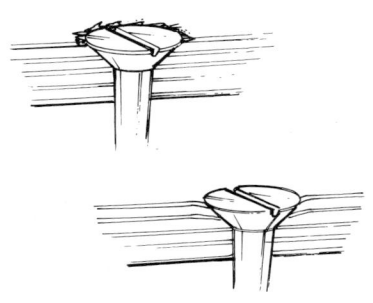

FIG. 58. *Countersinks in plywood will produce a ragged hole. Far better to let the screw head pull down into the top veneer.*

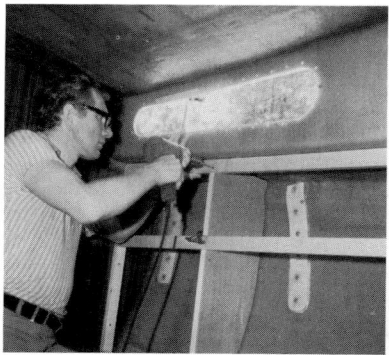

PHOTO. 11. *This vertical divider is 'hung' on the woodwork and has been cut clear of the moulding. When glassed in it will form a triple role; divide the locker space, separate the bookshelves, and act as a 'knee' to stiffen the side deck.*

PHOTO. 12. *The back of the dinette taking shape. The divider shown in PHOTO 11 has been glassed in to the hull. Note the chain plate pads.*

PHOTO. 13. *Once the t & g has been assembled dry it then has to be glued into position. I found a 'yankee' screwdriver just the tool for the many hundreds of screws that I had to drive home.*

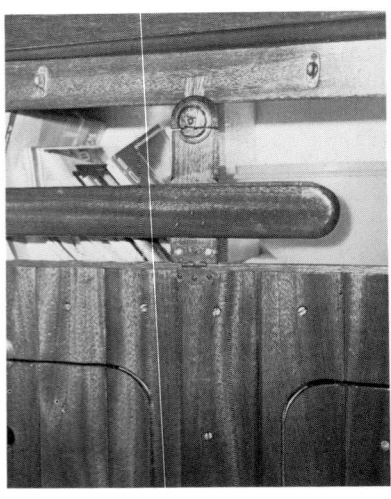

PHOTO. 14. *These bookshelves at the back of the dinette have a fold-down fiddle. The turn-button fabric fasteners are for the root-berth that is occasionally used to give an extra sleeping place.*

avoid hardspots when it was glassed-in (Photo. 11) and the hull and plywood both needed roughing up to provide a key for the resin to hitch into. This roughened area extended inwards for about four inches (100 mm) on the plywood and for about five inches (125 mm) along the hull on either side of the plywood. Masking-tape was used to hold newspaper in place to prevent splashes marking the furniture. See page 57 for a full description of working with resin and glass.

The bottom and side of the chain-locker were lined with plywood 'wear-plates' glassed in place with several layers of CSM; thus the chain is not bearing directly against the hull and any wear, or fretting, will not weaken the structure of the boat. You may feel that that is being excessively cautious—I don't! A limber hole fitted with a plastic pipe takes any water from the chain-locker down into the bilge.

When working with wood it looks neater if the nails, or screws are all in line and are also evenly spaced. It takes a few minutes longer but the end-result is that much better. The same thoughts apply to lining up the slots of any screws you use—horizontally along the boat, or up-and-down in vertical members. A simple marking-out gauge for screws can be made from scrap as figure 53 shows.

I used a lot of tongue & grooved mahogany matchboarding throughout *Solitaire* and with brass oil lamps throwing a soft light around the cabin and the gentle warmth from the stove it looks really nice. T & G is however, a very time-consuming material to use (Photo. 12) Each piece which goes into the furniture has to be positioned, measured, cut, then assembled dry to enable its mating plank to be fitted. Then when the item of furniture is finished it has to be numbered and taken

apart—then reassembled with glue. All the screwheads—I used 1 inch No. 8's or 1½ inch No. 8's throughout—should be lined up 'yacht style' (Photo. 13). As I said—all very expensive on time compared to using sheet materials. When ordering up woodscrews it is as well to standardize as much as possible since bulk-buying offers savings. As a rule of thumb the length of screw you need is three times as long as the thickness of the material you are screwing through—9 mm × 3 equals 27 mm or just over 1 inch.

All the time that this fitting of individual planks was going on there was a constant mental re-examination of the job in hand to see if it might interfere with some subsequent stage in the fitting-out programme. For instance, if you are planning to use a glassed-in plastic pipe to form a conduit, or duct, for the electrical services, then it needs to be among the first items fitted—not the last when you will have difficulty making a neat job.

Then there are those short-cuts which only become apparent in retrospect. Take the galley for example: the cabin sides and much of the boat have been clad with plywood (4 mm) to help the 'old-world-charm' look. But in addition to using plywood to mask the cabin sides I also used it to make the locker fronts for the galley. The cabin side panels are in fact held in place by the fastenings which go through the sheet acrylic (Perspex) windows and I could have continued those plywood panels down into the structure—thus forming the locker fronts as figure 59 and photographs show. The resulting job, apart from looking neater, would also have been cleaner and quicker. The same method could have been used to make the lockers behind the dinette if I had dispensed with the bookshelves (Photo. 14). As it was, the only place I put this method to use was in the small cave-lockers over the double berth in the forepeak. (Photo. 15).

Did you catch that reference back there to using the window fastenings to hold the cabin side panels too? That's an example of thinking and planning ahead.

Throughout *Solitaire* all the bunk tops, work surfaces, shelves and other horizontal areas were made from 9 mm outdoor grade plywood. Where the furniture touched the inner hull and deck mouldings it was glassed-in using no less than three layers of 1½ oz (450 gm/m²) CSM on each side. If only one side was accessible then I used five layers with one of them applied and pre-wetted before positioning as figure 68 shows. Each layer of CSM overlapped its predecessor by 1–1½ inches (25–32 mm) to avoid stress concentrations.

The saloon, or main cabin, table, is also the chart-table and is cantilevered about a vertical hardwood plank 5 × 1¼ inch (130 × 31 mm) which is fitted to a block at

Marking out bulkheads

There are several methods used for taking off shapes and by far the easiest is to ask the moulding supplier for a tracing off his set of templates. I jest, of course, for when it comes to fitting bulkheads and other members into your custom-interior I doubt that he will have templates that coincide exactly with your needs.

My favourite method is by measurement. This is time-consuming, but with practice gets faster and certainly gives good results. (Photo. 16).

Start by erecting a vertical post marked off with lines at six, or three-inch intervals (150 or 75 mm). The post is wedged into a position that approximates closely to the front edge of the bulkhead. When it is lined up, using a square and a rule measure across to the hull and note the results. (Photo. 17). If you haven't a long rigid rule then fix an extending rule to a batten with a couple of bits of masking tape. The resulting measurements should then look like figure 60. You will see that as you come down towards the bilge the points measured off span an

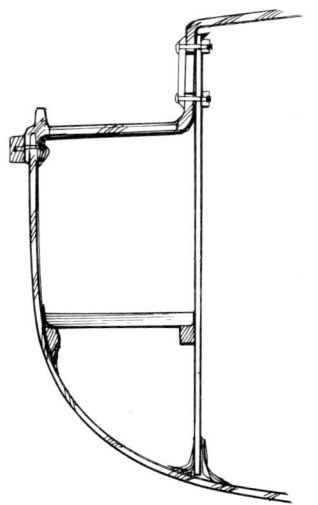

FIG. 59. *Had I thought long enough about it I would have realised that the cabin trunk lining timber could have been extended down to form locker fronts.*

PHOTO. 15. *In the forepeak the cabin-lining timber has been carried down from the deckhead to form these cave lockers. The strips against the hull are landings for the hardwood slats that separate the occupant from the hull.*

PHOTO. 16. *You will be very lucky indeed if your custom-interior coincides with the bulkheads that the builder normally fits. Arriving at the stage shown here took a considerable amount of measuring and cutting. When bonded to the hull this bulkhead will be clad with t & g planking.*

the deckhead and braced into the dinette structure at the bottom. The plank, or strut, plays a dual role for as well as being the table support it also braces the hull and deck in an area which otherwise could have flexed under load.

The strut is shaped to provide a vertical grab-hold, corresponding to one opposite in the edging of the galley bulkhead. The photographs on page 77 show how it is arranged.

increasingly large distance—often too wide to be much use. So instead of horizontal measurements you will need to take them vertically (Photo. 18). Once again a system of station lines is used.

You may measure directly with a rule or with a bob-line which is measured afterward.

The drawing, rules and square are then used to transfer the shape to the plywood sheet (Photo. 19). If

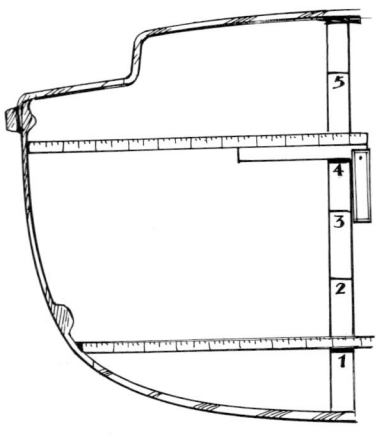

allow a bit extra
for 'adjusting'

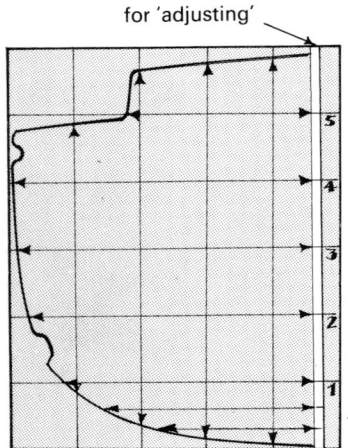

FIG. 60. *Measurements in two planes may be used to reproduce the shape of the hull with a reasonable degree of accuracy.*

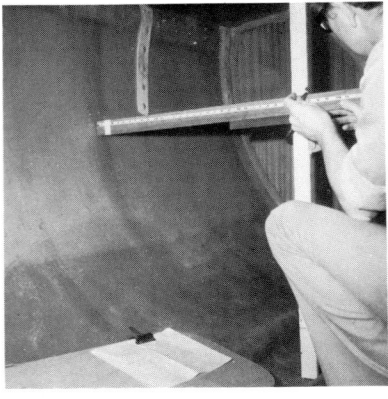

PHOTO. 17. *Once a vertical datum has been positioned and wedged into place then a series of grid measurements may be taken to determine the shape of the hull—and thus the required shape of the bulkhead.*

PHOTO. 19. *The measured data must then be transferred to the plywood before it can be cut out. It may be a wise precaution to cut well clear of the line and offer it up to the hull for final fitting if space and shape allows.*

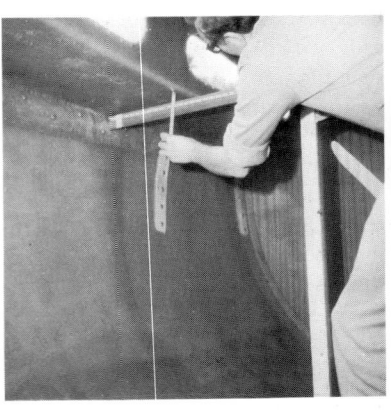

PHOTO. 18. *Vertical measurements on a fairly close grid are needed around complicated shapes—where there are straight lines such as here under the side decks only one measurement at either end is necessary.*

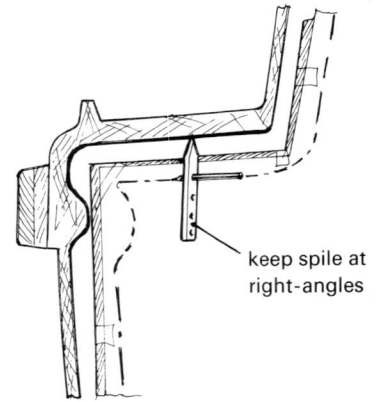

keep spile at
right-angles

FIG. 61. *Spiling can be used to take off complicated shapes, or around congested areas, where a large number of closely-spaced measurements would otherwise be needed.*

you are uncertain of the accuracy of any points when it comes to joining them up with fair curves then you will need to go back and measure once again. Wood is very expensive so it really pays to eliminate wasteful errors. Even when you are certain of your curves it is as well to cut a little clear of them and finally fit the bulkhead with plane and spokeshave. Note that the fit needs to be a little 'slack' if hardspots are to be avoided, but even so a reasonable fit is still needed for good results.

If one is dealing with a fairly complicated area, such as in the bows, or around the side decks then there are several ways to take off shapes; measure using one inch (25 mm) station lines; bend a piece of stout (soft) wire around the shape or use a shop-bought adjustable template, or spile the shape off.

The bent wire method is self-evident. Old wire coathangers are about the right gauge and if you leave one in a garden fire until its ashes are cold it will be very malleable . . . but very dirty.

Spiling requires a board covered in paper—ceiling lining paper is very cheap. The board is held square to the relevant part of the hull, using patches of masking tape with pencil marks to enable you to relocate as required. A spile is then used to transfer the shape onto the paper. A spile, if you are not familiar with it, is simply a short length of wood pointed at one end and with a series of holes through which a pencil is poked. Make a note of which hole you use so that no errors are introduced into the next step. This is to take the paper with the shape drawn on it and pin, or tape it to the plywood (or hardboard if you are making a template) then using the spile—with the pencil in the right hole—transfer the shape back onto the plywood as the drawing shows. Spiling requires a certain knack mostly to do with keeping the spile at rightangles to the surface it is following—but results can be very good. (Fig. 61).

If none of the methods outlined so far suit then I can recommend the fabricated method. This is more involved but gives one a physical representation of the shape of the bulkhead.

Erect a pair of uprights and then a couple of horizontal battens as shown. Cut scraps of hardboard by laying a short length of it against the hull, finding the greatest amount of daylight between its edge and the hull and transfer the shape direct using a spile. Rough out and adjust with the jigsaw until it fits and fasten to the battens. Continue until the shape has been produced. A somewhat lengthy method but guarenteed to give you

the correct shape, and well worth considering before you scrap that large, expensive sheet of teak-faced plywood. (Fig. 62).

Bulkheads may also be reproduced by means of a 'tick stick'. One end of the stick is positioned against the hull while the other end rests on a vertical board and is scribed around. When the 'master' is completed it is placed on the plywood and the stick accurately repositioned; its end is then drawn around. When the series of 'ticks' are joined up with a fair curve a faithful representation of the hull is reproduced. (Fig. 63).

One further method of determining the shape is possible but only if you have a detailed set of lines drawings and a table of offsets, complete faith in the craftsmen who made the original plugs from which the moulds were taken, and sufficient draughtsmanship to do your own lofting!

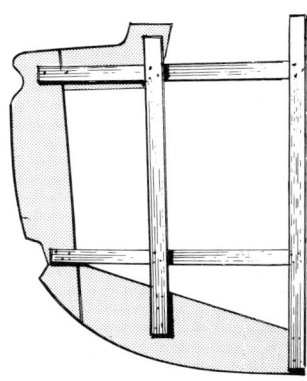

FIG. 62. *If you doubt your ability to get a good fit then scraps of hardboard, or cardboard, could be used to create a shape in stages. Much better than wrecking an expensive sheet of plywood.*

WARRIOR
With a long straight keel and a roomy centre-cockpit the Warrior is designed by Angus Primrose. She may be rigged as a sloop or yawl and sleeps seven. An after-cockpit version of the same hull is also available as the Voyager. Builders are Trident Marine Sales, Cranleigh Road, Portchester, Portsmouth. Part-complete options of both are available.

Length overall   35 feet
Length waterline   26.4 feet
Beam   10.5 feet
Draft   5 feet
Displacement   12,320 lb
Ballast   5,100 lb
Sail area   437 square feet

Some more thoughts on wood

One important thing to remember when fitting-out from scratch is the economies which are available in buying wood if you go about it properly. By that I am not referring to buying a tree off the local forestry commission. If you buy timber from your supplier 'off the saw' you will save some cash, and oddly enough some labour too. I suppose that last statement is a slight exaggeration but look at it this way; if you want to glue a piece of wood you have to rough up the faying surface if it is already nice and smooth. If it has a saw finish then you only have to run the plane over the three other surfaces. If, however, you plan to glass a piece of wood into the hull then it needs to be rough all over . . . so you may just as well standardize your buying.

During my last fit-out I found 10 ft lengths of 2 × 1 inch just right. Mind you it pays to prime the yard-hand to let you sort out the good from the rubbish; too many knots, sapwood, shakes and splits etc, will lead to waste of both time and material.

Having bought the wood I gave it a couple of coats of a suitable preservative—one containing zinc naphthanate in white spirit for preference. Never use a cheap copper-based one for it could affect the resin if not fully dried out. The reason for putting on a preservative is simply that those lumps of wood may already have within them spores just waiting for the right conditions to launch a fungal attack, and if that wood has meanwhile been entombed in a resinglass shroud. . . . This of course means that all the fasteners of deck fittings

which pass through bonded-in reinforcing blocks (as they should) must be well sealed with a rubber-type mastic to prevent water entering the block. Once it does there is no way it can escape and rot could soon set up.

Figure 64 shows longitudinal stringers in the forepeak and elsewhere throughout the boat. They serve a dual function—they act as attachment members for other fittings and also as hull stiffeners.

If they were used only as stiffeners one could employ paper ropes, or PVC or polyurethane foam strips to provide formers over which top-hat sections could be built up.

Some early production resinglass craft were re-inforced with ABS waterpipe as formers. These hold out the promise of simplification since running a tube around compound curves found in a hull, would, unlike a rectangular sectioned piece of timber, always present the same shape. (Fig. 64). However the use of such tubes is not to be recommended for one is simply building in a buckling point along the entire length of the resinglass reinforcement—even though matting over them is relatively easy. The only way to prevent this failure is to build up the gap with a generous fillet of putty or microballoons and resin.

Why will it buckle? If one considers a normal top-hat section it is apparent that the side walls are ideally placed to withstand normal loadings. But if one were to build a top-hat section with a deep longitudinal notch then that would be the point at which buckling could develop. This would happen with a glassed-in tube as figure 64 shows.

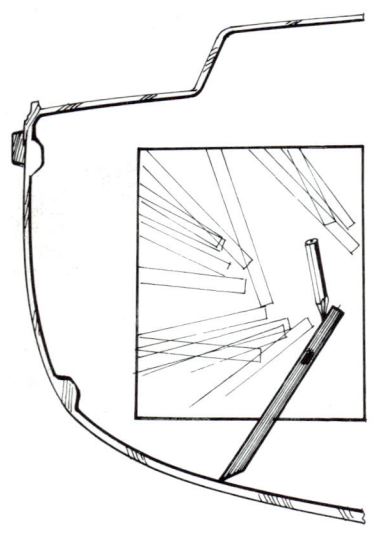

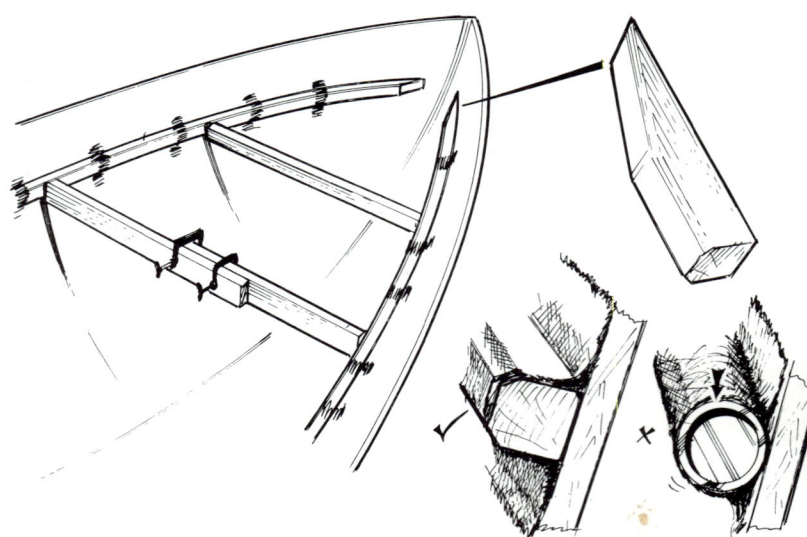

FIG. 63. A 'tick-stick' can give surprisingly good results since marks may be grouped closer around complicated shapes.

FIG. 64. Wooden stringers have to be 'sprung' against the hull and held there while patches of CSM cure off. Note the feathered ends which prevent stress-risers, and also the use of 'coffin-cut' sections to enable the CSM to form around them. Tube reinforcements tend to buckle under load.

The actual shape of the wooden stringer has to be considered. In practice it is difficult to persuade CSM to go around an outside 90 degree bend with ease (hence the temptation to use tubing). Give it two such rightangle bends in a couple of inches (50 mm) and the job becomes impossible. This means that the outer corners of the stringer must be well-bevelled off. I cut mine on a circular saw with at least a half-inch (12 mm) flat and met no resistance at all when glassing over them. I did experience trouble when shoring and chocking long lengths of 2 × 1 inch (50 × 25 mm) against the hull. Doing it single-handed in the forepeak of my Atlanta 8.5 reminded me of that classic cinematic scene repeated in so many Laurel and Hardy films—the routine with a piece of sticky paper. . . . I would no sooner get one strip positioned against its pencil marks when the other end would reach for the deckhead under the pressure of the shores. I suppose I was too ambitious trying to get them down each side of the hull at the one time. In the end

they *were* wedged in place! Athwartships shores were made up using two short lengths of 2 × 1 (50 × 25 mm) held together with clamps. This makes their length infinitely variable and if allowed to arch slightly while using one clamp they exert a fair load when forced down horizontally just before the other clamp is nipped up tight. I found that nails through their ends were necessary to prevent them skidding off the stringer.

Roughing up, degreasing and matting-in (Photos 20–25) follow the methods outlined on page 57. Even though I am fairly used to working with resin and glass I still find the smell of styrene distasteful, while on the other hand the use of acetone in a confined place endows one with a certain feeling of lightheadedness. Thus as much ventilation as possible is required—or you might end up imitating Charlie Chaplin and his famous bucket scene—only this time with catalyzed resin instead of water!

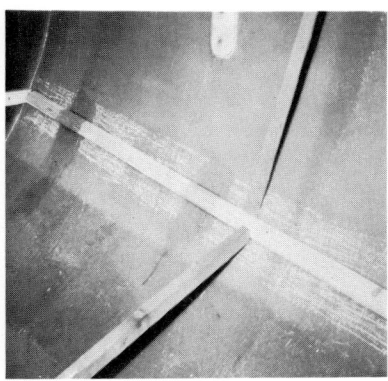

PHOTO. 20. *This wooden stringer serves two jobs—it forms the core of a top-hat section which stiffens the hull, and also acts as a landing to which furniture may be screwed. Buried timber such as this needs to be treated to prevent rot.*

PHOTO. 21. *Once the stringer has been 'tacked' in place the surrounding area needs to be roughened up and degreased to take the resin and glass. Here a scratcher is being used.*

PHOTO. 22. *Masking the adjacent area with old newspaper prevents unsightly runs of hardened resin down the hull. The first coat of resin is applied. Note the container.*

PHOTO. 23. *Precut pieces of CSM are then applied to the wet resin. A certain amount of 'hand-work' is necessary, and each piece of mat should overlap its neighbour.*

PHOTO. 24. *More resin is painted on, and as it penetrates the mat becomes nearly transparent. The stringer has its corners cut off to allow the mat to form round.*

PHOTO. 25. *You might just about pick out the knots in the wooden stringer . . . three layers of CSM have been put on and rolled. The job is just about over and its time to clean up the tools before everything sets.*

Bonding in bulkheads

When bonding-in (or glassing-in) bulkheads it is essential that you take care not to form a 'hard spot' for that is where even the normal stresses encountered when sailing could cause the hull laminate to fracture (Fig. 65). One occasionally sees local hull distortions from bulkheads fitted too tightly against the inner hull in the belief that a close fit is best. Polyester resin shrinks slightly on curing and this, combined with a very close fit, may pull the bulkhead so tightly into the hull laminate that it actually distorts it. Apart from the fact that it looks bad, it is also an invitation for the hull stresses to concentrate at that point: if they are high enough the laminate will fail around that area. To eliminate any tendency for that to happen, the bulkheads should be cut slightly small and bedded on PVC or polyurethane foam for preference (Fig. 66). Alternatively you could hold them away from the hull with thin wedges and trowel in a good sized fillet of a light putty—microballoons in resin.

Yet another alternative—and one I favour for cheapness—is to cut strips off fibre insulating board. This is sold by builders' merchants in 8 ft × 4 ft sheets with a thickness of about just over ½ inch (12 mm). Used instead of PVC it is quite satisfactory.

Where the bulkhead is against the hull at least two layers, and preferably three of 1½ oz CSM should be used to reinforce the hull locally (Photos. 26–28). The fillet of putty should be of a good radius—a sharp corner is an invitation for the reinforcement to fail under stress. The same desire to avoid hard-spots and stress concentrations means that so far as structural members are concerned there should be no abrupt changes in section. Instead they should feather away—and that applies to layers of reinforcing CSM too. If the edges of the bulkhead are rebated, or feathered as figure 67 shows, a very neat job can be produced. Note that each layer of CSM should overlap the underlying one by 2 inches (50 mm). The amount of CSM used varies from hull to hull but would approximate to ½ of the hull lay-up at the waterline.

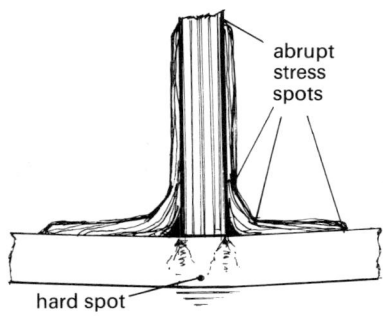

FIG. 65. A badly fitted bulkhead. There will be a tendency for the hull to flex about the hardspot, and possibly even fail, if the lay-up is relatively thin.

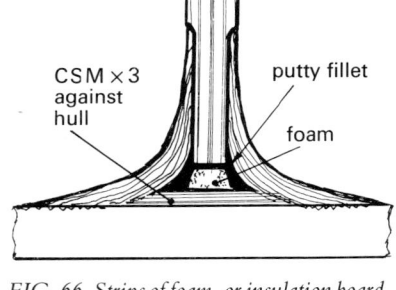

FIG. 66. Strips of foam, or insulation board, between hull and bulkhead prevent a hard-spot developing as the resinglass bonding shrinks. If the CSM is let into a rebate then a very neat job can be made.

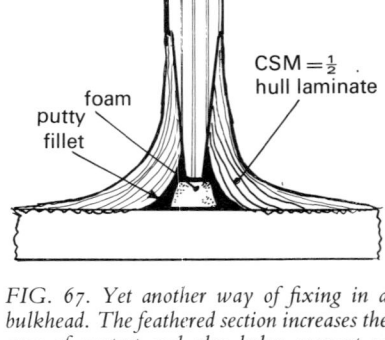

FIG. 67. Yet another way of fixing in a bulkhead. The feathered section increases the area of contact and also helps prevent an unsightly build-up of resinglass.

PHOTO. 26. Its worth saving up bonding-in until you have a goodly amount to do. Here the galley bulkhead and longitudinal stringer have been positioned and work is about to start.

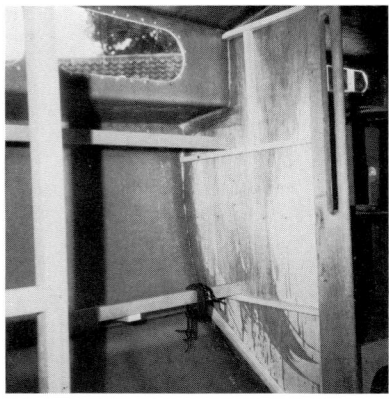

PHOTO. 27. What a mess! This shows just what happens if you don't bother to mask up. The stringers on the bulkhead are positioned to take the t & g planks which are yet to be applied.

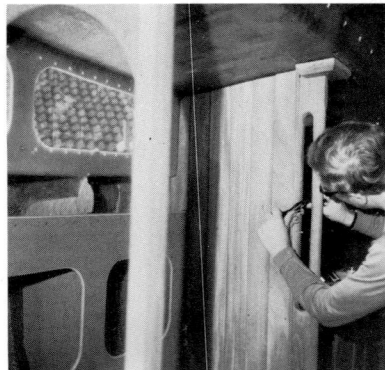

PHOTO. 28. The same bulkhead as in Photo 27. It has been clad and work is finishing on the vertical hardwood grabrail. Note the cladding finishing short of the deck head moulding. The gap will be hidden by the liner.

Figures, 68, 69, 70 are other methods which may be used to bond-in bulkheads and/or furniture. Where it is impossible to get to both sides of the furniture then Figure 68 shows a possible bonding-in method. Two or three layers of CSM are applied to the hull and the 'back layer' is pre-wetted and stuck on to the back face of the furniture member which is then positioned. Three or four layers of CSM are then applied to complete the matting-in operation.

Figure 69 illustrates a made-up, or kit, settee which can be bonded to the hull on both sides. In Figure 70 a strong web is laid-up and the bulkhead, or furniture is bolted to it. The same drawing shows a foam-cored section to which the bulkhead is 'glued and screwed' using an epoxy adhesive.

How to use resin and glass

The following notes are intended to dispel any doubts you may have about the materials and techniques you are about to use for the first time. The use of resin and glass seems to be shrouded in an unnecessary muddle of mumbo-jumbo and much advice is offered—sometimes by people who have had little practical experience. My own dabbling began when I worked in a pattern-maker's shop during the transition from plaster casts to those made from resin and glass fibre. Inspired by my daytime occupation I set about building a pram dinghy in a hardboard female mould screwed to the dining room floor. This grotesque failure—a total weight of 140 lb (63 kg) for a massively overbuilt 8 footer (2.4 m)—was my initial attempt at boat building in this material. Some twenty-odd years later my pioneering spirits have been suppressed and I have gathered a reasonable amount of information the hard way. I offer it in the hope that it will benefit you and steer you away from costly mistakes.

* * * *

Polyester resin as used for laminating—the work you will be doing—is best bought pre-accelerated (see *Safety* notes). It needs only the addition of the catalyst in the correct proportion before it starts to set. Once the catalyst has been added the process is irreversible—so don't hang about. The amount of catalyst to be added to the bulk resin depends mainly upon the ambient temperature. If the weather is cold more catalyst will be needed to affect the cure (up to 4 per cent), than on a good hot day (1 per cent). The addition of fillers (not really recommended except for putty) will also call for more catalyst, while if one is encapsulating ballast then a very slow curing mix is needed to prevent the exotherm damaging the mould-ing. (In fact a cold-curing epoxy resin may be better used for that particular job).

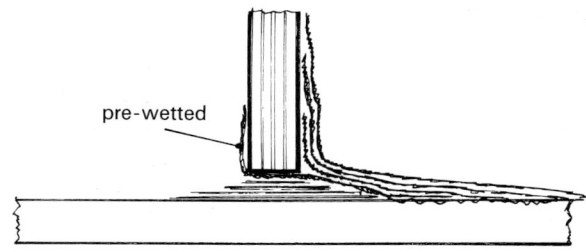

FIG. 68. *It is sometimes impossible to get behind an item of furniture to allow the matting-in operation to be done properly. Here a single layer of CSM has been pre-wetted and applied to the hidden face. The main bonding is made on the exposed face as before.*

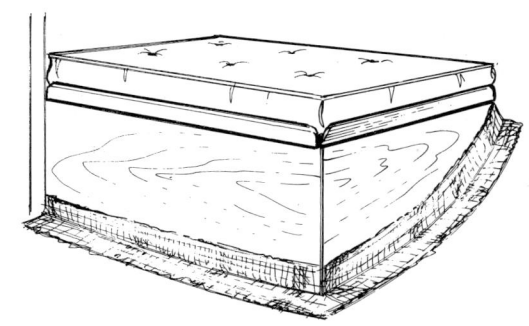

FIG. 69. *Normally three layers of 1½ oz (450 gm/m²) CSM is sufficient to bond-in any furniture. Note that if performed correctly such an operation also encapsulates any end-grain and so prevents water penetration.*

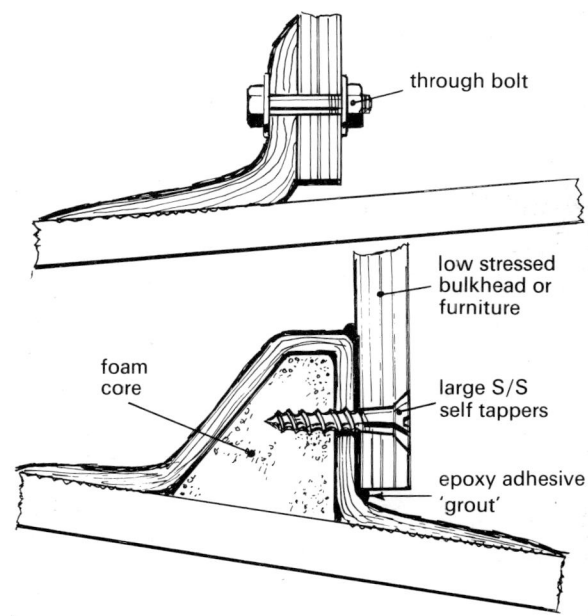

FIG. 70. *Two more methods of fixing in bulkheads or furniture. Through-bolts could also be used on any of the previously outlined methods.*

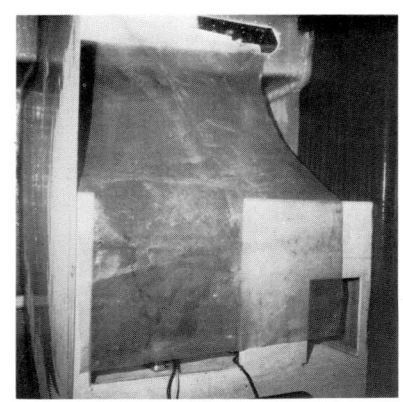

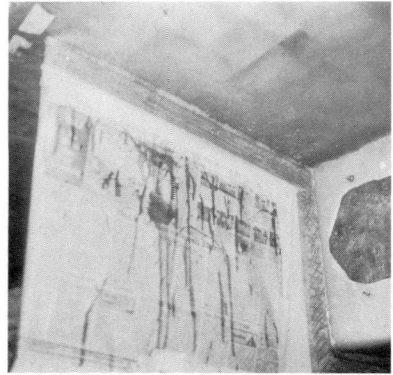

PHOTOS. *29, 30. If you must work when the temperature is much under 50°F then some form of gentle heat will be necessary. Black heat only should be used and a 'tent' helps to confine the heat to where it is needed.*

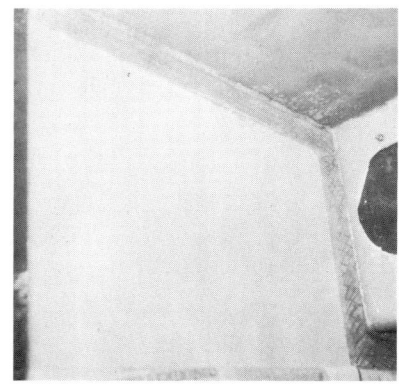

FIG. *71. Holes drilled through the bulkhead may be used to take lengths of rovings and thus considerably reinforce the attachment.*

PHOTOS. *31, 32. This bulkhead will be visible when completed and so it has been carefully masked up. The wood has been scored to allow the resin and glass to hitch on. By itself polyester resin is a poor glue.*

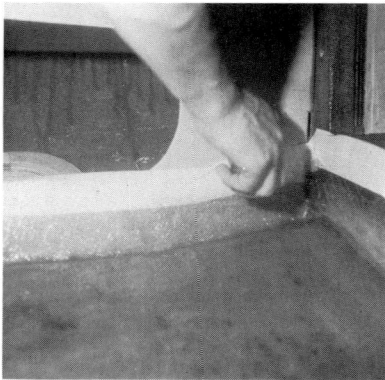

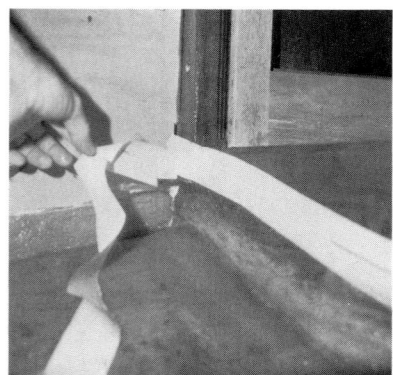

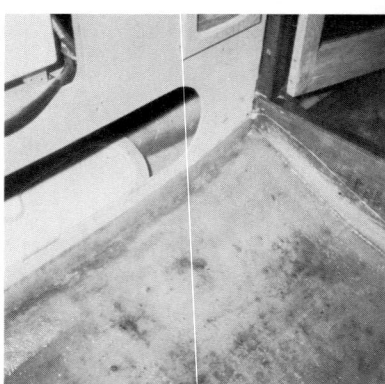

PHOTOS. *33, 34, 35. If you can time it just right then the lay-up may be cut with a sharp 'scalpel' and peeled away. The masking tape is used to provide a clean edge and is clearly seen through the 'rubbery' layers of resin and glass.*

The observant reader will have seen that it is *heat*, or rather *temperature*, which is the dominant factor together with *mass*. This is because polymerisation (setting) produces heat from within the resin. The hotter the mix (or the outside temperature) the faster the resin will set. Use a 4 per cent mix on a hot day and the pot-life of the resin will be a sparse few minutes; the resin will start to gel and set in the bucket (mass) generating so much heat that the bucket, if made from plastic, will actually start to melt. So tip it out at the gel stage and spread it thin to prevent trouble.

One has to be aware also of the other side of the coin. If you were to use a 1 per cent mix on a cold day the laminate would only partly cure due to loss of the styrene, and what curing did occur would be over a time-scale of hours (Photos. 29–30). Polyester resin contains about 35 per cent of the monomer styrene and it is this material which during the setting process is converted into polymers. If the resin contains less than 25 per cent styrene it will not cure properly—a positive blessing during laminating. While laying-up, some of the styrene evaporates out of the surface (smelling like old town gas). Once it has gone it cannot be replaced from within the laminate, and so the surface will remain tacky after the rest of the lay-up has cured. In fact it remains tacky for days and the blessing is that it then makes a good chemical bond if you add another layer of resin and glass fibre mat.

When I write about a 'percentage mix' of resin and catalyst I am in fact referring to parts *per* hundred and not parts of a hundred. A subtle difference I agree and a 4 per cent mix would be 100 parts by weight of resin *plus* 4 parts by weight catalyst. Fortunately for us the specific gravity of the catalyst is around 1.13—so very nearly 1 that we may ignore the fraction. Thus the catalyst is more accurately added by volume than by weight. The following table gives a reasonably accurate means of introducing the right amount of catalyst.

1 per cent—$4\frac{1}{2}$ cc per pound—10 cc per kilogram of resin.

2 per cent— 9 cc per pound—20 cc per kilogram of resin.

3 per cent—14 cc per pound—30 cc per kilogram of resin

4 per cent—18 cc per pound—40 cc per kilogram of resin.

As it cures, polyester resin shrinks by between 5 and 8 per cent depending largely upon the time taken to cure. Because of shrinkage, bulkheads, thin engine-bearers and narrow floors and webs should never be fitted directly against the hull. To do so would cause a discernable 'hard-spot' on thin hulls, and a hidden stress point in more robust lay-ups as previously explained. Bulkheads in the bows of seagoing sailing and motor boats should be installed on strips of foam as previously outlined. Then, when out at sea, the action of the boat slamming will not cause the hull to flex against a solid, hard edge, leading ultimately to failure.

Like good painting, good laminating owes much to initial preparation—which needs completing before the bucket of resin is catalyzed! Both surfaces must be prepared to accept the resin and glass. That means that the hull is well scratched-up and degreased with acetone. The bulkhead, if wood, will need roughing up to make a mechanical key for the resin and glass to hitch into. In a heavily loaded area a series of through-holes (essential in metal), or dimples into which the glass can be worked are necessary. If through-holes are used then lengths of rovings should be poked through before glassing-in commences. The lay-up on either side of the bulkhead should be from one-third to one-half hull thickness in that area (Fig. 71).

Before applying the CSM and resin, mask the bulkhead and surroundings with masking-tape and sheet polythene, or even with old newspapers (Photos. 31–32). Then when the lay-up has reached a 'rubbery' stage, about 45–60 minutes after you finish work on it, it can be trimmed back with a very sharp knife to the still-visible masking-tape. The whole lot is then peeled away to give a nice clean professional-looking job (Photos. 33–35). Do not be tempted to trim the lay-up too soon. The resin goes through a gelling stage into something that resembles old cheese before finally setting hard. If you try cutting it when it is still very soft you may only succeed in pulling it away from the bulkhead.

Each strip of mat should overlap its predecessor by at least an inch (25 mm) although 2 inches (50 mm) is better, and the final lay-up should extend about five to six inches (125–150 mm) out from the bulkhead. Note that these overlaps naturally prevent a 'step' developing and give a smooth stress transition.

Engine bearers and wide floors with large load-spreading areas in contact with the hull do not need foam inserts under them if they are bedded down on two or three layers of CSM first. In robust hulls, lightly loaded members such as bunk fronts do not need foam under them—leave them wedged slightly away from the hull and glass-in from both sides. (See also figs 68–69).

Putty can be bought, but as outlined under *Materials* it is much cheaper to make your own. Mix a quantity of commercial talc or microballoons in pre-accelerated resin. Stir it in a container until it resembles window putty and when you want to use it take out a lump give it a fairly generous amount of catalyst (6–7 per cent) and mix thoroughly. The actual amount of catalyst to add comes with experience, but tends to be twice or three times what you would need for straight resin since you want it to go off fairly quickly. If it starts to look lumpy, clean up you tools and mix up a new batch.

Polyester resins, unlike epoxies, are not harmful in themselves to your skin, provided you take a few precautions. First, a good oil-proof barrier cream must be used. Work it well into finger nails and the webs between the fingers. Before any resin sets wipe it off with a special resin-removing cream—your supplier will have one.

As I said earlier you should wear coveralls or your very oldest clothes and look upon them as being disposable. Once resin gets on them it is impossible to remove. Dry cleaning is no good and while prompt action with acetone might save the day (or your trousers) remember that acetone attacks some modern man-made materials. So wear old clothes and throw them away when they get too bad.

Acetone is a strong solvent and while it may very occasionally be used for cleaning hands, constant exposure will remove the vital oils from the skin and ultimately lead to dermatitis. A good hand cream is therefore recommended—your wife will have some!

But there is still a role for acetone when fitting out—for degreasing areas of the hull, and for cleaning tools, brushes and rollers. It is best to have two containers. Use the first for the initial wash, the second for the final rinse. Special brush and tool-cleaning fluids are available but I find it simpler to stick to acetone. In the end the first container will have so much resin in it that it will 'gel'—throw it away and start a new one, promoting the rinsing container to 'first-wash'. Acetone is completely miscible with water—thus a water barrier to prevent evaporation is impossible. Instead cover the jar with a piece of plastic material secured by tape, or a rubber band. If a wire grid of chicken-mesh is made to fit the bottom of the bucket like a trivet, the tools can be left standing in the acetone and any resin will drop out and fall through the mesh (Fig. 44). It is important to remove all the acetone from the tools before using them again—especially rollers, for the acetone will thin-down and weaken polyester resin. Remember too that acetone gives off fumes that are dangerous in two senses—avoid breathing them too much and never smoke while laminating or using acetone.

It is important that laminate does not end up with too much, or too little resin in it relative to the glass content or it will be a weak lay-up. The weight ratio between glass reinforcement and resin in the laminate should not be greater than 25 per cent for mat (25 per cent glass, 75 per cent resin), 40 per cent for cloth (40 per cent glass, 60 per cent resin) and 50 per cent for woven roving (50 per cent glass, 50 per cent resin). A resin-rich laminate is a brittle one, while one containing too little resin has poor

weather resistance. Note that when working on vertical surfaces the resin may need thickening with pregel paste to make it more thixotropic and prevent it draining away to leave a resin-starved area. Remember that the resin which is allowed to drain away will end up forming a resin-rich area somewhere else.

It is sometimes necessary to pre-wet the glass fibre reinforcement before it is applied to the hull; for instance when working overhead. This is easily done if the CSM is layed upon a sheet of waxed plastic kitchen laminate, or even a piece of glass, from which it may be peeled after the resin has been painted on. The CSM is then positioned by hand and a resin-wet brush is used to stipple it into place and to work any trapped air through the layer. A going over with a small 3 inch (75 mm) washer roller will complete the lay-up. Grooved, or washer rollers are needed to do this since dabbing and stippling with a brush is not so effective for its bristles simply splay out under pressure. You need a downward force of about 10 pounds (4.5 kg) on the roller to remove the air. The roller should be moved sedately about for if you roll too vigorously then instead of squeezing out the air bubbles you run the risk of introducing more, resulting in a weak lay-up and not the stronger one you are seeking.

While it is possible to apply resin with a lamb's wool roller it is impossible to consolidate with it. Should you try you will simply end up with a bow wave of resin which will be picked up and deposited astern of the roller. Any bubbles in the laminate will remain. (Fig. 44).

As previously noted under *Materials* cheap plastic buckets or ice-cream containers make ideal resin pots. For small quantities use cut-down plastic bottles—never those cups sold in vending machines—those made from polystyrene will melt away. It is helpful if the container is of the semi-see-through type of plastic. Then, after the first batch of resin has been weighed the container may be marked on the outside and subsequent batches poured to this mark.

Use a new container for each batch of resin. Remainders of resin will contaminate a new batch and reduce its pot-life. Three containers used consecutively are ideal—the first will have cured before the third is finished. Old, hard, resin can be knocked out of soft buckets with a flat stick. Use a syringe or patent dispenser for the catalyst and mix thoroughly with a power stirrer—taking care not to form a vortex and suck large amounts of air into the resin.

It cannot be stressed too often that you must take care when handling these chemicals for they pose a serious health risk if not used correctly. Always try to buy pre-accelerated resin. If the catalyst and accelerator come into contact they explode. If you have to apply accelerator then treat the whole drum—do not add it drop-by-drop to small batches. Read all instructions carefully and keep all materials well out of the reach of children—large and small. (See also under *Safety*).

Fastenings in resinglass

Fitting out a moulded hull from scratch gives a great deal of pleasure, but requires a certain amount of mental gymnastics when it comes to doing things in the correct order. As I have said, deck fittings need to be put on at the outset of the project so that you can work around their internal reinforcing pads and inside fasteners. The work itself is not exacting, and it is made easier if you have a clear set of drawings to show where individual items are fitted. However, should you be doing your own thing then you need to ponder long before you start with the drills. Let me give you a 'forinstance'. The sheetwinches on *Solitaire* were intended to fit on moulded plinths which already contained plywood reinforcements. Not being a firm believer in the efficacy of woodscrews I decided to throughbolt them—a job made doubly hard since I had already fitted a hardwood capping piece to the top of the cockpit coaming. This capping is easier on the eye and better to hang on to when the going gets rough, but because it was there I had to fit a similar thickness of wood to the plinth—otherwise the bottom-action winch handle fouled. Meantime I had blanked off the end of the starboard quarter-berth to form a cockpit locker division. And at the same time I had squared off the end locker with another piece of plywood neatly glassed in place. Now the snag was finding someone small enough to get into the locker, and strong enough to do up the nuts securing the winch on that side. Fortunately the other locker opposite is large enough to admit me! The same problem was met with the bolts for the stern pushpit and also the cleats and fairleads. I am lucky that my wife is both small and good-natured and still supple-enough to contort her frame into the lockers.

Deck fittings (apart from planning them in at the right time) offer several other problems with resinglass—problems that one is not really aware of when working in wood.

Take simple through-bolts. Using a modest sized machine screw—5/16 Whit (or perhaps M8 metric) one can easily generate a compressive load in the order of half a ton or more. Now the thing that a resinglass laminate likes least is being compressed, particularly if the surface is a resin-rich gelcoat. Apply a localised load like that under a small washer and the resin is crushed. The more you try to tighten it, the looser the fastening becomes!

This can be magnified by the fact that the interior of the moulding will be rough and local 'pimples' on the surface will turn to powder under such loads. Thus it is essential to have over-sized washers—the larger the better. They need to be at least 2.5 times the diameter of the fastening and for small sizes a factor of 4 should be used. Even so, metal backing plates may be preferable. The thickness of the washer should be about one-tenth of the bolt diameter and fastenings should never be sited less than three times their diameter from the edge of the laminate. Naturally all the components in the fastening system need to be electrically compatible if corrosion is to be prevented. Note that self-tapping screws are suitable only for lightly loaded items, can be used only for secondary bonds, and even then only if the laminate is thicker than 1/8 inch (3 mm). If using self-tappers smear them with an epoxy adhesive before driving them into their pre-drilled holes.

Pads behind all fittings are essential and sometimes pads should be used outside too. Care should be taken to select the right kind of timber. Hardwood pads could cause bumps in the surface of the laminate to crush and one is faced with two alternatives; interspersing a thin rubber or neoprene gasket between the two, or else a piece of resined mat (Photo. 36). If the latter is employed then the fastenings should be drawn up only moderately tight—and fully tightened when the resin has cured.

PHOTO. 36. *Pads should be used under fittings—and on occasions outside too. This hardwood pad under the mast is fastened down with eye-bolts which subsequently could be used to take turning blocks or the ends of halliards.*

This tendency for resinglass to crush has to be catered for externally as well if the gelcoat resin is not to crack. Use something like a polysulphide rubber sealing compound under all deck fittings. Be generous and once again the bolts should only just be nipped up—then fully tightened after the synthetic rubber compound has fully cured into a gasket. Alternatively a special tape-like gasket may be available from your chandlers.

The reason for advocating the use of a relatively expensive bedding compound instead of one of the more traditional 'grease' mastics is that a fitting under load tends to rock. If the sealant grows old and hard—or if you had bedded the fitting down on something like polyester resin, then the resulting compressive loads would crush the resin gelcoat. Alternatively, if a very soft mastic were to be used then this material would be forced out under load leading to crushing by subsequent loadings which could also cause the bolts to start working in their holes. (Fig. 72).

One word of warning about copper (and copper-bearing metals) used in conjunction with polyester resin; it prevents it from curing! Thus you have to be careful about such fastenings and fittings if you intend glassing them in, or inserting them in a wet-assembly. Equally this applies to bronze sea-cocks and skin-fittings.

Personally, I believe that the best backing material for deck (or hull) fittings is marine-grade plywood. Since the veneers in a piece of plywood run across each other there is no tendency for the backing pad to split as might a piece of hardwood—oak, or mahogany for example. Also, strength-for-strength, one shows a considerable gain; for instance a 3/8 inch (10 mm) thickness of plywood roughly equals an inch (25 mm) thickness of 'treewood'.

That leads me to the subject of sandwich decks (Photo. 37). As previously mentioned moulders sometimes use a core material of balsa or foamed plastics to form a light, stiff sandwich. This type of material suffers from the fact that it will permanently deform (i.e. crush) under quite modest local compressive loads—our 5/16

inch (M8) fastener could crush the sandwich flat unless large pads were used to spread the loads. Of course there is an exception or two to this 'rule'; PVC 'Airex' foam will accommodate a modest amount of compression and return to its original state—fine for localized impact loads, but not for throughbolts. Another exception is where the core material is in fact solid-plywood and other woods are sometimes inserted to reinforce special areas, under the mast for example.

There are several methods which may be used to fasten through a sandwich deck. Firstly if the fitting is only lightly loaded (and can one ever guarantee that?) then one could simply use large pads on either side of the sandwich to spread the loads—which will not only be those exerted by the fasteners, but also be the working load coming into the fitting—take for example a fairlead. (Fig. 72).

If the fitting has a sufficiently large base area—and very few of them have since they were primarily designed for use on wooden boats which are not so sensitive to crushing—then the easiest way is to drill the through-holes oversize by at least half an inch and then use tubular packing pieces around the bolts and a large pad underneath. The only real problem with this method is that the packing pieces, which may be hardwood, brass, stainless steel, or Tufnol, must be made to the correct length. (Fig. 73/1).

An alternative, and similar method, is to drill the holes for the fastenings through the sandwich and the counterbore up from underneath to remove the inner laminate and the core material, but leaving the thicker outer laminate intact. Polyester putty (talc, not micro-

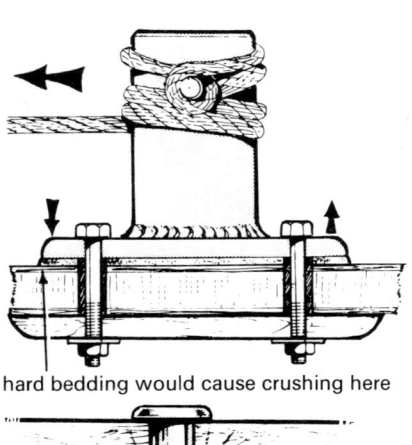

hard bedding would cause crushing here

FIG. 72. Care must be taken when using fastenings in a resinglass laminate. Pop-rivets are a particular menace and the temptation to use screws should also be resisted.

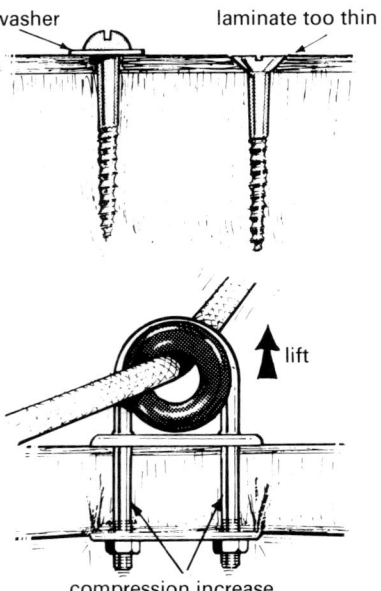

washer   laminate too thin

lift

compression increase

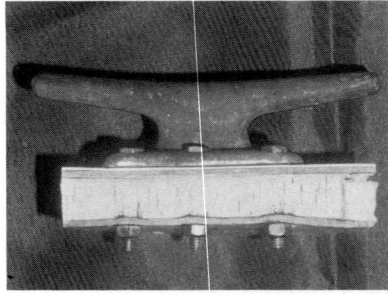

PHOTO. 37. The modest sized bolts used to fasten this cleat have started to crush the laminate—and that is before any real load has been applied. Even a large backing pad is not the ideal solution.

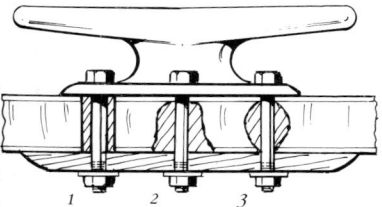 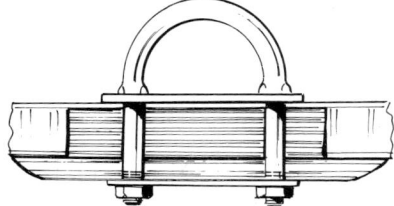 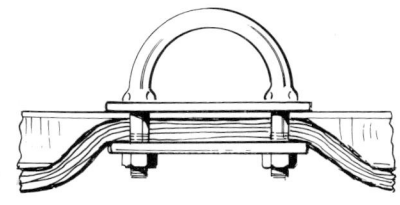

FIG. 73. *Three alternatives to prevent crushing in a sandwich deck. (1) Large diameter sleeves. (2) Solid pads of 'putty' applied from underneath. (3) Putty pads made by scooping out the core and refilling. Stout wooden backing pads are essential in all cases.*

FIG. 74. *Even a simple U-bolt needs backing up if it goes through a sandwich laminate. The core must be removed, and one solution is to replace it with a matching plywood pad, backed up by another, larger pad, to spread the loads.*

FIG. 75. *An alternative method is to lay up resin and glass equal to at least twice the thickness of the outer laminate. Each successive layer should overlap by a minimum of an inch (25 mm) all round. Taper off to avoid stress points.*

balloons) is then used to make good the large hole. The bolt can be pushed through and the deck fitting lightly fastened down. Needless to say the bolt will need greasing, or taping to protect its threads, and the backing pad should have been made when you first drilled the holes. (Fig. 73/2). Once the putty has cured the assembly may be stripped down and re-assembled with proper bedding compounds.

A variation on this is to drill the hole(s), scoop out the core material, re-fill with putty and then, if you have judged things correctly, insert the bolt as before. Or you can wait until the putty has cured and re-drill the hole(s). (Fig. 73/3).

Yet another way is to remove the inner layer of resinglass over an area two, or three, times the area under the base of the fitting. Then scoop out the core material—easy for foam but more difficult for balsa—and replace with a piece of plywood assembled wet on resinglass. Then glass over the area and extend it as you do so to a thickness at least equal to the outside laminate. Make up a large-sized wooden pad and then drill through for the fitting as before. (Fig. 74). This method is perhaps the best for fastening down foredeck mooring cleats and bits which are too likely to be heavily loaded.

There is a variation to this method; instead of inserting a piece of plywood use layer upon layer of CSM and resin. Each layer of mat should overlap the underlying one by at least an inch (25 mm) all round (Fig. 75). This is perhaps easier than the previously described method and has the additional merit of not introducing a hard spot. For a minimum I would suggest four layers of $1\frac{1}{2}$ oz CSM, and I feel safer with five or six.

There is a temptation to use builders' type cavity fittings in sandwich lay-ups and these are to be avoided even for the most lightly loaded fitting for they may encourage the top laminate to pull away from the core material. Should water then enter, the laminate, if balsa, could start to rot. Expanding screw inserts *could* be used

below-decks to fasten headliners—but that is about all.

Another source of temptation is offered by hollow, or 'blind' pop-riveting systems. Initially you might imagine that they would work quite well, and in point of fact they do. However, the rivet grips because the mandrel expands it before it breaks off. This expansion crushes the surrounding resin in the lay-up and lets the rivet work loose. If the hole has been drilled too tightly then star cracks will radiate out from the heads of such rivets used in thin laminates.

Similarly, anyone used to working in metals might assume that tapped holes might be used in certain places. I would be extremely cautious about this approach for the laminate will not accept a fine thread form, and around about $\frac{3}{8}$ inch Whitworth in a laminate about half an inch thick would be the minimum starting point—and you'll not meet many of these situations.

In some lightly-loaded areas—the headliner once again—you *could* use self-tapping screws if the lay-up is more than one-eighth of an inch (3 mm). The hole size needs to be nicely judged—a little on the tight side since the resin will crumble, and a smear of epoxy adhesive on the threads will improve their holding powers too. Even so wooden battens attached to the raw deckhead with patches of CSM would produce a better job with less likelihood of subsequent troubles.

Holes through the laminate should not be counter-sunk; the thickness will invariably be too thin to let you sink the head of the fastener without seriously weakening the area under its head (Photo. 38). Similarly a row of fastenings should be staggered and well spaced out—at least four times the diameter and never closer to an edge than three times the diameter.

I wrote earlier that resinglass laminates do not like to be compressed. While that is true I must also point out that they like tension even less since this introduces the possibility of delamination through shear. It was once thought that superior boats could be built entirely of woven rovings: such a hull would be lighter and stronger. And so it was, until the layers of reinforcement started to part company. It is for this reason that layers of CSM are always used to sandwich roving mats for the CSM can be worked into areas which would otherwise be resin-rich and relatively weak.

The most obvious example of tension in the hull would be found around the chainplates. To eliminate any possibility of failure in the laminate, the chainplates need to be as long as possible; at least half as long again as those you would use on a wooden hull. They must also be well-backed with inner pads, or straps (Photo. 39). Through-bolts must be used to prevent failure through shear, and if the backing straps can be hitched into a bulkhead or knee, so much the better. (See also Fig. 51).

Work for a winter's evening

Keeping several jobs on the go at once is a recipe for getting afloat quickly. Down-time in one area means that you can move to the next and generally keep things moving along. I started cutting out grabrails before I had installed the engine. But I had fitted the cockpit drains and left the seacocks poked through their holes in the bottom of the hull—even though the pads were yet to be fitted under them! It is all a question of juggling jobs and keeping as many in the air as possible.

Early on I had the good fortune to acquire some hardwood floorboards—it's amazing what friends will turn up with! They were six to eight feet long by $4\frac{1}{2}$ inches wide and $1\frac{1}{4}$ inches thick (1.8–2.4 m, 110 × 30 mm). Figure 76 shows how I arranged to cut a pair of grabrails with the very minimum of waste. Once again the jigsaw came into its own and I found that the thin metal-cutting blades worked best on close-grained hardwood. At the 'corners' I drilled holes to enable the blade to change direction. This is only necessary along one grabrail for once one is cut out it obviously becomes much easier to cut the other (Photo. 40).

Dimensions are a matter of personal choice and again much depends upon the material sizes available. Figure 76 shows the basic dimensions I used and the resulting shape looks right for the boat (Photo. 41). When it came to fastening them through the sandwich decks I opted for spacer tubes and long stainless wood screws through a long continuous plank underneath (Photos. 42–44). They were bedded down on a rubber-type mastic and not varnished—just lots of teak-oil and wood preservative.

Needless to say cutting them out was only the start of the job for they had to be planed, filed, filled and sanded—all those curves (Photos. 45–47). Still it was a satisfying job which saved the cash I would have needed to buy those dreadful looking stainless tube confections.

But do you need grabrails? I find that most of the time they are in use as additional toe-rails and thus the plank-on-plank type (Fig. 77) might have been just as effective and more economic in terms of time and money. That's the fun of fitting out—its up to you to make these decisions.

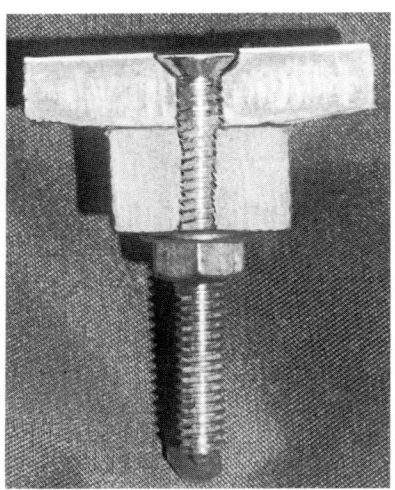

PHOTO. 38. *Very often the laminate is a great deal thinner than this—and even here it is really too weak to take a countersink. The area of resin under the head will crumble unless somehow the area is greatly increased. The same goes for woodscrews and pop-rivets which expand and crush the resin.*

PHOTO. 39. *Inner pads and throughbolts are essential for chainplates—which also need to be much longer than would be commensurate with a wooden hull.*

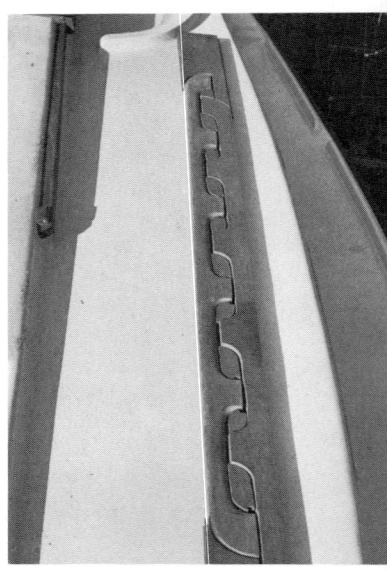

PHOTO. 40. *Two into one will go if the proportions are right. This shows the hardwood grabrails that formed the basis of many evening's winter-work.*

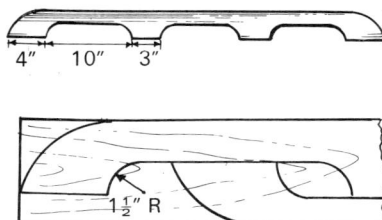

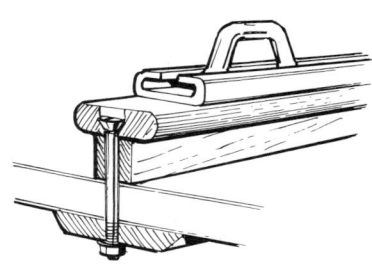

PHOTO. 41. *Its looking good! The windows have been cut and stuck in with tape and the finished grabrail is offered up for effects. Robust dimensions are in keeping and allow the rail to be grabbed without losing skin to the decks. . . .*

FIG. 76. *Two grabrails out of a single plank. Proportions are a matter of choice— but those given look about right.*

FIG. 77. *Plank-on-plank grabrails are quick and easy to make. With a wide flat top it should be possible to incorporate a stout stainless steel sail-track which could contain a special slide to take a safety harness clip.*

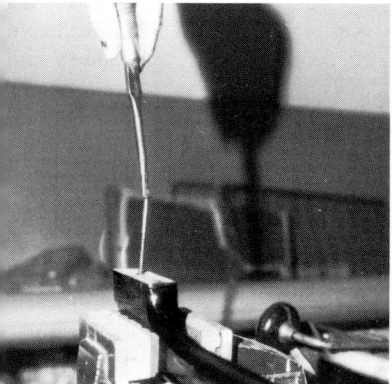

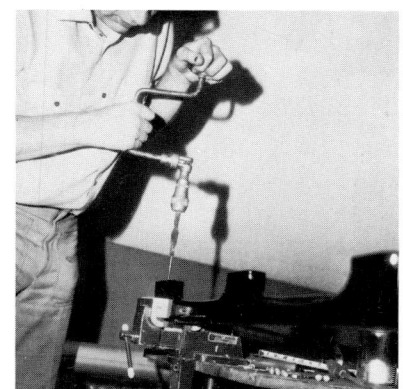

PHOTOS. 42, 43, 44. *Very large woodscrews are almost impossible to screw home with a 'driver'. A screwdriver-bit in a ratchet-brace is an improvement, but I found it easier to 'tap' the holes first using an identical steel screw in a tap-wrench. (The vice jaws are soft rubber).*

PHOTOS. 45, 46, 47. *All those curves . . . metal-cutting blades are best for hardwood and it pays to keep all tools as sharp as possible. The Black & Decker Workmate, really was a 'mate' for it used to go into the boat and 'hold one end. . . .'*

5

Laminating deck beams

The compression loads in the mast of a 28 footer with average sail area can be considerable. Given steady sailing conditions they come out to about $1\frac{3}{4}$ tons (1750 kg). Pitching, or sudden squalls, the weight of which must be absorbed by the rigging until the boat either heels, or accelerates, can easily increase that figure to about $3\frac{1}{2}$ tons (3,500 kg). I had had the builders fit two partial bulkheads into *Solitaire's* otherwise empty hull. Her deck is a resinglass and balsa sandwich, except where the deck-stepped mast stands. There the balsa is replaced by a large piece of marine plywood. I had arranged that the $\frac{3}{4}$ inch (20 mm) bulkheads should come directly under the mast, just forward of the main-shroud chainplates. The starboard bulkhead comes right out to the centreline of the boat and all I had to do was hitch the tops and bottoms of the bulkheads together to produce a 'ring' bulkhead ideally positioned to absorb both the compression loads of the mast and the crushing forces exerted on the hull by the rigging. (See also Fig. 33).

On a conventional boat, that is a traditionally wooden one, there would be a strong beam arranged under the mast's tabernacle plus a vertical framework of posts standing on horizontal floors braced longitudinally to absorb the loads and distribute them into the rest of the structure.

I therefore decided to join the bulkheads at the top with a laminated hardwood beam which would measure two inches by three (50×75 mm). (Photo. 48). At the bottom I would use a softwood floor measuring $1\frac{1}{2} \times 9$ inches at its deepest (38×230 mm) (Photo. 49). The deckbeam is shaped to closely follow the underneath of the deckhead, and to avoid hard spots it is bedded on two layers of $1\frac{1}{2}$ oz (450 gm/m²) CSM. Six 5/16 inch (M8) bolts through the beam and bulkhead, aided by a resorcinol glue as opposed to the cheaper urea-formaldehyde glue used elsewhere below decks, provide a strong arrangement. The bottom floor is similarly glued and through bolted and is matted to the hull with three layers of CSM each side where possible, and five layers elsewhere.

PHOTO. 48. *The laminated hardwood beam is glued and through-bolted to the part-bulkheads under the mast. The door jambs swell out to help support it and also stiffen the bulkheads against buckling. This is a very heavily loaded area.*

PHOTO. 49. *This robust beam sits on foam and is bolted to both part-bulkheads. When glassed into the hull it gives a very strong link in a critical area.*

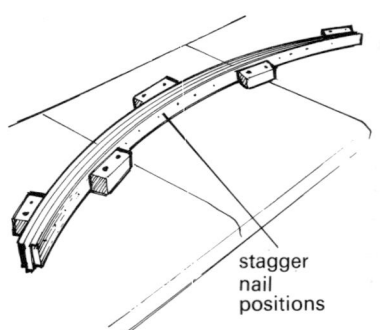

stagger
nail
positions

FIG. 78. *Deck beams may be formed using a simple jig with wooden blocks, or metal angle-iron brackets, bolted to a strong base.*

PHOTOS. 50, 51, 52, 53. A water-mixed urea formaldehyde glue was used to laminate the deck beam. Fast work and a lot of clamps were called for, and the inner laminates were also nailed. I left it in its jig while planing up—something of a chore since the grain kept shifting ends.

▲
PHOTO. 54. There is also a hardwood plank, or strut under the mast and it is fastened to the forward face of the bulkhead. A strong resinglass 'knee' is moulded at the bottom.

Laminating the deckbeam was rapid and the finished result looks good too (Photos. 50–53). Instead of laying the seperate slats of wood on deck and weighting them down until the glue had cured, I had to make up a jig on which to laminate the beam (Fig. 78). The shape was spiled off on to a piece of hardboard which was used to draw the full curve on to a plank which had been protected with polythene. A necessary precaution or you may end up with the beam glued to it! Blocks of wood, or angle iron if you wish, are then screwed to the plank to coincide with the curve required. The first strip of hardwood, which like all the others measured 2 inches by 5/16 inch thick, was nailed to the blocks to form the first curved layer. All the other strips were then applied with glue on one face and nailed from the centreline out to the edges. The final layer of wood was only glued, and this hides the heads of the nails previously driven. When all was clamped up the surplus glue which squeezed out was carefully removed. If it is left to set it quickly blunts the plane-iron. Planing called for care with much changing of ends for it is impossible to arrange the strips so that the grain is running all one way. Once planed the beam was cut to the hardboard template, due allowance being made for the increase in width of the cabin-sides over two inches depth. Then it was glued, matted and bolted in place. Once in position the rest of the doorway could be framed-up. This again is hardwood 2 × 1¼ inches (50 × 32 mm) wide and the vertical posts swell out into 'knees' at their tops to sit snugly under the laminated deckbeam (See also photo. 2). The main support for the mast comes from a hardwood plank 6 × 1¼ inches (150 × 32 mm) which is fitted fore-and-aft on the centreline, hitched to the bulkhead and to a 2 × 1 (50 × 25 mm) stringer (Photo. 54). This upright is also

PHOTO. 55. *Once the window line was decided upon it could be drawn on the cabin trunk and cut out. Airborne glass fibres should not be inhaled and a mask is essential. Once again metal-cutting blades in the jigsaw proved adequate.*

PHOTO. 56. *The Perspex was cut into small, more manageable pieces, and then marked out for individual windows. The resinglass cut-outs were used as templates with due allowance being made for the increased size required.*

glassed to the hull at the bottom and sits on a pad of foam to prevent a hardspot. Many layers of CSM were used to fabricate generous 'knees' all around down to the hull. The starboard bulkhead is reinforced against buckling by the bunk structures and framing in the fore-, and main cabins. This structure under the mast may seem excessive but remember that the original design employed two pairs of part-bulkheads and a longitudinal beam resting on them.

Custom-made boat windows

I like lots of windows on boats, but they have to suit her lines and this, as any designer will tell you, can be very difficult to achieve—it's almost as hard to get as a nice-looking sheer-line. When it came to the windows on *Solitaire* I decided to depart from those used by the builders which to my taste gave an insuffient total area. To get the lines right I experimented by drawing them out on sailing photographs and drawings supplied by the moulder. This gave a good impression of how she would eventually look compared to the designer's idea, and it is a method I strongly recommend. A nasty window can mar an otherwise attractive boat.

Estimates for custom-built windows in frames put them far out of my reach and so I decided to use clear acrylic (Perspex) windows each 3/8 inch (10 mm) thick bolted directly to the coachroof coamings.

The first job was to transfer the shapes and positions from the photographs on to the scale drawings. From those the holes in the coamings could be drawn, sawn out (Photo. 55), and the window material bought.

The openings were easily cut with a jigsaw and metal-cutting blades—blades with 18 teeth to the inch give a

useful working life. Resinglass is a hard abrasive material and you soon lose the cutting edge off saws and drills. Remember too that there will be dust flying about and wear a mask and goggles. Protect you hands and arms against the 'itch' with a barrier cream too.

Having cut the window apertures out I taped them back in place with masking tape until the windows themselves could be fitted. The acrylic sheet was bought via the 'yellow pages' and I also got around 300, 3/16 inch × 1½ inch (M5 × 40 mm) dome-headed machine screws, nuts and washers. These were used to fasten the windows in place.

When it came to cutting the acrylic it was once again a question of measuring twice and cutting once— it's an expensive material (Photo. 56). The window material was cut with the jigsaw, again with metal cutting blades— although those sold for cutting plastic laminates also performed well. I cut a few test runs on scrap acrylic to

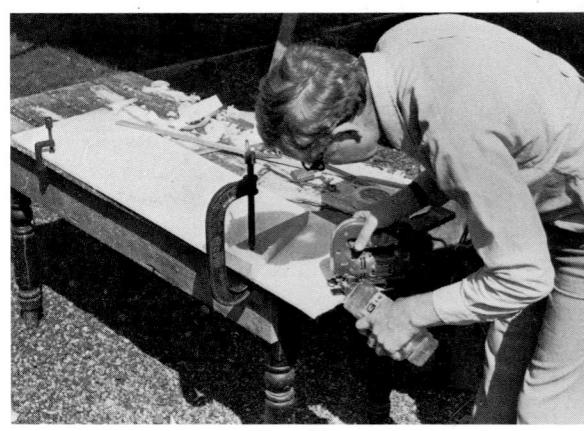

PHOTO. 57. *Sawing the Perspex called for water-cooling. Otherwise the debris melted in the cut and fused the material back together again.*

PHOTO. 58. Excessive overhangs should be avoided when cutting acrylic plastics. Note the paper masking and the indirect clamping which spreads the pressure over an increased area.

PHOTO. 60. With the protective paper still on I went around the edges of the windows cutting a large 45 degree bevel. A sharp corner could have damaged ankles. . . .

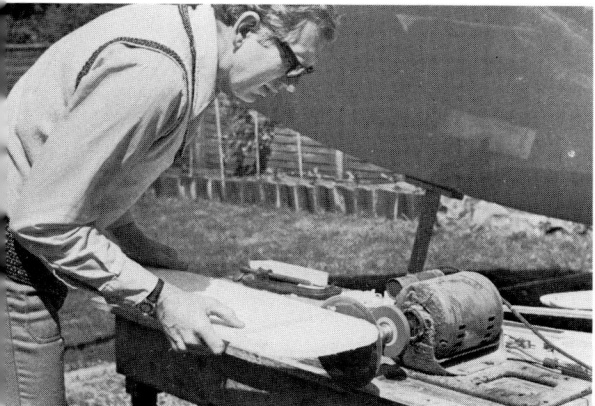

PHOTO. 59. A sanding disc in the chuck of this converted 'fridge' motor soon dressed the sawn windows. A fairly low speed is required to prevent heat build-up.

find out if snags presented themselves—and of course one did! Jigsaws cut on the up-stroke and their blades also generate a fair amount of heat. These combined to fuse the sides of the acrylic back together again after the saw had passed through the material. If I stopped cutting for even the slightest time the blade cooled down and became firmly embedded with every likelihood of breaking when the saw was switched on again.

During the cutting operation on the window acrylic a handy plastics bottle was used to squirt a small amount of water and detergent into the cut—while being careful not to get the same water into the jigsaw (Photo. 57). This kept things cool and the actual cutting operation was fairly fast. To prevent cracking it is essential that the acrylic is well-supported, and clamped, with not too much of an overhang during sawing (Photo. 58). At all times I was careful to preserve right up to the last

moment, the paper used to protect the surfaces of this relatively soft material.

Cleaning the sawcut edges was comparatively easy. I used a sanding attachment fitted to an old electric motor (Photo. 59). I also decided to bevel the windows around their peripheries. This is necessary not so much to feather the edge and reduce stresses at an abrupt stress-transition point, but to prevent damage to legs passing along the side-decks. A 45 degree cutter attachment in a power drill soon put a large bevel on all the windows (Photo. 60). The windows overlap the resinglass laminate by $1\frac{1}{4}$ inches all round (30 mm) and I arranged the fastening line $\frac{5}{8}$ inch (16 mm) from the edge, just clear of the bevel. These acrylic materials have a different coefficient of expansion from a resinglass laminate. Not much, but enough to cause stresses around the fasteners if one were to use countersunk machine screws. I used instead domed-head machine screws and drilled out the holes 20 thou (0.5 mm) oversized. When the windows were finally assembled I bedded them on a non-drying mastic which enabled them to move slightly as required.

The thinnest practical (safest) size of acrylic one could use for windows is 7/32 inch (5 mm) and this is suitable for windows less than 8×8 inches (200 × 200 mm). At the other end of the scale a window measuring 40×20 inches (1000 × 500 mm) would need a thickness of $\frac{9}{16}$ inches (14 mm). These sizes are for windows screwed or bolted directly to the laminate, or held by a timber-frame or by a car-type elastic joint. The latter method is my least favourite for given the flexibility of the acrylic sheet there is every chance of such windows popping in if hit with a large lump of solid water. Windows fitted in screens, or supported by metal backplates, could be a little thinner in section—or larger in area for the same section; 12×12 inches, $\frac{7}{32}$ inch (300 × 300 mm, 5 mm). Generally speaking it is better to err on the side of safety.

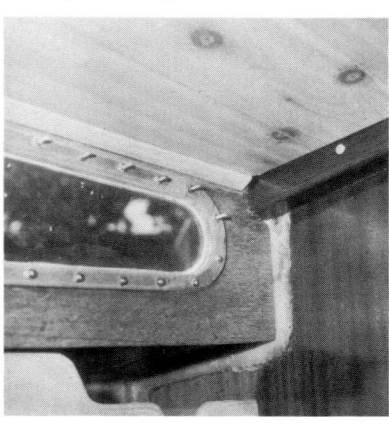

◄ *PHOTO. 61. The window is bolted through both the cabin side, the liner and also a wooden bezel. Note the lip which supports the deckhead liner.*

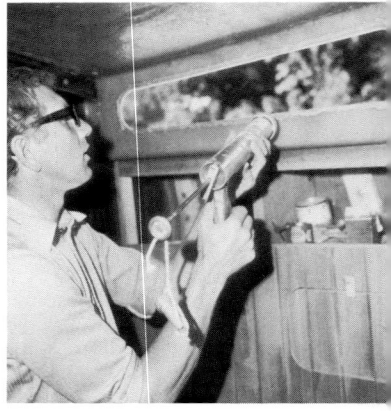

PHOTO. 62. The cabin side liner was ► painted, and assembled on mastic, to prevent the possibility of water finding its way down the back. Many coats of varnish were applied around the sides and window aperture.

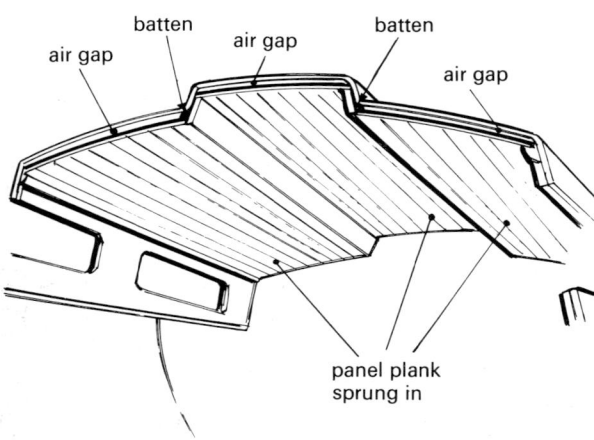

FIG. 79. This is how I fixed Solitaire's headliner. The air-gap, combined with the sandwich deck moulding, gives good insulation against both heat and coldness.

Note that while windows from polycarbonate, plate glass, laminate glass or other materials with comparable characteristics may be used, ordinary window glass should not!

One of the prime considerations I concerned myself with during the fitting out programme for *Solitaire* was to hide as much as possible of her resinglass interior, ending up with a 'traditional' look in a modern hull. To this end the cabin sides have been lined with plywood, and inch-wide (25 mm) wooden bezels were fitted around the window apertures. (See also Fig. 79). A thin strip of wood was nailed and glued to the top edge of the side panels and angled to support the deckhead lining. The cabin side panels are held by the same bolts that are used to fasten the windows and I took the trouble to make certain that these bolts coincided with the centreline of the bezels (Photo. 61). Washers and nuts complete the

job. This is another example of thinking ahead for those strips destined to support the head liner had to be fitted before the side panels were installed (Fig. 79). Even so, had I thought about it a little more I would have realised that the windows could have been held with far fewer throughbolts since woodscrews could have been screwed into the window bezels—the total thickness of wood available being $\frac{3}{4}$ inch (19 mm).

The backs of all the plywood and timber which would be difficult, or impossible, to paint later were given two or three coats of metallic pink primer and the interface between the cabin side liner and the resinglass was well larded with a mastic (Photo. 62). Condensation forms on the inside of windows and I was loath to think that this freshwater might cause rot to start in these lovingly-varnished cabin sides. Incidently I retained all those cabin-side cut-outs; who knows, I might one day want to go 'blue-water' and they could be refitted as 'storm shutters!

Louvred doors for air flow

Ventilation is a very desirable asset—even in a resinglass boat which should not rot of its own accord. Having said that, there is nothing nice about a damp, dank, mildewed cabin, so during fitting-out I made provisions to encourage total air-flow.

For instance, all the locker doors have an inch diameter (25 mm) finger-hole drilled through them. This dispenses with the need for bought-in pull-handles. These holes have been removed from the ordinary by lining them with short lengths of annealed brass tube gently persuaded to bell out with a cross-pein hammer and a large metal ball (Fig. 80). Brass button-on-a-plate catches are used for the locker doors and this small amount of brass together with rich-looking varnished

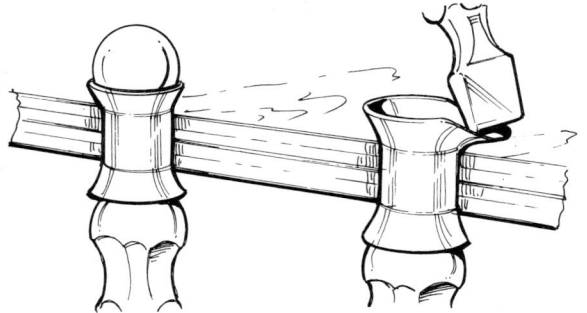

FIG. 80. *Lined finger-holes 'lift' an otherwise drab locker front. Annealed copper, or brass, tube can be worked cold without too much difficulty. Even so it is worth practising on scrap first. . . .*

mahogany, is easy on the eye. The only thing to remember about fitting similar brass tubes, is that the stubs used should not be cut too long—twice the thickness of the wood is just right.

Brass and copper, can be softened (annealed) by heating in a gas flame to around 500°C and, if you are in a hurry, quenched out in cold water. How do you judge the temperature? Rub the hot metal with a dry stick of white-wood (pine) and when the stick starts to char the temperature is about right.

As well as ventilating fronts of lockers, several holes, again one-inch diameter (25 mm) have been drilled through the vertical webs comprising the locker sides. Also the divider at the end of the quarter-berth, which also forms the starboard cockpit locker, has been left a little short at its top—again to assist ventilation. The ends of quarter-berths often suffer from lack of ventilation. I have slept on boats in such berths and woke to find the bottom of the sleeping bag decidedly damp—in fact 'wet' might be a better description. A hit-and-miss ventilator, or a mushroom-type let into the cockpit-well which can be made watertight when under way—always solved the problem.

The doors to the forecabin and WC compartment on *Solitaire* are louvred (Photos. 63, 64). These doors are based on small cupboard doors bought in the highstreet. The hardwood extensions, carefully colour-matched are glued and screwed and their 'joints' made by drilling and inserting dowels at slight angles to each other. (Fig. 81) (Photo. 65).

Hardwood dowels are hard to find in timber-yards. You can make you own very simply—any size you

PHOTOS. 63, 64. *Doors on Solitaire were based on hardwood louvred cupboard doors which were extended to the size needed. Matching hardwood was used to frame them up using a waterproof glue and dowels.*

PHOTO. 65. *Side-members were screwed to the doors, but screwed and dowelled to the bottom cross-member.*

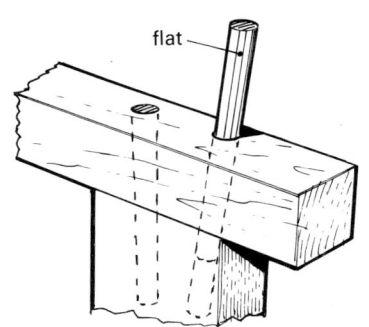

flat

FIG. 81. *Instead of chopping mortice and tenons I used stout dowels, glued and driven home in pairs.*

PHOTO. 66. *T & G panels were used to infill at the bottoms and they sit in recesses made up using mitred quadrant. Note the carving . . . easier than planing off.*

PHOTOS. 67, 68. *Plywood 'doughnuts' were used to pack out the space between the deckhead and its liner. They were through-bolted to the mushroom ventilators and a 'wet' assembly with lots of mastic prevents any possibility of leaks.*

PHOTOS. 69, 70, 71. *This decorative 'kitchen' material comes in 8 ft × 4 ft sheets and also in a variety of types. Used throughout as a headliner in Solitaire, I have also met it in several British and Continental craft. Glossy 'plastic' finishes are available.*

FIG. 82. *Pairs of wedges can provide a positive clamping action. Remember that too much pressure may produce a glue-starved (and hence weak) joint.*

PHOTO. 72. *Hardwood slats in the forecabin make a cosy berth even more comfortable. Varnished, and contrasting with the white paint behind, they are pleasingly functional and removable for cleaning.*

like—by knocking roughly-shaped sticks through holes drilled in a piece of $\frac{1}{4}$ inch steel plate. When you are using dowels it is essential to put a flat along them to allow air and glue to escape as they are driven in—for their holes need to be nicely sized; too tight and you might split the timber, too loose and you put too much dependence on the glue. If you drive the holes in pairs so that they converge at about 20 degrees, then the dowels apply their own clamping action. Large sash-cramps were a help when framing up the doors but not essential—I could easily have made do with the DIY type shown in figure 82.

The bottom of the doors were filled with panels of tongue and grooved mahogany matchboarding to suit the rest of the cabin (Photo. 66). They were edge-glued and their endgrains covered in thin hardwood strips glued and nailed in place. Small hardwood mouldings are used to keep the panels in the frame.

One important consideration with louvres is that you fit them the right way round, if you do not then you can see through them!

Deckhead ventilation has been achieved by the use of three strategically-placed ventilators. They all started life as simple mushroom ventilators, but those amidships—one over the galley, the other over the table—were converted into Dorade-type units by the use of simple resinglass mouldings.

The mushroom ventilators measure 4 inches (100 mm) on their inside diameters, and by searching the chandleries I was able to mate them up to four-inch diameter opening inspection covers. The outer ring of the cover makes a nice-looking bezel, hiding the sawn edge of the headlining material. Doughnuts of plywood pack out the distance between the resinglass moulding and the back of the headliner (Photos 67, 68). I have retained the centres of the inspection covers for they jam into their surrounds thus providing a watertight seal. This allows the mushroom vents to be sealed off completely—an added safety factor for although these vents are particularly cheap they also have a weakness—tread on an open one and you will very likely break the threaded crosspiece. To prevent any chance of water entering between the plywood rings and the headliner I assembled all the various parts 'wet'. By this I mean that all the various bits and pieces were well-smeared with a suitable mastic as they were fitted.

The actual headlining material is a 'mock' tongue & grooved wallboard, sold to decorate kitchens. It comes in 8 ft × 4 ft sheets of shoddy-looking plywood 4 mm thick. The 'planks' are in fact a vinyl paper machined through to give the appearance of proper treewood. This sounds worse than reality and your local timber-yard may carry a range of it—shades are from white lime, through teak down to rose-wood. I lined out the whole deckhead with three sheets and I have since seen it used commercially in two ranges of boats in the UK. Plank widths are irregular and thus have to be 'handed' to give a regular look to the deckhead. Some idea of the actual installation is given in figure 79, and also in the section devoted to making windows. The reverse faces of the headliner were well painted with metallic pink primer and after four years show no sign of trouble—despite my initial misgivings about quality (See also photos. 69–71).

Needless to say all the electrics have been run under the deckhead where possible. The one-inch (25 mm) air gap between the back of the headliner and the resinglass and balsa sandwich moulding helps enormously to prevent condensation in the winter. It also aids in keeping her cool in the summer.

The lockers under the berths have been sub-divided with slats, again to help ventilation, and the sides of the hull adjacent to the berth in the forepeak and the quarter-berth have been given a 'ceiling' (to use the proper term) of mahogany slats. These measure $1\frac{1}{4} \times \frac{5}{16}$ inch (32 × 7 mm) and are very easy to fit; in addition they improve the comfort of the berths and the looks of the boat. They are located on four or five vertical members cut from 2 × 1 (50 × 25 mm) puttied against the prepared hull and firmly held in place with several strips of $1\frac{1}{2}$ oz (450 gm/m²) CSM. The slats are screwed with cup-washers under their heads to facilitate subsequent removal for cleaning and re-varnishing of the boat. The least air-gap between the slats and the hull is one-inch (25 mm) (Photos. 15, 72).

Before the slats were finally screwed in place the inside of the hull was locally painted—once I was certain that no more bonding was to take place. This is important, for most paints affect the adhesion of polyester resin and will have to be ground away completely before bonding could take place. (See notes of *Painting*.)

More notes on wood

The following timbers are all suitable for use in a marine environment and while some are annotated as being only '*moderately durable*' note that this relates to a standard test conducted by the British Timber Research and Development Association in which an untreated 2 × 2 inch stake (50 × 50) is driven into the ground. The timber chosen is heartwood—since this tends to rot the quickest. In those extreme conditions a '*moderately durable*' species would rot away in 10–15 years. '*Durable*' spans 15–25 years, while '*very durable*' covers more than 25 years. Even '*non-durable*' takes 5–10 years to rot. This of course applies to timber which has been properly seasoned.

Afrormosia

Yellow/brown with brown markings Moderately easy to work, finishes smoothly. Glues and polishes well but tends to split in nailing. Stains in contact with steel. Very durable, very stable. Also known as Kokrodua. 43 lb/ft³ (688 kg/m³)

Agba

Pinky brown or light brown, works glues and nails well. Stains and polishes satisfactorily. Also known as Tola. bleaches lighter than teak 32 lb/ft³ (512 kg/m³).

Ash

White with possible pink hue. Perishable. Works easily, glues, bends and finishes well. Takes polish and stain 43 lb/ft³ (688 kg/m³).

Danta

Reddy brown possibly with pin-knots. Works fairly well but may dull tools. Glues, bends and finishes well. May split when nailed 46 lb/ft³ (736 kg/m³).

Rock Elm

Pale brown, straight grain. Non-durable. Screws, nails and glues satisfactorily. Finishes smooth, stains, varnishes and paints well 44 lb/ft³ (704 kg/m³). (Not to be confused with American White Elm or Swamp Elm).

Wych Elm

Matt brown (British) Straight grained, non-durable. Easy to work, screws, nails and glues well. Also finishes, stains and varnishes well 42 lb/ft³ (672 kg/m³).

Iroko

Reddy-brown, very durable, moderately easy to work. Finishes well, screws, nails and glues satisfactorily. Irregular grain may cause distortion—otherwise stable 40 lb/ft³ (640 kg/m³).

Mahogany (African)

Reddy-brown, moderately durable. Easy to work, finishes well, stable, screws, nails and glues well. Darkens on weathering 35–44 lb/ft³ (560–704 kg/m³).

Mahogany (American—Honduras)

Light reddy-brown to straw. Durable, stable, easy to work. Screws, nails and glues satisfactorily. Stains, paints and finishes well 34 lb/ft³ (544 kg/m³).

Makore

Dark reddy-brown to pinkish, very durable, works moderately with dulling, screws, nails and glues well. Finish very good 39 lb/ft³ (624 kg/m³).

Oak

Light to medium brown, durable, stable. Screws, nails and glues well. Stains in contact with steel. Texture uneven and coarse 45 lb/ft³ (720 kg/m³).

Sapele

Reddy-brown to pinkish, moderately durable, lacks stability. Screws, nails and glues well. Finishes excellently 35–43 lb/ft³ (560–688 kg/m³).

Teak

Medium to golden brown, straight grain, very durable, very stable. Screws, nails, glues well. Nails may split near edges. Moderately easy to work 41 lb/ft³ (656 kg/m³).

Utile

Purple to reddy-brown, striped grain, durable, fairly stable. Works fairly easily with some dulling, screws, nails, glues satisfactorily. Better than Sapele 34–37 lb/ft³ (544–592 kg/m³).

Softwoods

All these mentioned are suitable for use below decks in situations where they are not likely to be constantly soaked in water. Use suitable preservatives if completely covered with resinglass.

Cedar

Reddy-brown no resin, soft, durable, stable. Very easy to work, screws, nails and glues well. Finishes good. Stains in contact with steel 24 lb/ft³ (384 kg/m³).

Douglas fir

Orange-brown to reddy-yellow, moderately durable, moderately stable. Works well, screws, nails and glues satisfactorily. Resin and raised grain may cause trouble with finish. 33 lb/ft³ (528 kg/m³).

European Larch

Orangey-reddy-brown, durable, moderately stable. Easy to work, screws, nails and glues well. Finishes satisfactory. Resin pockets 35 lb/ft³ (560 kg/m³).

Pitch Pine

Pale yellow-brown, durable. Resinous pockets make for hard working. Fairly hard to screw and nail. Needs care for good finish. Straight grain, hard, strong 41 lb/ft³ (656 kg/m³).

European Redwood

Light reddy-brown to yellow-brown, moderately durable, stable, Easy to work, screws, nails and glues well. Stains, varnishes and paints satisfactorily 31 lb/ft³ (496 kg/m³).

Sitka Spruce

Light pink-brown with high sheen, non-durable, stable, works easily, screws, nails and glues well. Fine finish, varnishes and paints well 28 lb/ft³ (448 kg/m³).

Plywood

This versatile material with its high strength-to-weight ratio is excellent for fitting-out with. Ideally one should use marine plywood of good quality and in the UK this means that it should conform to BS 1088. Stamped on every sheet should be the Kite Mark of the British Standards Institution together with the words 'BS 1088'. The maker's mark will also be shown. Plywood sheets are available simply with 'BS 1088' stamped on them, but that is no guarantee that you are getting true marine plywood: look for the kite mark.

Plywood to BS 1088, the proper type, that is, should not show any open gaps or open defects in the outer veneers. The maker is allowed to fill gaps during the manufacturing process with a closely-fitted inlay, and a few sound knots are permitted together with the occasional worm-hole in the core—but only if the latter is running at rightangles to the surface.

Core material may contain a greater percentage of knots and worm-holes but the joins between sheets of veneers should not be greater than 20 thou (0.5 mm) wide. A ready-check is to examine the edges of the sheet to ascertain the size of gaps. Special plywoods are available with a greater percentage of the grains orientated in one direction—these being suitable for rudders and dagger boards etc (Photo. 73).

Having written the above it is worth restating that exterior grade Weather and Boil Proof (WBP) plywood is quite satisfactory for fitting out resinglass craft. True the timbers used may not be as durable as those used for Kite-marked BS 1088 timber, true the gaps and knot holes may exceed the British Standards specification. But it is also true that this material has been successfully used all over the world to build large cruising catamarans to the design of James Wharram—some of which have notable voyages to their credit.

WBP plywood is available in the same-sized sheets and thicknesses as that made to BS 1088, but generally seems to have slightly inferior-looking exterior veneers. However, chosen with care—paying particular attention to the edges of the sheet where gaps may be seen in the core veneers—the exterior-grade plywoods are quite adequate for internal joinery. If in doubt increase the thickness to the next available size.

Plywood is commonly available in 8 ft × 4 ft sheets and thicknesses are given in metric sizes—the nearest inch equivalents are shown in the table:

1.5 mm ($\frac{1}{16}$ in.)	15 mm ($\frac{5}{8}$ in.)
3 mm ($\frac{1}{8}$ in.)	16 mm ($\frac{5}{8}$ in.)
4 mm ($\frac{3}{16}$ in.)	18 mm ($\frac{3}{4}$ in.)
5 mm ($\frac{3}{16}$ in.)	19 mm ($\frac{3}{4}$ in.)
5 mm ($\frac{1}{4}$ in.)	22 mm ($\frac{7}{8}$ in.)
9 mm ($\frac{3}{8}$ in.)	25 mm (1 in.)
12 mm ($\frac{1}{2}$ in.)	

Plywood should be stored flat to prevent it from warping and it is important to prevent the end-grains from absorbing excessive amounts of water during storage. This means that the sheets should never be stood on edge in situations where they are likely to get wet—leaky sheds, conservatories, etc. Bonding-in seals the end grains.

Note that rain spots will mark plywood sheets and this can in some instances show through several coats of varnish. If plywood gets splashed when you are bringing it home the only thing to do is give a wipe all over with a wet cloth—this may raise the grain but the surface can be restored with sanding (Photo. 74).

Special faced plywoods are available and your supplier will advise on availability. Similarly he may also be able to supply larger sheets on request—up to 10 ft × 5 ft max., although generally speaking the standard-size is adequate for most fitting-out projects.

◄ *PHOTO. 73. These cabin doors lift off and are put away when its time for sea—or she is locked up on her mooring. They are really plywood panels mocked-up with hardwood surrounds. The Perspex windows have been set on wet varnish—a very good seal.*

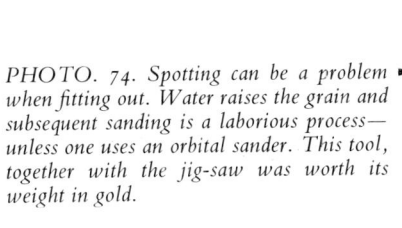

PHOTO. 74. Spotting can be a problem ► when fitting out. Water raises the grain and subsequent sanding is a laborious process— unless one uses an orbital sander. This tool, together with the jig-saw was worth its weight in gold.

Designs for tables

Depending upon the type of layout you choose the table will vary in size—if it is a dual-role table that must also be used for chartwork then the minimum size should be 28 × 22 inches (710 × 560 mm) for that will take a once-folded chart. A flat top sized at 30 × 25 inches (760 × 640 mm) is better, and the same dimension would also suit a drawer chart-drawer.

Folding cabin tables are fairly easy to arrange. They need a strong middle section which may be no more than six inches (150 mm) across—although ideally the bottoms of the side-members need to swell out to about 12 inches (300 mm) to provide increased lateral area in contact with the cabin floor and stop the table rocking. Such tables can have pull-out stays, or fold-round 'knees' to keep the table sections in the raised position. The table itself can be fastened to the cabin-sole by means of brackets and thumb-screws—a nice arrangement since it will allow you to take the table out into the cockpit for dining *al fresco*. The centre-section may incorporate a shelf and fiddle to keep bottles in—or the top of the centre-section may be lifted out to reveal a small 'drinks locker' (Fig. 83).

Hinges used need to be fairly stout, as do the staying arrangements, for people moving about in small boats often bear-down quite hard on surfaces and fitments.

Occasionally one sees boats which have their cabin table supported about a pole which runs from deckhead to sole. This pole may be structural in the sense that it is keeping the hull and deck apart—or at least lending some support—or else solely provided to take the table. There will be a sliding bracket with long knee and the table is then fixed to the knee (Fig. 84). Such a table has its merits as well as its drawbacks. Firstly it is easy to make and install. It is also capable of swivelling around (in the horizontal plane) to any desired angle—and it can also be adjusted to a comfortable height. Its support tube provides a somewhat slippery hand-hold and, in my opinion, tends to dominate the cabin through sheer ugliness. Perhaps that is simply because the builders who adopt this method also use a stark plank of plywood to form the table. A box section table with chart stowage would be an improvement as would perhaps a satin-finished tube instead of the commonly used chrome-plated type.

A slight variation on this is to use two such tubes and slide the table up and down them. This lets you use a deep box section and even folding table 'wings' as before (Fig. 84).

The table we decided to use on *Solitaire* (Photo. 75) had to be a multi-role one; we had to eat off it, use it for chart-work and then lower it down to form the basis of a double-berth. Complicating the design was the fact that

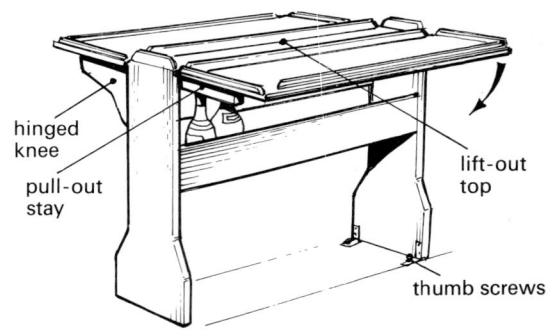

FIG. 83. *Cabin tables are a blessing if they suit the interior. This one folds down to reduce overall size and so make passing through the boat that much easier.*

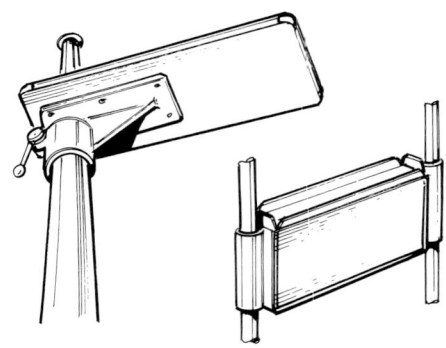

FIG. 84. *Sliding the table about a post (or posts) means that some form of positive lock is necessary. A single-pole calls for a very substantial knee.*

we had a half-bulkhead opposite it and I considered that to even things up we needed to support the deckhead with a post of sorts. Since we were going to have a post it then seemed sensible to use it to also support the cabin table. Figure 85 shows the basic dimensions for the table and the seating. All the joinery was 2 × 1 inch (50 × 25 mm) softwood hitched to existing members as much as possible, and glassed into the centreline of the hull. Mahogany t & g cladding with 12 mm plywood tops embodying the usual lift-out access panels completed the sitting accommodation.

The table was a little more complicated in that the post about which it slides is rectangular in section. The table is made from a combination of softwood, oak, plywood and teak, giving a chart stowage depth of 2 inches (50 mm). One end of the compartment has been divided off to take rolling-rules, pencils, dividers etc. (Photo. 76).

The sliding arrangements for the table are simple but effective. The post is hitched into the bottom of the dinette 'floor' which in turn is glassed to the hull. This lets any compression loads to be well shared out without creating a hard-spot. The top of the post is recessed into a

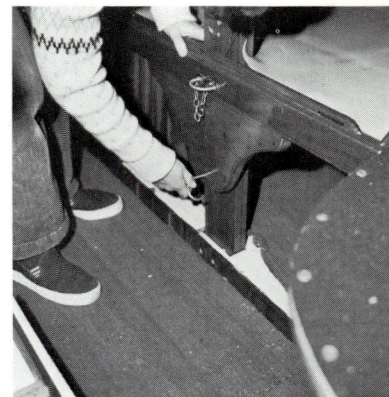

PHOTO. 75. *It might just look like an ordinary boat-table but it had to serve in a number of roles. . . .*

PHOTO. 76. *Back-flap hinges keep the top of the table flush for chart-work. . . .*

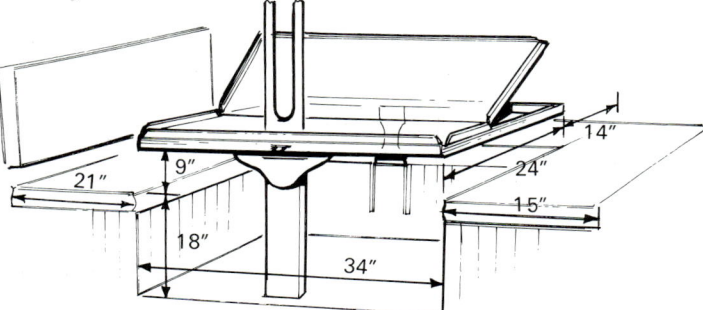

FIG. 85. *Solitaire's dinette table is built around a hardwood plank. It also serves as a chart-table. The top portion of the plank is cut to make hand-holds—much safer than slippery metal tube. . . .*

PHOTOS. 77, 78. *The plank about which the table is hung is fixed into the dinette structure at the base, and into a special hardwood pad at the top. It is slotted above the table height to make a grabrail.*

generously sized hardwood block, fitted, padded and throughbolted via external backing pieces—once again to spread the loads for if there is one thing resinglass dislikes it is concentrated point loads (Photos. 77, 78).

About the post is fitted a 'chute' fabricated by screwing and glueing two slotted wooden blocks to the bottom plywood of the table. A large laminated knee gives athwartships strength, while the fore-and-aft rigidity is provided by an oak 'double-knee'. The depth of the 'chute' is an inch (25 mm) greater than the width of the post—anything 'undersquare' (less than the thickness of the post) would tend to rock and cause the table to bind.

Above the raised height of the table the post is slotted to make a vertical grabrail suited to the physical heights of all users—quite unlike those handrails set into the deckhead which are fine for tall adults but useless for vulnerable children.

A sliding leg set in guides is fitted to the back face of the table and this supports the table when it is lowered for its bedtime role (Photos. 79, 80, 81). The height of the table is adjustable in one-inch (25 mm) increments by means of a series of holes drilled in pairs to take a $\frac{5}{16}$ inch (M8)

U-bolt. Another separate pin is used lower down to help locate the table horizontally and prevent it rocking in that same line about the post, for a certain amount of slop between the post and the chute is necessary for free movement. Lines scribed on the post help with alignment.

The success of this table for chart-work is undisputed, once that is, we overcame the fact that a near-centre hinge-line (with back-flap hinges) allowed spilled beverages to seep through onto the stored charts. A blackberry coloured Solent surmounting a chocolated large scale chart of Cherbourg, adds interest, if not flavour! A loose-fitting piece of soft vinyl flooring now covers the table-top and gives time to mop up spills. It is worth noting that this slightly resilient surface improves pencil work—something that should come as no surprise to a draughtsman. . . .

Visitors destined to sleep on this table have eyed it with a certain amount of interest, if not dismay. However its efficiency is vouched for the following morning by their reluctance to rise without first being bribed with a mug of tea!

Above the dinette is provision for a simple root-berth

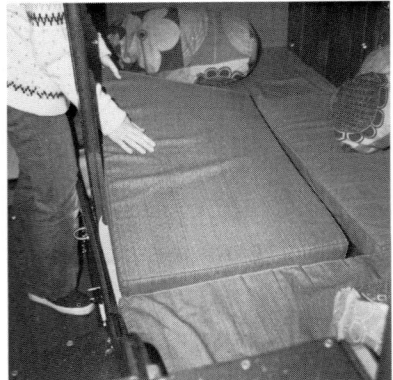

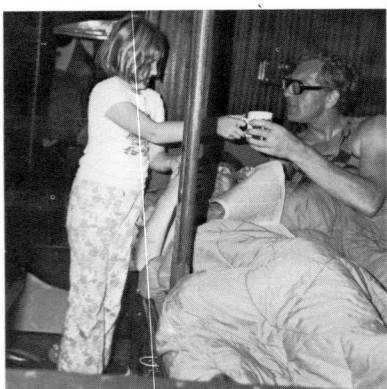

PHOTOS. 79, 80, 81. When lowered for its sleeping role, the table is supported front and back. A matching infill cushion fits on the table-top and once assembled the whole thing is very comfortable.

PHOTO. 82. Over the dinette is a fabric root-berth. It's pole-ends fit into plywood brackets, and the inset drawing shows how a square sectioned pole could be used.

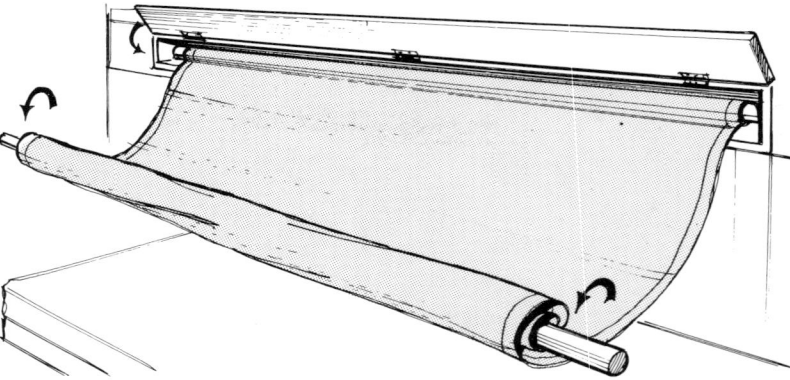

FIG. 86. Instead of cramming in too many permanent berths it may be better to provide occasional sleeping arrangements such as a root-berth. alternatively a metal pipe-cot could be used.

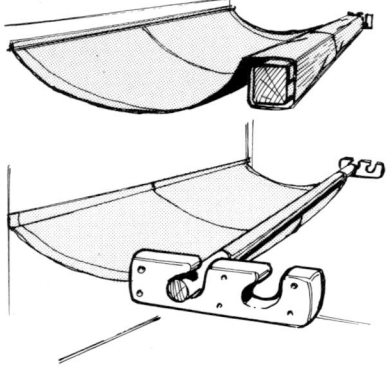

FIG. 87. With a fabric root-berth special end-brackets may be used to increase, or reduce, sag.

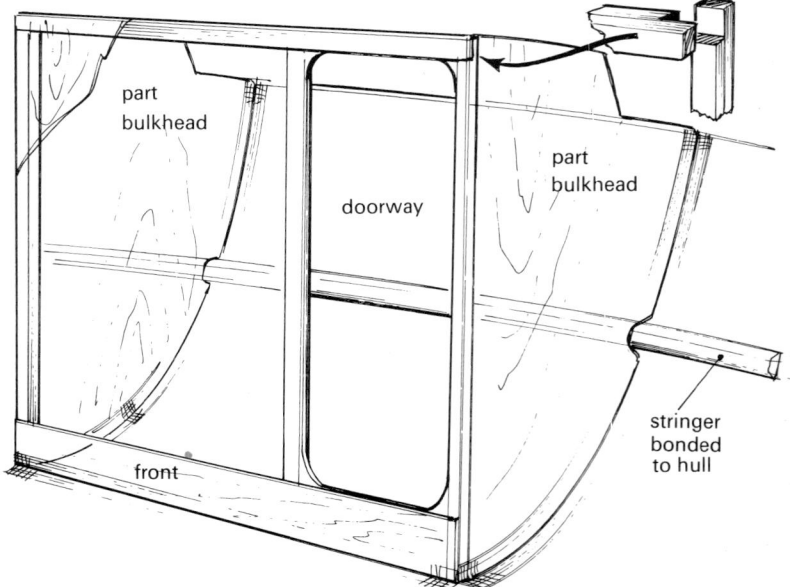

part bulkhead

doorway

part bulkhead

front

stringer bonded to hull

FIG. 88. If the design allows, then a small cabin could be worked in between a pair of bulkheads . . . it need only be as long as a single berth. W.C. compartments under the mast are commonly arranged between bulkheads.

(Fig. 86). Root-berths were once all the rage (just like gaff-rings and boomed staysails) but they are seldom seen today on production boats. I had intended to build one in when I first designed the cabin—but was dissuaded by the thought that we were never likely to sleep more than five, or six—the odd one sleeping on the cabin sole which measures 6 ft × 18 inches (1.8 × 460 mm). The basis of a root-berth is something like a stretcher. It has a stout 1½ inch (37 mm) ash pole and a couple of metres of plasticised fabric. Many of these materials may be both glued and stitched for added security. The ends of the pole fit into recessed blocks of wood screwed to opposing bulkheads (Photo. 82). The shape of these blocks is such that the weight of the occupant pulls the pole into the locked position. If one so desired the end blocks could have alternative positions to introduce, or remove, sag in the material (Fig. 87).

Alternatively, a square-sectioned pole can be used and it can be rotated to add or subtract material to suit the berth user. The outer edge of the root-berth material is fixed to the side of the hull joinerwork by means of patent turn-button fasteners pitched on 9 inch (225 mm) centres. The berth needs a weathercloth at least 12 inches (300 mm) high. Lanyards are used to tie the weathercloth, or leeboard, up to stoutly fastened eye-plates.

Figure 54 shows a typical settee berth and illustrates just how simple the structure can be. The ends of the berth may be partial—or go right up to the sidedecks, or even to the deckhead. Carefully cut from plywood they must be notched around the stringer and any other reinforcements. A strip of 2 × 1 inch (50 × 25 mm), notched for a halving-joint is then glued and screwed to each, taking care that it is positioned so that the berth top will end up horizontal, and at right-angles to the waterline. The plywood divider(s) are notched at the top to suit the stringer and also have a strip of 2 × 1 (50 × 25 mm) along the top face to lend support to the bunk top. The side panel has pieces of 2 × 1 (50 × 25 mm) both vertically and horizontally. The vertical members allow the end panels to be secured and the longitudinal 2 × 1 member forms the support for the berth top plywood panel. Note that while the top panel may flex under your weight, once it is screwed in place around its outside it will stiffen up considerably. A fiddle should be left on the front and end panels so that the berth cushion is held in place. Top access holes have a 'ring' of plywood to support the lift-out lids and these 'rings' may be complete pieces of plywood, or more likely two D's joined with two straights. Plenty of glue and clenched-over nails will produce strong lips. The ends of the berth and its front, plus any dividers should all be well bonded to the hull as previously described, and take care that all is painted or varnished before final

assembly makes such tasks doubly-difficult. I adopted the practice of painting inner locker faces with polyester resin while I was bonding them in. This seems to have been quite effective and in fact darkens down the plywood to a matt varnish effect. Where plywood will be seen it is a wise precaution to mask up to prevent unsightly resin-runs and splashes.

Working between a pair of partial bulkheads enables you to fit in those areas which either need a lot of 'wall' area, the chart table and navigating area for example (Fig. 28); safety—the galley (Fig. 25), or privacy—the WC (Fig. 88).

The bulkheads must be carefully marked out by one of the methods previously outlined and set into the hull true both in their vertical alignment, and parallel if fitting of other components is to be accomplished without too much hassle. Initially you might find it easier just to secure them in place with putty before assembling the rest of the structure 'dry' and then dismantling completely before bonding-in. This will allow you to approve (or otherwise) the looks and such personal preferences such as work-top height. A chart-table (Fig. 28) should have its working surface at an angle of about 15 degrees, other surfaces should be set horizontal.

Once again the basic framework material is 2 × 1 inch (50 × 25 mm) and only very simple woodworking is required. Unless, that is, you decide to fit drawers!

If you are fitting a door to the WC it will obviously need a well-framed-up doorway—jambs and all (Fig. 88). These could be 2 × 2 inch (50 × 50 mm) or made-up from two pieces of 2 × 1 inch (50 × 25 mm) glued and screwed together. The doorway will need a lintel, of about the same scantlings and a step-over web at the bottom will give the single door something positive to close against and at the same time brace the bulkheads. Alternatively you may decide to arrange two half-doors which when opened out from the WC compartment doorway effectively close off the fore-, and main-cabins.

The cockpit-well will need supporting for it is a fairly highly-loaded area—four or five adults could impose static loads of 800 lb (360 kg) or so, and this could be higher as one jumps down into it. The easiest way to reinforce the bottom of the cockpit sole itself is with a sandwich-panel of end-grain balsa or foam. Hopefully that is what your moulder has already done for it is no fun working upside down in confined places with resin and glass. If he has not done a proper job then I would be tempted to use instead of a sandwich an 'egg-box' made up from a series of longitudinal and cross-webs matted both to the underside of the sole and to the hull. Even if the sole has been reinforced with a sandwich it will also need side panels taken down to the hull to prevent the possibility of 'swaying' and flexing. These side panels of plywood also help make the cockpit lockers and act as braces for the quarter-berths as (Fig. 89) shows.

In a berth an 'air-height' of 18 inches (460 mm) inclusive of an allowance for a 4 inch (100 mm) mattress is the minimum to aim for.

Here, as elsewhere, there will be a compromise for should you decide on, say, a height of 24 inches (610 mm) over the top of the berth then its width will be considerably reduced. Note that with some modern boats with very high freeboard and shallow cockpit-wells it may be possible to work in a double-berth under the cockpit sole as in figure 90.

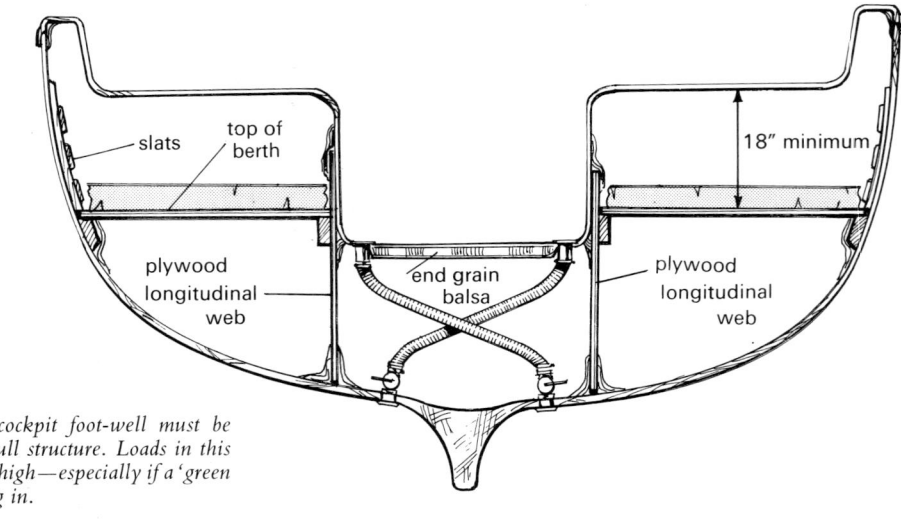

FIG. 89. *The cockpit foot-well must be braced into the hull structure. Loads in this area may be very high—especially if a 'green one' comes rolling in.*

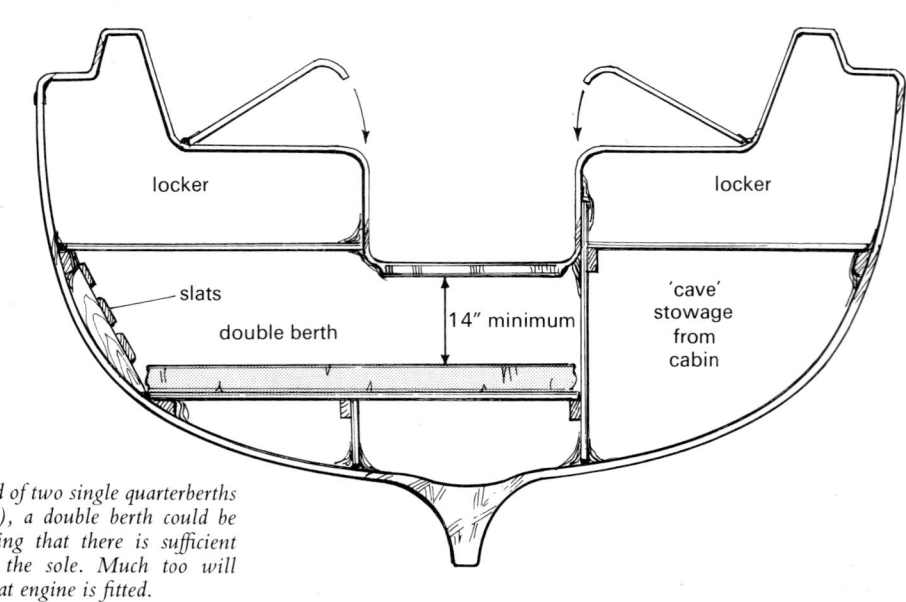

FIG. 90. *Instead of two single quarterberths (as in FIG. 89), a double berth could be arranged providing that there is sufficient clearance under the sole. Much too will depend upon what engine is fitted.*

6

Berths

Elsewhere in this book I described alternative layouts—some of which made use of a settee-berth which converted into a double as required. The easiest way to achieve this is to use a structure as shown in figure 91. It makes use of a series of 3 × 1 inch (75 × 25 mm) slats which are arranged so that they slide between themselves when the front panel is pulled forward. Naturally some provision must be made to accommodate the extra cushion that such a berth requires and this may be used either as a backrest, or more probably as a double-thickness settee cushion—thus making a very comfortable seat. A bonus when sleeping on the open slats is the good ventilation under the mattress, keeping it cooler than its solid plywood counterpart. Use a hard polyurethane varnish on the slats, an ordinary one will quickly spoil with the sliding action.

Elasticated webbing, sold for upholstery work, can also be used to make very comfortable berths (Fig. 92). It needs to be stretched nice and taut to start with, otherwise when you sit down it will sag excessively. The berth structure must be strongly made for the 'point' loading can be quite high and a load concentrated at one place will cause the webbing to exert a strong inward pull on its fastenings. A rounded hardwood batten with plenty of screws and cup-washers can be used to trap the webbing, which could also be of the non-stretch woven Terylene type as used for car seat-belts. It may need a stitch or two where the 'wefts' and 'warps' coincide to stop gaps developing, but generally speaking, if the tension is correct no stitches will be required. Note that a three inch thick (75 mm) mattress or less could be used with this type of berth.

Other types of structure can be used for berths. For instance a snug sea-berth can be made by using longitudinal slats of 2 × ¾ inch (50 × 18 mm) over a series of cross-webs. The degree of curvature should not be excessive for comfortable sleeping—something like 4 inches (100 mm) over 24 inches (600 mm) is about right (Fig. 93).

Alternatively a flat berth top can be made more

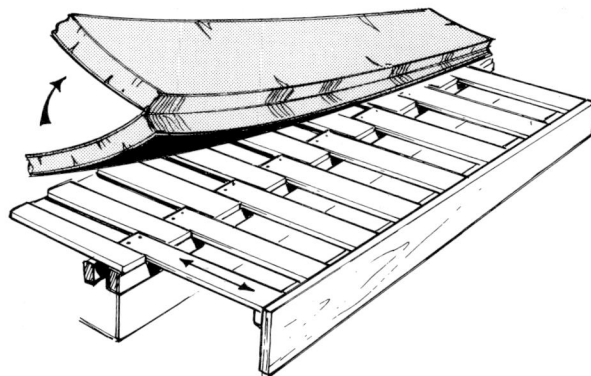

FIG. 91. Double-berths that are based on a settee can be arranged in a variety of ways—this one makes use of sliding slats.

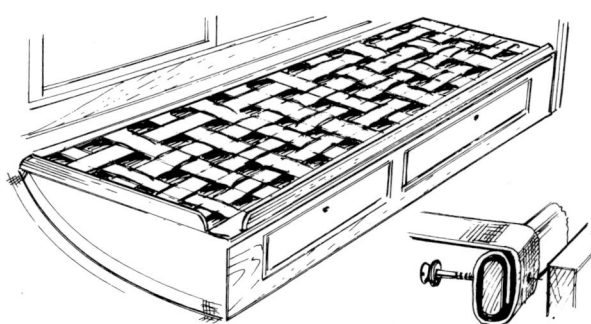

FIG. 92. Webbing makes a very comfortable berth and allows a thinner, 3 inch (75 mm), mattress to be used.

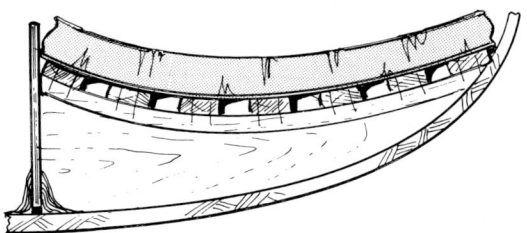

FIG. 93. Berths are much more comfortable if they conform to the human frame. A thin mattress on a curved slatted bunk feels much better than the same mattress on a hard, flat, surface.

comfortable by having a hinged bunk-board permanently fitted to it. When not in use this is folded flat under the mattress and when required unfolded to positive stops. This, together with a fabric lee-cloth, makes a very secure passage-berth out of an otherwise untenable settee (Fig. 94).

Hanging lockers and wet-lockers for oilskins may be worked in as required. They may be between partial bulkheads or built-in against such a bulkhead. Once again only a simple framing up is required and the front could have a narrow louvred door, be left open to give maximum ventilation, or be closed off with a zipped plasticised fabric 'door'. We have a canvas 'door' to *Solitaire's* hanging locker, or wardrobe, and when we are underway this can be fastened in place by means of large press-studs. We do this to prevent spray or splashes coming in through the forehatch wetting our clothes—although since we have our double-berth almost under the forehatch we are especially careful about letting water enter! Wooden and plastics hangers are to be preferred to those jangling (cheap) wire ones, which also tend to leave white marks on clothes.

The actual dimensions of a hanging locker are much smaller than you might at first imagine (Fig. 95). For instance a man's jacket and trousers on a hanger require a space of 18 inches (460 mm) by a drop of 3 ft (910 m) and a depth of 12 inches (300 mm) will accommodate about seven suits—not that you are likely to ever want to travel with that amount of apparel! Even so a depth around this amount will allow you to hang up shirts and blouses which will then arrive fairly 'wrinkle-free'. Good ventilation is important in the hanging locker if mildew is to be kept at bay—or you could go to the other extreme and insert your clothes into shrouds of plastic bags (dustbin liners) so that as much air, and hence moisture, as possible is kept off them. We use this method on *Solitaire* and find it works well for periods up to a month or so.

Cabin floors, or more correctly 'soles', pose two fitting problems. Firstly should they be firmly glassed in place? This method has the dubious merit (in this case) of simplicity, for all that is required is a suitable-shaped plywood panel, which is prepared and matted in. This type of sole will prevent a small amount of bilge-water slopping about the boat—but it will also prevent any water on top of it draining into the sump where it can be attacked with the bilge-pump. Also a fixed floor means that in the event of an accident you will be prevented from rapidly checking the hidden area at a time when speed is essential.

With these points in mind I suggest that it is wiser to adopt the second method; more work is involved, for the sole will need supporting at its edges, and with a wide floor area, webs across the boat will also be needed (Fig. 96). These webs, or 'floors' may be cut from fairly thin plywood, say 6 mm, with their tops thickened to provide an increased bearing (or 'landing') surface. Webs should be well matted to the hull and it could be advantageous to completely encapsulate them in CSM and resin to protect them from constant immersion.

Whatever the method adopted the best material for

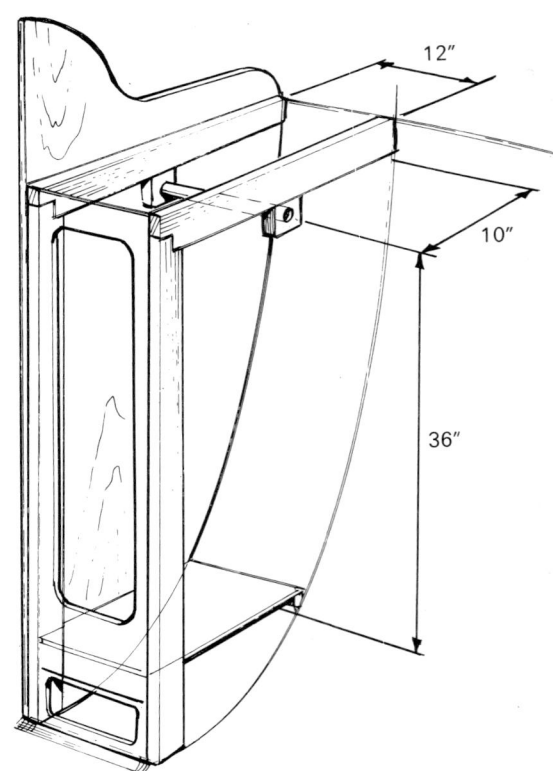

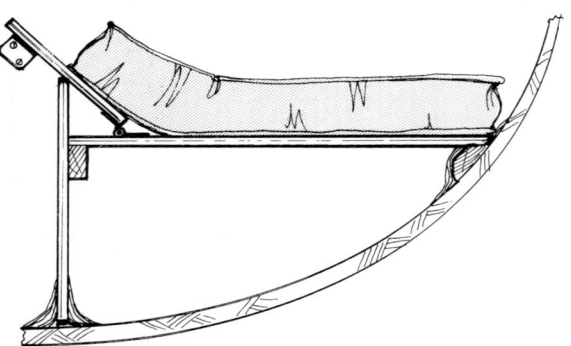

FIG. 94. A fold-out bunk-board can add curvature to a flat berth and make it more comfortable. When not required it stows under the mattress.

FIG. 95. A wardrobe, or hanging locker, with these proportions will take all the clothes you need for a longish cruise. Plastics hangers are better than wire ones, and a door is a matter of choice—but a good airflow keeps mould away!

the sole is plywood, a thickness of around 12 mm is minimum, and I would suggest proper marine-grade plywood, for you need something dimensionally stable and able to withstand repeated wettings without damage. The end-grains need to be adequately protected for it is there that water will enter the plywood. For safety and ease of handling the sole should be arranged in conveniently sized panels—something around 2 foot (610 mm) is right, and the webs should be arranged to coincide with the ends of these sections. On *Solitaire* we have fitted teak slats along the sole to provide a fairly non-slip surface; exposed once the carpet is taken up and we are underway. That is one of the nice things about a resinglass boat, the bilge does not get too wet, and thus carpets are feasible if you chose a fairly short-pile synthetic with a woven /latex backing. Avoid foams for these backings invariably seem to sop up water like sponges and never seem to dry out.

A variation on the teak slat scheme is to make the cabin sole a 'feature' by using narrow teak slats laid and payed with a black polysulphide rubber. Or you could choose contrasting woods, say ash and teak, which with black stripes (paying) between, could look very smart. A strictly functional approach would be to stick down a patent non-slip surface material to the plywood sole.

Should it appeal there is something to be said for building into the sole a 'dust-pan'. Cabin sweepings are fed into this and then picked up with the pan and taken out for disposal.

More winter work

Racks can be easily made and fitted to add interest around the boat. They can be fixed permanently or arranged on 'key-holes' so that they may be lifted free and carried out to the cockpit, or on to the cabin-table as required. 'Key-hole slots are easy and cheap to arrange, for they need only a large-size dome-headed woodscrew (Fig. 97). A hole is drilled through the bottom of the rack and this is then extended to make a slot which has a sliding clearance on the shank of the woodscrew. Used in pairs this form of attachment is surprisingly secure and has the additional merit of being quick to make.

As figure 98 shows, racks can be used for glasses and mugs if they are of compatible size. The depth needs to be at least one-third the height of the glasses—and the

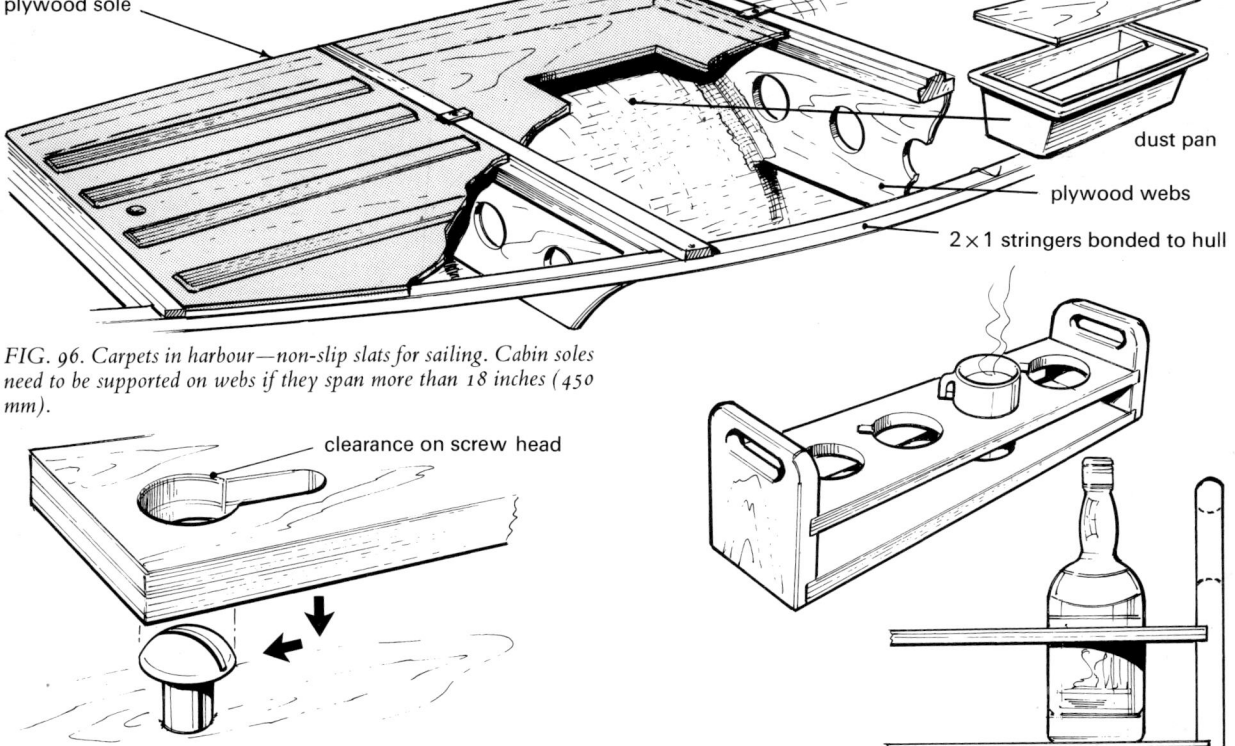

FIG. 96. Carpets in harbour—non-slip slats for sailing. Cabin soles need to be supported on webs if they span more than 18 inches (450 mm).

FIG. 97. Pairs of 'key-hole' slots can be used for many purposes. Vertical key-holes could be used to install semi-permanent equipment such as echo-sounders, and radios, in various locations around the boat.

FIG. 98. Keeping several jobs on the go is the key to a quick launching party. This mug, or glass rack, crafted in teak would enhance any boat.

same sort of measurement applies to bottles too. Take care though not to make the clearance too deep if you are using mugs for you want to be able to grip their handles.

A 'pilot-berth rack' (Fig. 99) can in fact be used anywhere around the boat. Apart from the obvious use of having somewhere to park one's glass or mug, there is also a need for stowing those small items which are easily lost in cavernous lockers—a watch, keys, small coins and the like.

These racks and other items shown elsewhere have the great merit of being easy to fabricate and if 'treewood' such as teak is chosen then they can elevate the eye-appeal of large areas of featureless plywood—especially if the same wood is used to face-up locker fronts etc.

Once you get into 'production' then, apart from the racks around the galley, you could also make a sink-cover which doubles as a bread board on one face and perhaps a chopping board on its other (Fig. 100). Book and magazine racks (Fig. 101) can be quickly made and any left overs used to make a 'navigator's tidy' to take pencils, rule, dividers etc (Fig. 102). If you drill holes

into a solid block of teak this will make a very simple but effective pencil holder.

Naturally this type of work should be regarded as a fill-in between other, larger parts of the fitting-out operation. There is a temptation to make lots of these 'nick-nacks' some of which may eventually be thrown aside as you come to see that they could just as easily be built in to the rest of the boat's furniture.

To oil, or not, is again a matter of personal preference, as is painting or varnish. Eggshell (matt) finish varnish can look attractive and may be achieved either by means of special varnishes or by matting down well-cured ordinary polyurethane varnish with fine wet-and-dry. Most oily woods such as teak will need their surfaces degreasing before they will accept varnish properly. I would recommend a two-pot polyurethane varnish around the galley and cabin tables, because it dries extremely hard-wearing and is resistant to unsightly marks left by very hot pans, mugs etc. Mind you it takes more effort to apply this varnish—but the extra trouble is worth it.

FIG. 99. A small thing—but the numbers of boats I have been on where there is no where to store small personal things.

FIG. 100. A sink cover that doubles as a chopping, or bread-board, is another easy item to make during those long winter evenings when working with resin is impossible. Note that the bottom piece of wood needs to be a very snug fit in the sink Once you get going then a magazine rack, or binocular bin are child's play. Card-table baize makes a good lining material.

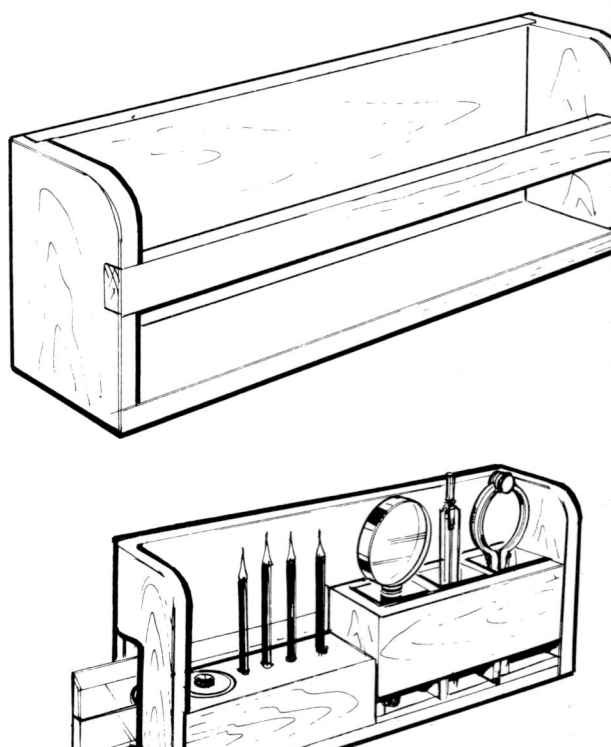

FIG. 101. Bookshelves and a nav' rack can take the bareness out of an otherwise empty bulkhead.

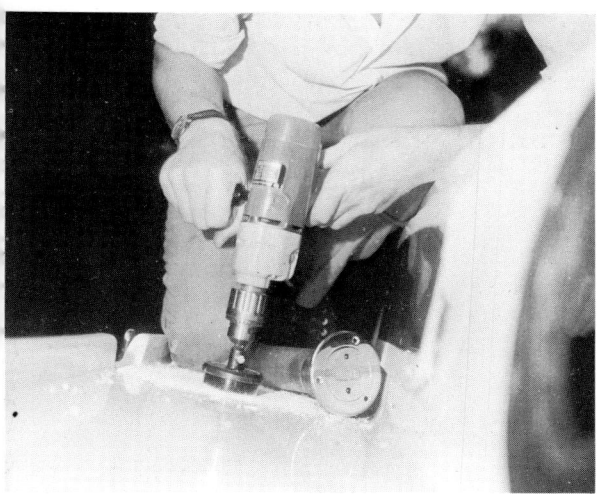

PHOTO. 83. *The cheapest hole saws are quite good enough for drilling through resinglass laminates. Although here it is being used for the deck filler plate, it will zip through the hull for the sea-cocks with ease . . . and cut plywood too.*

On seacocks and skin fittings

It might be thought that a resinglass hull and superstructure are waterproof, and in a practical sense that is so, but the gel-coats used are in fact microscopically permeable. The lay-up will take up about 1.5 to 2.5 per cent of water if the boat is afloat the whole year round. After that proportion has been reached the further amount of water absorbed is, in most cases, nil.

The exceptions would be where the gel-coat is very thin, or very porous due to air-bubbles, or if there is an undercured layer which has allowed its pigment to leach out, so forming galleries through which water can reach the rest of the laminate. It might be supposed that the actual polyester resin is waterproof—and once again it very nearly is—it is the microscopic glass fibres that draw water into the lay-up by capillary action.

How you may protect your hull is dealt with later on, but this business of capillary absorption, or wicking, means that any hole cut through the laminate should be properly sealed so that the raw edges do not present an easy waterpath. Obviously those holes below the waterline are more critical in this respect than deck-fittings—which, if they leak—will soon let you know by the drips that fall on to you!

To some extent the bedding compounds that are used to make skin-fittings watertight will also seal the cut resinglass. However, although a large flange inside the hull, or even large nuts and washers, may keep water out, it is quite possible for there to be a water-path into the skin itself.

The correct procedure is to drill the hole to take the skin-fitting, then degrease, and paint the cut laminate with gel-coat resin. It need not be a waxed gel-coat for it matters little if it stays tacky. You may need to shield the area around the hole with masking-tape to keep it clean, but generally speaking a coat or two of gel-coat carefully applied with a small brush is sufficient.

Note that cheap hole-saws may be used to drill those large holes needed for WC outlet and cockpit drain skin-fittings—around 1¾ inches (45 mm) diameter (Photo. 83). The flanges of the fittings need to be bedded on a rubber-type mastic; fastenings should be lightly nipped up, and fully tightened when the mastic has cured to form a gasket. Some seacocks are supplied with integral skin-fittings and these may sometimes be found with dome-headed coach-bolts supplied as standard. These fasteners with their square section under the head are obviously designed for use with wooden hulls and any attempt to use them in a tight hole in the resinglass laminate will cause it to crack locally (Photos. 84, 85). Thus you are left with the problem of either drilling the through-holes oversized; filing the square section off the bolts, or filing out the holes through the hull square to match the bolts. Working single-handed the third option is probably the best!

The quality, or perhaps the lack of it might be more correct, of seacocks and the occasional skin fitting, leaves

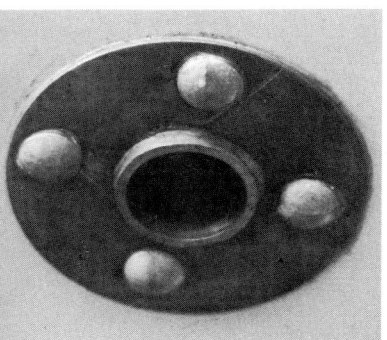

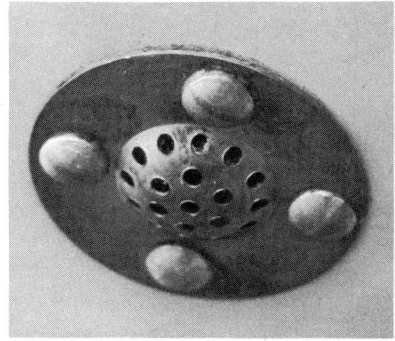

PHOTOS. 84, 85. *Both these sea-cocks were supplied with bolts and outer ring and rose. Unfortunately the bolts were designed for use with wooden hulls for they had square portions under their heads. Coach bolts should not be used with resinglass—they will crack it as they are drawn home.*

PHOTO. 86. What a mess! This sorry looking sea-cock assembled here for the benefit of the camera was not only full of sand cavities, but lacked locknuts on the top flange, had internal apertures that did not line up, and just look at that lip which is bound to cause a blockage. The bolts supplied were brass. . . .

PHOTO. 87. A burr-cutter in a power drill soon gave a smooth transition from outside to inside diameter—almost like tuning up a cylinder head—but worth the effort.

PHOTO. 88. The blacked-in portion shows just how much metal had to be removed before the hole in the plug matched that in the body when the cock was turned to 'ON'. Once again a good radius was worked-in to ease the flow around nearly a rightangle.

much to be desired. Mostly they are sand-castings—often full of blow-holes (Photo. 86). The one notable exception are those from Blakes of Gosport, England, who many years ago invested in a set of matched metal moulds in which their seacocks are cast to close tolerances. Of course, not all seacocks are bad—some are simply indifferent; as are the boat builders who fit common brass gate-valves of the sort used by plumbers. Brass should not be used for such an important job for it contains within itself the seeds of its own destruction—copper and zinc have a built in galvanic 'fizz' which will, in a relatively short while, cause the fitting to fall apart. Do not think that resinglass boats are immune from galvanic and electrolytic troubles. Turn to page 119 for a full explanation.

Nor are boats intended for freshwater use protected from these problems for most 'freshwater' is in fact polluted!

I bought my seacocks from two sources, and what a sorry sight they were. They all suffered— I had seven in two sizes—from at least one design fault, and all were guaranteed to give trouble of some kind or other! Take for instance the outlet seacock on the WC plumbing. Now anyone will tell you that a sudden change in diameter of a pipe carrying a mixture of water, paper and human excreta, is likely cause a blockage. Yet any standard seacock for use with a $1\frac{1}{2}$ inch (37 mm) pipe chokes the bore down to $1\frac{1}{4}$ inches (30 mm) at the very

point where its waste has to be coaxed around a 90 degree bend. So the very first thing to do with your 'factory finished' seacock is to take out its insides and ease out the bore of the spigot to remove the step. Burr cutters in a power-drill are the answer. Wear goggles to protect your eyes from those flying needles (Photo. 87).

Having sorted out one blockage, on to the next! On all my seacocks I found that the hole through their taper-plug failed to line up exactly with the hole through the spigot. Thus there was a lip which, in some cases, was as much as $\frac{1}{8}$ inch (3 mm) high—or wide—against which a blockage was likely to pile up (Photo. 88).

The cure again is very simple. Insert the taper-plug and align the 'ON' position marks. Scribe around the bore and remove the plug and go to work. Remember that this time a radius to ease flow around those 90 degrees is desirable. While you are about it remove all those nasty burrs and flashes which should properly have been eliminated during the factory fettling. What I find annoying is that if the hole had been cast slightly larger in the first place there would have been no need for these 'tuning' operations.

The next point to consider is just how well the male and female tapers mate together. Clean well, smear the plug with fine carborundum (valve grinding) lapping paste, insert, and give it a few half-turns. Lift the plug, move it through 90 degrees and give a few more half-turns. Remove from the body, and if there is less than a

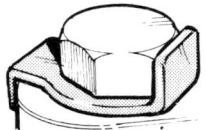

PHOTOS. 89, 90. On the last lap—if you will excuse the pun! It is essential that the plug and body are a close fit, otherwise they will have to be tightened down to prevent a leak—and then you won't be able to turn the handle! At least half an inch (12 mm) of lapped surface at top and bottom is required.

FIG. 102. Tab-washers must be used whenever it would be dangerous for the bolt (or nut) to work loose. Some sea-cocks are made with no provision for wiring or locknuts.

PHOTO. 91. These bolts need tab-washers to prevent them working loose. Remember that they cannot be tightened down hard or the plug will not turn. Such bolts will soon work themselves out through engine vibrations, etc. and leave a gaping hole.

half inch (12 mm) wide band of mating surfaces at top and bottom, carry on lapping until there is (Photos 89, 90).

Once again it should not be left to the careful fitter-outer to go through these antics. The manufacturers should be able to set his machines to within half a thou or so!

Having lapped in the components, strip down and thoroughly clean to remove the grinding paste; paraffin seems to work best. Smear the plug with a good underwater grease and reassemble.

That simple job presents another area of contention—or bad design. Unless the top flange of the seacock is provided with bolts with locknuts it is impossible to set the device up correctly. If nuts *are* fitted then one only has to tighten down the bolts evenly until the plug becomes hard to turn. Back both bolts off by about half-a-turn, hold them still and nip up the nuts. The plug should now rotate sweetly. It may be advantageous to use one of those anærobic resin glues on the threads to lock them up chemically—however if you assemble everything well-greased the use of this material is suspect and I would not put much trust in it.

That the plugs should turn easily is important for it means that the distaff members of the crew should have no difficulty in turning them on and off each time the WC is used. One thing for sure—an hour spent at this stage with nice clean components is worth many foul hours playing 'plumbers' to trace a blockage which, if the designer and manufacturer had done their jobs properly, would probably never have occurred!

What about those other seacocks, inlets, sink wastes, exhaust, and cockpit drains? In fact they pass only water with the minimum of solids. All they will need then is lapping-in and setting-up correctly.

What if there are no lock-nuts? Well, like me, you will just have to make up locking washers and put them under the heads of the bolts; turn one tab up against a flat on the hex' head, and the other down over the seacock's top flange (Photo. 91) (Fig. 102). Do not ignore this advice. I heard of a chap who did, and running-in his badly-installed engine the bolts vibrated out and left him with a 1¼ inch (30 mm) hole through the bottom of his boat.

One last thing. Make up some suitably tapered softwood plugs and hitch one with a length of non-rot line to each seacock. Should you need it you will have the wherewithal to seal the hole if it ever falls apart.

Custom 'ironwork' is easy

One of the largest areas of saving hard-earned cash is the boat's 'ironwork'. If you cost out those stainless steel items such as pushpit, pulpit, cleats, stem-head fitting

PHOTO. 93. Six stanchions and their bases custom-made to suit. They were cranked in slightly to stop that splayed-out look that one often sees. The 'ironwork' was assembled and checked before sending away to be galvanized. Seeing it in position gave me a chance to add on those small items which are so necessary—brackets for the nav' lights for example.

PHOTO. 92. Solitaire reaching in a smart breeze. Note the stanchions, pushpit and steps up her mast. The headsail boom is in the foreground, and it is controlled via a single sheet working over a wire-span across the deck behind the forehatch.

with roller and stay attachments, chain-plates, stanchions and fairleads the total will frighten you. Then sit down and add the cost of all those stainless steel fastenings which you will need to bolt them on with!

I came to the conclusion that I could make everything *Solitaire* needed for a sixth of that total—and in addition I planned to fit a tubular platform to her bows to extend the foredeck working area and allow me to work in a cutter sailplan (Photo. 92).

Galvanized mild steel water pipe is a universal sort of material which together with some flat strip, angle, and box-section was used to fabricate all I needed. There was the additional ever-present bonus, that I could custom-make these fittings to my own preferences. Take the stanchions for instance . . . (Photo. 93).

I am rather long in the leg and the near-standard UK 24 inch (600 mm) rail catches me exactly behind the knee. Thus my stanchions and rails are 27 inches (690 mm) high—much safer!

Then again I object to the thin diameter of wire that is invariably used for lifelines. To avoid this I have welded short pieces of pipe to the top of each stanchion through which 1¼ inch (30 mm) circumference pre-stretched Terylene rope passes. This is much kinder to rub against and not so prone to hidden corrosion (and subsequent failure) as is plastics-covered galvanized wire. NATurally experience has shown that these ropes need protecting from chafe—but there is enough clearance

for the rope to be locally 'wormed, parcelled and served'. Attachment at either end is by lanyards through a hard-eye splice. That allows the top line to be moved as need be, or as old salts would have it, 'freshen the nip'.

The stanchions themselves were very simple to make (Fig. 103) (Photo. 170). I used ¾ inch (20 mm) nominal bore pipe (outside diameter 1⅛ inch—28 mm) set into 2 × 1 inch mild-steel box section bases. The box section was cut at an angle to allow bolts to enter the base-plate, and the pipe was let through a suitably sized hole in the top face (made by drilling lots of small holes and chiseling out the centre). One good weld all round the top face fixes the pipe in place. If you do not have access to a small electric welder, then I am sure that you will be able to find someone who will weld them up for a reasonable fee. Alternatively you might consider buying a small unit which you could sell when your work is finished.

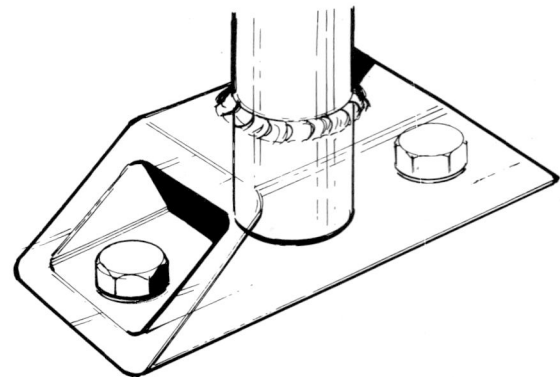

FIG. 103. Rectangular box sections make a good starting off point for stanchions. Add a length of tube and you're almost there!

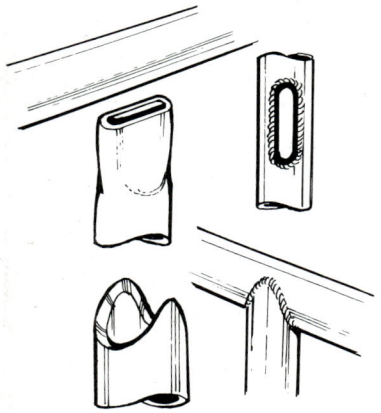

FIG. 104. *Fitting pipe-to-pipe calls for some accurate cutting. I chose to slightly flatten the tops of vertical tube members so as to form a rectangular lozenge which makes welding a great deal easier.*

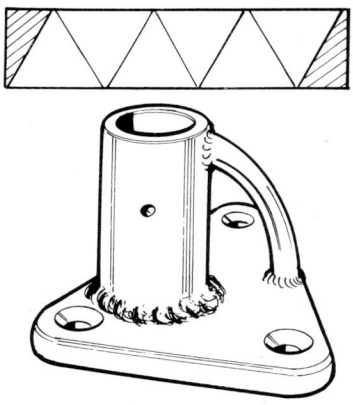

FIG. 105. *Custom-fabricated stanchions and their bases are a matter of choice. Provision can be made to incorporate a number of design features to meet specific requirements.*

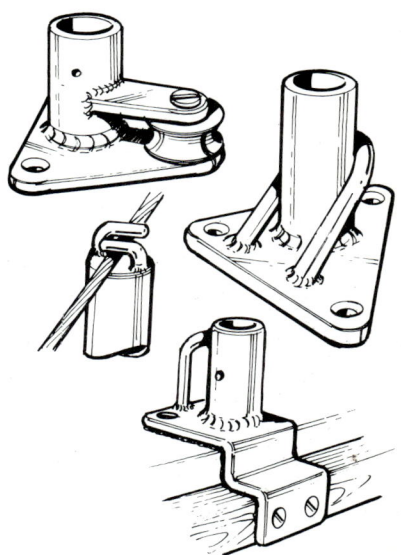

Half way up my pipe stanchions I put a flat area by inserting the pipe in a vice and squeezing. This increases the width of the pipe without weakening it, and allows a small hole to be drilled through to take a centre wire (not rope this time . . .). The hole-size was adjusted to take a short stub of copper pipe to make a ferrule and thus prevent the wire fretting on sharp edges. The ferrule was inserted after the stanchion was galvanized. (See later).

When it came to welding all those pieces of pipe together I remembered a tip from my youth that greatly simplified things. It applies to all those occasions when one wants to weld together two pipes at right angles to each other (Fig. 104). Place the open-ended pipe adjacent to the weld in the vice and pinch it to form a lozenge. This gives two flat, straight welds (plus two nearly square ends) instead of a complicated fitting job and then rising circular welds (or else large gaps which must be filled—and that is poor practice!). Note a stanchion should have at least one bolt through the inboard toe of its base, and be capable of withstanding a load of 150 lb (70 kg) applied horizontally to the top of each stanchion. This means that the laminate and under-deck backing pad must be well-fitted and amply dimensioned. Now although I chose a standard box section for my stanchion bases there is no reason why you need adopt the same design. Figure 105 shows several alternatives. Sizes may be altered to suit specific requirements, as may the addition of special features such as sheaves for turning blocks, or stout 'eyes' for a safety harness, or snatch-block attachments. Having started making simple stanchions there is no reason why you should not progress to producing 'gateway' types which need the addition of a second leg, or strut to enable a gap to be opened in the safety wires without

weakening the structure. For although stanchions need to be firmly fixed and stoutly made to accommodate those mis-uses as when coming alongside another boat with too much speed on, it is the end attachments of the wire that are very highly loaded when a body is hurled against it. Figures 106 & 107 show some other items which may be easily fabricated.

I used the same basic materials to make up the pushpit and pulpit—with the exception that the pushpit legs terminate in flat feet (2 × 1 inches (50 × 25 mm) by $\frac{1}{4}$ inch (6 mm) thick. The pulpit was a bit more complicated since it is directly on top of a tubular bowsprit (Photo. 94). Short stubs of smaller diameter pipe were welded to the bowsprit and the legs of the pulpit fit over these. The reasons for this arrangement are two-fold; ease of assembly and galvanizing. The final attachment of the pulpit to the bowsprit was by means of small diameter ($\frac{3}{16}$ inch—M5) throughbolts through the legs and stubs.

Bending pipe of small diameter—and 1$\frac{1}{8}$ inch (28 mm) is small diameter in the pipeworld—is easy (Photo 95). There are several 'rules of thumb' which are a help when it comes to calculating lengths of pipe required. Firstly, the minimum radius that one can achieve without recourse to sophisticated gear is equal to 5 or 6 times the outside diameter of the pipe. Anything tighter and you run the risk of kinks. The length of pipe needed to go around a 90 degree bend is approximately 1.75 × the radius. The radius being measured to the centre of the pipe. For a 180 degree U bend take three times the radius. For angles other than 90 and 180 degrees the formula is: radius × inclusive angle (in degrees × 0.018. Incidentally those rules apply equally to bending flat metal.

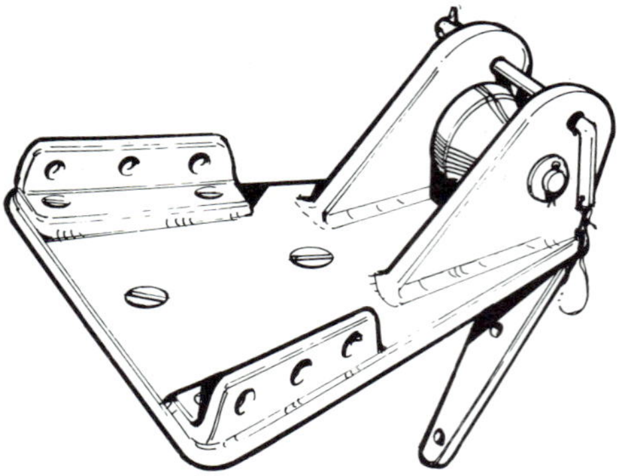

FIG. 106. Stemhead fittings are invariably too small and under-engineered for serious cruising. The use of easily obtainable components such as a trailer keel-roller offers some considerable savings in time and money.

PHOTO. 94. Short stubs are welded to the tubular 'bowsprit' and the legs of the pulpit sit over them. The teak slats on the deck give a good footing in an otherwise slippery area.

PHOTO. 95. Bending small pipe is easy. A hole in a plank lets you pull it round as required without kinking or forming a series of flats. Ordinary galvanized waterpipe has dozens of uses when it comes to 'ironwork'.

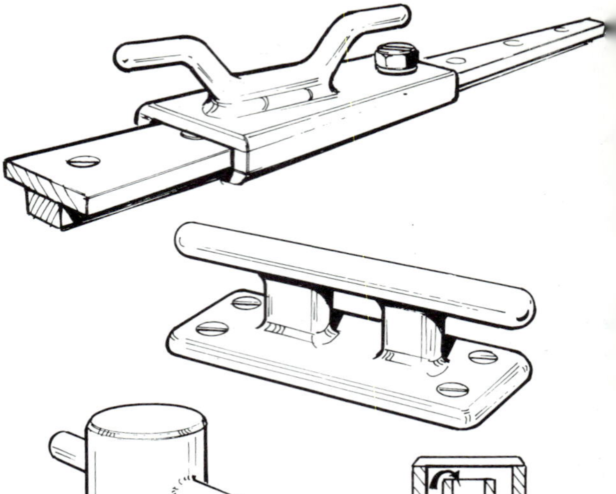

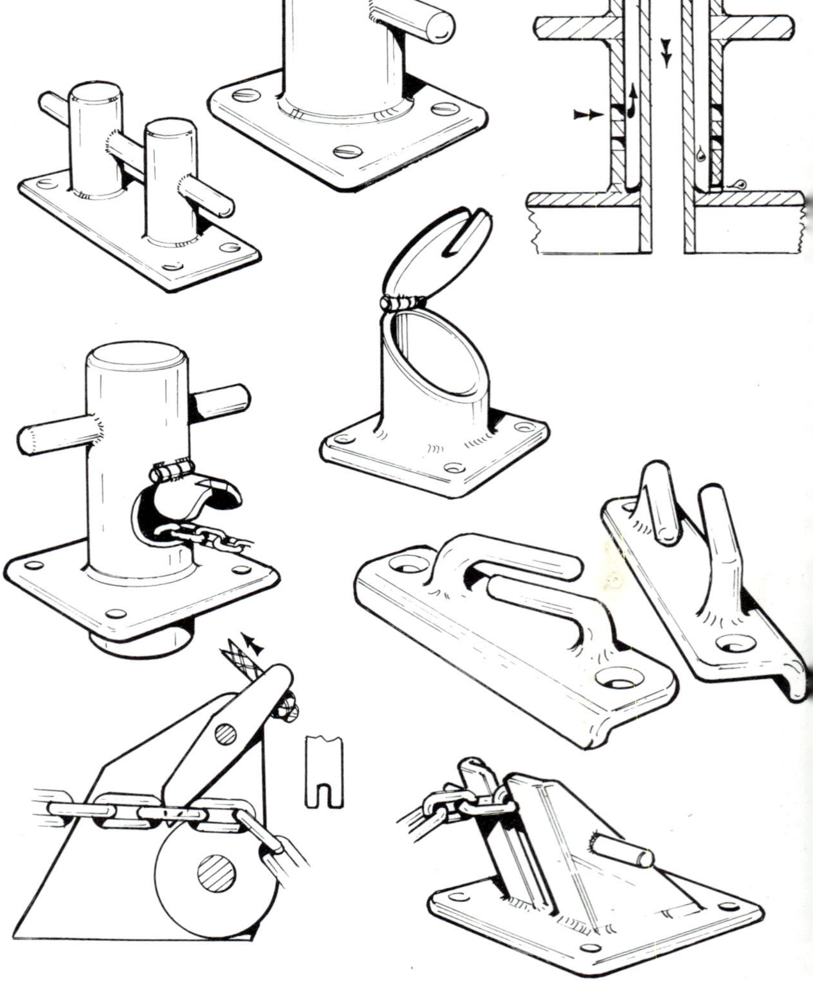

FIG. 107. Almost any fitting you see in your chandlery, or marina, can be duplicated at home—often in an improved version. Some items cannot really be copied and will have to be bought—but even sail track can be assembled from two flat sections.

PHOTO. 96. *Bending large steampipe such as this is really a two-man job. It will go round without kinking if the inner part of the bend is cooled while the outer part is kept red hot to enable it to stretch.*

Bending the 1½ inch bore (37 mm) steampipe for the bowsprit called for improvisation. A friendly tree with a double-trunk took the bend to just under 90 degrees cold. A garden bonfire was then needed to heat the pipe about the middle. A Spanish Windlass across the open end of the U did the rest (Photo. 96). Naturally I introduced a slight kink but fortunately it came exactly where I planned to fit the attachment plate and angle-iron for the outer forestay.

While I had the fire going I also flattened, as best I could, the ends of the pipe so as the enable me to bolt them through the rubbing strake. When it came to fitting this bowsprit to the boat I was caused some headaches—several likely solutions were discounted because they needed unattainable engineering facilities. In the end I opted for a pair of half inch (12 mm) bolts through the rubbing strake—arguing with myself that the likely loads would be accommodated by the rubbing

strake and the fact that behind it the hull and superstructure are joined together mechanically with nuts and bolts, and also chemically with layers of resin and glass fibre material. Large internal backing pads are used to prevent the bolts crushing the laminate.

In addition to the end-bolts the bowsprit is also supported by a crosspiece of 1½ × 1½ × ¼ inch (37 × 37 × 6 mm) angle welded to a stemhead plate which is bolted through a moulded-in 'kingplank' under the deck. The inner forestay attachment is also incorporated in this arrangement (Photos. 97–99).

A similarly dimensioned crosspiece of angle bridges the forward end of the bowsprit. Teak slats are bolted to these angle-irons and also to a teak filler-piece screwed to the rubbing strake. I have gone on at length about this bowsprit, which I admit is a strictly one-off job, for it shows just how far 'custom-fabrications' can go with the very minimum of equipment.

My welding soon progressed from the proverbial 'chicken scratching' to reasonable weld runs. The literature supplied with the welding set outlined various welding methods but I was fortunate in having remembered (from the days when I could weld reasonably well) tips that will be of value to someone following along this rewarding path (Photos. 100–102). Figure 108 highlights some causes of bad welding and also the action needed to produce good results.

First the choice of electrodes. I found 10 swg (3 mm) best for all the welding—mainly because I was using a thickness of metal an eighth of an inch (3 mm) or more. However, continuous welding with these rods can exceed the ability of a small welding set to cope—I found I had to spend long periods for the thermal cut-out in my Black & Decker F320 to cool and reset itself.

Welding electrodes work well if they are warm and

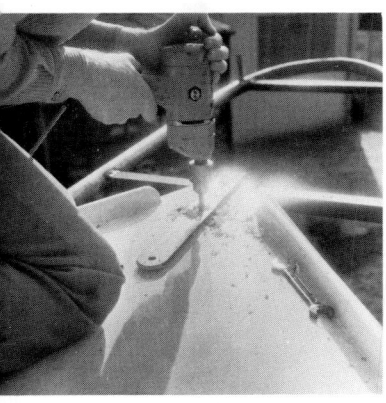

PHOTO. 97. *Underneath this attachment for the bowsprit is a moulded in 'kingplank'. Even so I used another, larger internal backing pad. This strap extends down the stem and is again through-bolted.*

PHOTO. 98. *And now for the proof-load test . . . there is also a tubular bob-stay (seen resting into the ground) which transmits the tension in the forestay into the hull.*

PHOTO. 99. *Before it could be sent away for galvanising all the holes for items such as these teak slats had to be drilled. Although galvanising is self-healing extreme damage may start it rusting—and in this context extra holes are extreme damage!*

PHOTOS. 100, 101, 102. If you wind the cable around your arm like this the weight of the cable is removed and it is thus easier to maintain the steady hand needed for good welding. A relaxed frame of mind is also essential. Note the crank in the electrode which lets me get into an awkward spot at the right angle.

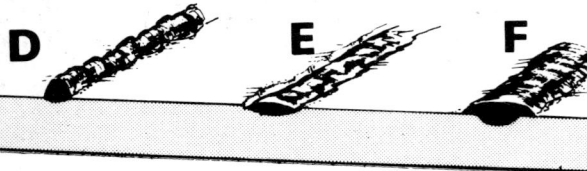

FIG. 108. (A). Good clean weld, even ripples and steady arc. (B). Splatter—damp electrode/long arc. (C). Small weld bead, sometimes undercut—travel too fast. (D). High narrow bead, little penetration—current too low. (E). Wide flat bead, undercut— current too high. (F). Wide bead, excessive metal, overlap—travel too slow.

A bent electrode lets you get into difficult corners. Using a brick as a 'scratch block' makes striking the arch that much easier.

dry. Ten minutes under the cooker grill works wonder and dries out any moisture that may be present in the flux coating. Storage in a warm, dry airing cupboard is ideal.

An old brick may be used as a 'scratch block' to remove the shell of flux that is sometimes left at the end of the welding rod. This shell prevents the arc being readily struck and maintained. Do not be too eager to remove the slag with the chipping hammer. Let it cool off and it almost falls away.

The zinc coating on the waterpipe adjacent to the weld zone gives off mildly poisonous fumes when it is heated excessively—although given good ventilation these fumes are not really troublesome. Even so, I filed and ground most of the zinc off before welding, and tried to weld in the open as much as possible.

If you need to wear spectacles—and I do—then use an old pair. You will only get them splattered. If you do not wear spectacles then I would strongly recommend that you wear clear-glass goggles behind your face shield.

Deck-boots are dangerous—large lumps of molten metal and slag will sometimes drip off your work, and being very hot will burn your feet if not protected. Open Wellington boots are an open invitation to trouble unless trouser are worn outside. Even then the rubber offers no protection. Leather Oxford-style shoes are a shade better—old army boots are best!

The welding process involves considerable heat, so wear gloves and never be in too much of a hurry to pick up newly-welded metal.

If you have an assistant then instruct him (her) to look away. Ultra-violet rays are given off by the arc and these can damage the eyes. 'Arc-eye' is very unpleasant and easily avoided. It inflicts the affected person with watery, prickling eyes, which are exceedingly sore. Bathing with special eyedrops and resting in a shaded room are the cure—your doctor will advise. But it is far better to be aware of the potential danger and take avoiding action.

Get your assistant in trousers—my long-suffering wife lost several pairs of nylon tights through sparks flying about. This also applies to the welder. A cotton coverall is desirable—a thick cotton shirt and woollen jumper second best. Remember that most man-made materials, nylons, Terylene etc, melt when very hot and could melt into your flesh. Take care.

Tack all the various components together first and try them in place on the boat before finally welding. If you are working on a wooden bench or table then a piece of asbestos sheet, or even an old tile, will prevent the table catching fire directly under the weld. Be aware of the fire risk, an extinguisher, or a bucket of water might save the day!

As confidence grows so will your welding technique. I must confess that I spent some time filing and grinding my earlier welds—kidding myself that the result would look neater after galvanizing. In any case, all traces of flux (slag) must be removed for an adequate zinc coating to be deposited.

How welding works

Electric arc welding is a fusion process by which the surfaces of the metal pieces to be joined are melted by the heat of an electric arc (Photo. 103). The current for the arc is provided by a transformer working off the single-phase (domestic) supply. The arc—or prolonged spark—is made between two terminals in an electrical circuit—the tip of the welding electrode and the workpiece (which is connected back to the transformer by an earthing clip). The heat generated by the arc is around

6,500°F—hot enough to instantaneously melt the electrode tip and a small area of workpiece metal under the arc. The actual filler metal is not deposited by gravity, it is driven across in the arc, and this enables one to make overhead welds. During the welding process the resulting molten metal mingles and is added to by the electrode filler metal (Fig. 109).

The welding electrode consists essentially of a metal rod, or thick wire, covered by a clay-like flux. This flux has two main jobs. Firstly it generates a cloud of gases which protect the molten metal from oxygen and nitrogen present in the air we breathe. Both these elements are detrimental to the weld for they will combine with the molten metal to produce oxides and nitrides which will weaken the weld and also make it brittle. The flux also produces a slag which covers the molten metal and protects it from contamination while it is cooling.

PHOTO. 103. Good welding comes with practice and the correct electrode size. It is no good attempting to weld thick pipe with very thin electrodes—or vice versa. Note the gloves which should be leather to prevent burns through heat and radiation.

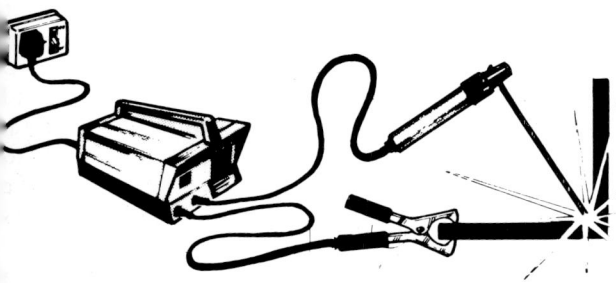

◄ FIG. 109. This is how the welding circuit is made. The return clip to the welding set should be positioned on clean metal or the arc will be hard to strike.

Welding faults probable causes

Bad appearance	A, B, C, D, K	A.	Current too high	G.	Arc too long
Undercutting	A, E, F	B.	Current too low	H.	Slag on electrode tip
Weld splatter	C, G, A	C.	Damp electrode	I.	Poor earth connection
Striking difficult	C, H, J, I	D.	Erratic manipulation	J.	Voltage too low★
Porosity	B, G, E, C	E.	Electrode movement too fast	K.	Lack of practice
Slag hard to remove	C, A	F.	Electrode angle wrong		

★It is worth noting that I occasionally had difficulty in getting a good weld around about lunchtime on Sundays. The voltage may have been too low due to all those roasts!

Beating a salty environment

Having fabricated all that lovely 'ironwork', you must protect it from the ravages of the salt sea! The recommended method is to have it hot-dipped galvanized—this is cheaper in most instances than electro-galvanising, or flame-spraying. Though if your 'Yellow Pages' show a flame-spraying outfit it is worth considering, for the process is relatively quick; you could opt for a saltwater-resistant grade of aluminium instead of zinc if you have used non-coated steels. Plastic coating is another method worth considering.

I chose hot-dip galvanizing since this process causes the zinc to hitch on to the underlying steel with a molecular bond—one which will not allow the zinc to peel away if it should become damaged—as a simple coating might.

Metal which is to be galvanized needs to be clean; light rusting is acceptable as is grease, for that will be removed in the acid pre-treatment baths. Domestic waterpipe is usually colour-coded with paint, and paint is the one thing that the process dislikes. Thus all my bits and pieces were cleaned up as needed with emery cloth to bright metal. Similarly, mill-scale and weld slag must be removed for good results. The former is easily removed by a few weeks natural rusting out in the open; the latter comes off a good weld almost by itself—most of mine were cleaned up with a collection of files and rotary burr cutters in a powerdrill.

Sealed lengths of tube must be avoided at all cost! These, when instantaneously heated up in a bath of molten zinc running at well over 450°C, can explode with terrifying results. Thus all sections must have a hole at each end to let the air and any trapped moisture out. Holes $\frac{3}{16}$ inch (4 mm) diameter are the minimum for one-inch (25 mm) bore pipes, and since hole sizes increase *pro rata*, I drilled $\frac{3}{8}$ (10 mm) holes in the components made from $1\frac{1}{2}$ inch (37 mm) steam pipe.

The actual galvanizing process is fairly straightforward. After acid pre-treatments and washes, the component is heated to make sure it is absolutely dry and then lowered into a large bath containing molten zinc (Photo. 104). Long, unwieldy objects such as my bowsprit and pulpit are dipped one end at a time, or even leg by leg, if the bath is too small. Unlike electroplating, hot-dipping does not simply plate the component with a thin layer of zinc. In the hot-dip process the zinc actually combines with the iron substrate giving a true bond. The actual layer of zinc is around 2–4 thou (0.1 mm).

Zinc protects the underlying metal by providing sacrificial protection for steel and iron—in other words it is an 'anodic coating'. The rate of oxidisation of zinc in air is extremely slow and even in salt water/air conditions it will last for many years depending upon the original thickness of the deposit. If the zinc gets scratched through to the underlying ferrous metal then it starts to corrode preferentially at a higher rate. The products of this corrosion in salt water (and hard freshwater) is a deposit of carbonate which effectively seals the surface and prevents further corrosion from taking place. However the rate at which corrosion occurs is rapidly increased with humidities over 70 per cent.

The effectiveness of the zinc layer can be further enhanced by the use of a chromate passivation treatment. But I decided to go one stage further and try to beat it completely. How well I succeeded is borne out by the fact that only after four summers afloat did *Solitaire's* 'ironwork' get a repaint—and even then it was solely for cosmetic purposes—of signs of rust there were none!

PHOTO. 104. Blakes at Gosport and Solitaire's 'ironwork' fresh from the hot-dip galvanising bath. With care the life of a painted coating is almost indefinite.

PHOTOS. 105, 106. Painting with modern materials calls for a close time-table. While the smaller items were getting their treatment in the garden the larger pieces were being painted in the garage.

Now although old paint interferes with the galvanizing process, a good paint scheme will protect new galvanising and extend its working life almost indefinitely. I decided to paint the newly galvanized components straightaway with a paint scheme suggested by International Paints. They recommended one coat of self-etch primer, followed by two coats of 707 primer for steel and light alloy, followed by several coats of two-pot polyurethane paint. The self-etch primer is a two-part preparation which chemically etches the surface much better than natural weathering. It does however, in common with many other chemical compounds of an active nature, give off unpleasant fumes, so lots of ventilation is needed. One thing I did discover is that to get the best from these modern paints one has to stick to a very close timetable.

So two hours each night for a week were set aside to paint the various bits and pieces until they looked like white enamel (Photos. 105, 106). Although I had some left-overs I found that 500 ml of each product was more than sufficient—and I painted the heads of all the fasteners too—for these were galvanized mild-steel—stainless seemed not only out of reach pricewise, but also unnecessary.

When it was time to fit all these items to the boat I used a 'wet assembly'. What this means is that copious amounts of mastic are applied to all the parts involved and the surplus cleaned up afterwards. Boatyards tend to skimp on the use of sealants and very often as a result annoying deck leaks develop under stanchions and the like. It's not so much the price of the materials they use—simply that it takes time to do the job properly and to clean up afterwards. Mastic coated tapes are available and these are a help but in my opinion there is no substitute for a good soft mastic smeared around the bolts as they are pushed home.

Neoprene sheet material with a fairly high density makes a good intermediate gasket if you smear both faces with mastic. So too do sections cut from old deck boots—of which I always seem to have a large number—thanks to a growing daughter!

Using modern mastics and sealants it is essential that the maker's instructions be followed closely for successful results. Remember too that you are dealing with nasty chemical compounds and that accidental smears in, and around the eyes need special care and attention. Keep them well out of the reach of children and dispose of spent tubes, waste, and solvent-soaked rags carefully.

7

Deck painting! No slip ups!

Once I had fitted all the various stanchions, cleats, fairleads and the like to *Solitaire* the autumn was fast approaching and I decided to get her decks painted—not all over, for white is a colour which keeps a boat nice and cool. I intended painting those areas of skiddy gel-coat which could prove dangerous underfoot. I chose to use a fairly pale green two-part polyurethane paint applied over an etch-primer; but first I considered other ways to improve the deck underfoot.

Take working around the base of the mast for example; there you are up on top of the cabin-top, swigging up halyards in a hearty manner while the ship heels to a good breeze. You see at once that a sound footing is required, and even if you sit down to your work like a prudent sailorman, you still need some grip in your contact with the boat. In my opinion a rough-loaded paint together with the very best deck-boots, are second best when compared to a series of raised teak-slats, which being raised, shed water quickly and also provide a purchase for your feet.

During fitting-out I had the good fortune to stumble upon a couple of teak firedoors—solid teak! Once stripped down to the various parts a local timber-yard—a very small one—cut some of the sections for me in to thin slats measuring $1\frac{3}{4}$ × $\frac{5}{16}$ × 5 ft (45 mm × 8 mm × 1.5 m) for just under the price of an ounce of tobacco! These slats were sawn, not planed, and I fixed them down to the deck around the mast by means of stainless steel self-tappers and a polysulphide rubber compound which promised to 'stick and seal'. The holes for the self-tappers were drilled out snug and a smear of epoxy adhesive—the five-minute-drying type applied just before the slats were bedded down. Four years later they are still perfect. The sawn surface, which was fairly finely sawn, has been scrubbed to a nice even texture, and the wood itself has bleached to a light straw. All very pleasing, and functional to boot!

The slats on the foredeck were laid to match those already fitted to the tubular bowsprit, and were added to improve that other dangerous occupation—weighing

anchor. There again slipperyness underfoot is a recipe for disaster, and even though I find it best to sit down with feet braced against the aftermost pulpit legs, it is still essential to be secure in the knowledge that the area is really 'non-slip'. . . .

The slats were fastened down on the same mastic as previously used and instead of self-tappers I opted for $\frac{3}{16}$ inch (M5) raised-head brass machine screws. Once again it is that sealant which squeezes out which is the valuable bit—for it indicates that the job has been well done!

Those deck areas to be painted were marked out with pencil and masking-tape. Note that some brands of masking-tape allow you to see pencil marks through them—Sellotape for one—the tape was then carefully cut back to the lines with a sharp scalpel.

When determining the areas it is worth bearing several points in mind. Shiny gel-coat is much easier to clean that rough non-slip paint, and although initially one might suppose that the entire deck area and cabin top might as well be painted, that is not so. For instance there is a tendency for dirt to collect alongside the toe-rail, and similar areas. Thus an inch (25 mm) of white gel-coat was left alongside them to make cleaning that much easier. Rainwater, plus its smuts and dirt, will run out through the gaps left by the moulders in the toe-rail adjacent to the stanchions and pushpit bases. So we left them surrounded with unpainted panels to ease cleaning. The wooden grabrails will need scraping down and oiling, or revarnishing from time-to-time; and so a thin white strip was left around them to save trouble later (Photo. 107). Likewise it is best to leave a white surround around all deck fittings so that should they need re-bedding you will be able to wipe up the sealant without difficulty. Pre-planning is the name of the game! Last but not least, the juxtaposition of these whites against the fittings and painted areas, add interest and highlights to the discerning eye—in other words she will look smarter for that little bit of forethought and care!

It took me two rolls of tape and three hours to prepare

the areas and arrive at the next stage. This was to degrease the decks with special Oil-Removing Fluid and water, prime them with an acid etch-primer, and apply a couple of coats of two-part polyurethane topcoat.

Acetone should not be used to degrease gel-coat for it has a debilitating effect on it. If the decks are free from waxes, release agents, and silicons, then water will lie in a flat film. If it stands proud in beads special treatment is needed: more details are given under *Painting Resinglass*.

Having degreased the decks I decided to thoroughly abrade those areas to be painted with an orbital sander and fairly-coarse grit (Photo. 108). This floated over the masking tape leaving about $\frac{1}{4}$ inch (6 mm) around the periphery of each panel to be abraded by hand. The reason for roughing-up was influenced by the fact that my hull had been out of its mould for over six-months

and the resinglass and gel-coat could be considered to be fully-cured, although in truth this process seems to take a year or more; the rate of cure tailing off to virtually nothing after about six months.

Once again I used International Paints' products and their Glass Fibre Primer has an intriguing chemical role. According to the makers it is apparently highly reactive and combines with free hydroxyl groups of chain molecules present in the undercured resin thus forming a key for the subsequent polyurethane paint scheme, the curing agent of which has an affinity for hydroxyl groups. I was doubtful that my decks by this time had any such 'free hydroxyl groups', and thought that even if they had a good mechanical key for the paint to hitch into could be an additional advantage.

Having roughened the decks, and carefully degreased them again, they were painted with the special

PHOTO. 107. *Leaving a margin of white gel-coat surface around all the fittings called for lots of masking tape and sharp scalpel.*

PHOTO. 108. *A coarser grit than would normally be used for hand-sanding is required by an orbital sander to achieve the same degree of finish.*

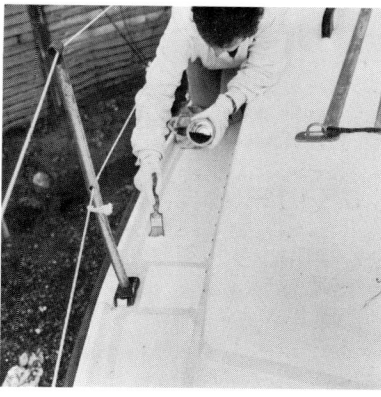

PHOTO. 109. *The special etch-primer links chemically with residual compounds in the gel-coat surface and also provides a chemical key for the two-pot polyurethane paint. Proper overcoating is important.*

PHOTO. 110. *When using a polyurethane paint it is essential to apply it in good 'round' coats and not brush it out too thinly. Note the mast step pad and eyebolts.*

PHOTO. 111. *While the painted surface was wet it was sprinkled with clean sand. This method is easier to control than a loaded paint which needs constant stirring to keep the grit particles suspended.*

PHOTO. 112. *As you can see here the decks were painted before the 'ironwork' was sent away for galvanizing and subsequent painting. This final coat is being painted on to lock the sand into the underlying surface.*

primer (Photo. 109). An early start is needed for this paint scheme since the Primer must be overpainted within 6–24 hours. Some $5\frac{3}{4}$ hours later I could contain myself no longer! Half the components of the two-part poly' were mixed with a power-stirrer, and then I had to wait 10 minutes for the bubbles to escape. I had calculated the approximate surface area involved and 500 ml was just enough for my 28 footer.

With the wind and the sunshine plus an air temperature in the upper 60°F's (19°C) I had to work fast to apply a good round coat (Photo. 110). The paint dries in about two-hours and fully cures over the next week, or so, depending upon ambient temperature. As I covered specific areas I sprinkled them with a fairly coarse non-slip grit (Photo. 111). This can be obtained from paint suppliers—or as silver-sand from goldfish shops. You can mix the sand straight into the paint, but previous experience suggests to me that a better job is achieved if the sand is applied separately from a shaker—a jam-jar with a multitude of small holes in its lid. Doing it this way means that an even layer of grit can be applied, but it also means that a second layer of poly' is needed to seal in the grit.

The two-pot poly' I was using may be overcoated after 6 hours—but more normally between 16–24 hours; and so the sealing coat was put on the next day (Photo. 112).

One of the reasons for using a two-pot poly' apart from the fact that these paints are tougher than the gelcoat and thus afford a high degree of protection, is that generally speaking the choice of deck paint colours is strictly limited. We wanted a nice light green—and were only able to obtain the desired shade by mixing up our own paint using white as the base. Note that this needs careful research for the second part of the paint scheme (i.e. the hardener) often has a different formulation depending upon the darkness, or lightness of the paint colour. It is also essential to mix up more than enough paint to complete the job for colour matching is very difficult. Note that ordinary enamels, and one-pot poly's may also be used to paint resinglass with—but the extra cost of the two-pot types is not, in my opinion, grounds for rejecting them for they are so much superior.

Various grades of grit sizes may be used, as may even coarser grades of silicon-carbide grits which give a surface akin to a rasp. Pumice, sawdust and wood flour may be mixed in with the paint to give a smoother, matt area more suitable for sitting on than those rougher, sanded surfaces—and also less wearing on the bottoms of water-proof over-trousers!

The efficaciousness of the system I adopted is borne out by the fact that four years after painting, *Solitaire's* decks were still functionally smart and non-slip, and yet to be over-painted.

Berth covers! Woman's work!

Don't get the idea that fitting-out from scratch is all man's work. There are some areas where, at the price of seeming to come over as a MCP, women can turn out a neater job—faster and better-looking than us mere males.

Take bunk mattresses for instance; the following section is donated by my long-suffering wife, and able crew-mate, Anne:

'Could you explain how your sewing machine works. . . .' This from a husband who knew perfectly well! *'You see, I want to machine up the covers for the berth mattresses,'* he went on somewhat hopefully. *'And having spent so much money it would be a pity if they turned out wrong. After all, I haven't been to all those evening classes on dress-making'.*

How the male mind works! Those evening classes he referred to resulted in one waistcoat, which, even when finished, didn't quite match any suit he possessed and was last seen covered in anti-fouling—being worn over a coverall to *'keep the chill off. . . .'*

True I have sewn curtains and cushions in the past, and a neighbour did once nearly talk me into re-covering our settee. *'It's easy once you get started'*, she had enthused as she casually draped a rather frightening amount of material over the back of her 'put-you-up'. So with an air of confidence I didn't really feel, I told the 'Captain' that I would run up something 'professional'—secretly hoping that my end-result wouldn't spoil the look of the super interior he'd made in *Solitaire*.

Polyether foam seems to come in three grades, 'soft' 'medium' and 'firm', suitable for cushions, sleeping, and sitting, respectively. Thus we had settled on 'medium' for the static berths and 'firm' for the dinette seats which converted into an occasional double-berth. Perhaps the only worry with polyester foam is that in its generally available form it burns readily, and like polyurethane foam, gives off large amounts of chokingly poisonous (isocyanate) fumes. While these foams may be made flame-resistant, it appears that the products of combustion from a foam so treated are particularly noxious if it really catches fire. So having listened to the 'skipper' while he patiently explained this to me, I resolved to be particularly careful while living on board.

The foam arrived in two sheets, erupting out of the car like some alien monster, to be dumped seconds later in the middle of the lounge. *'We may as well start at once'* said the 'skipper' briskly seizing a rule and bread-knife and before I could raise any objections we were busy measuring and cutting (Photos. 113, 114).

Actually it was a case of measuring twice—and cutting twice—once from each side of the foam. The

PHOTOS. 113, 114. Marking out and cutting the foam presented no real problems. It was cut with a fine-toothed saw-knife, dragged through the block.

PHOTO. 115. Being able to walk across the garden and try things like these foam blocks for size is a tremendous help to a quick completion job.

saw-toothed breadknife worked well as it was dragged through the foam at a shallow angle alongside a wooden batten. The cutting was so clean that we didn't even need to trim off any bumps. To my amazement the whole operation took less than half an hour, and our cut-out foam shapes fitted exactly when we took them across to the boat (Photo. 115). One highly delighted mate disappeared leaving me to try to pick up with the Hoover the millions of crumbs clinging tenaciously to carpet and curtains.

I had shopped for a suitable covering material with the brief that anything would be better than vinyl plastic covered cloth which tends to 'sweat' in the summer and sticks to bare flesh. Anyway, we didn't want to bring a 'caravan' look to *Solitaire's* varnished interior. Woollen upholstery fabric would have been nice for it is less than a fire hazard since it merely smoulders and to some extent is self-extinguishing. But the cost was prohibitive and the fact that the fabric could be only dry-cleaned—no quick washing out in the event of soup stains or the results of *mal de mer*—was a further drawback. So we ended up with Dralon, a man-made acrylic material sold under other brand-names such as Orlon, Courtelle, Acrilan, Dolon etc,. This material is said to have a high resistance to abrasion while staying soft, and it is available in a wide range of colours, prints and weaves. Its price is quite reasonable too.

As the material tended to fray I cut it out with pinking shears, but the sewing itself presented no difficulties. I used a fairly loose stitch and synthetic thread (Trylko). A cotton thread would have caused the seams to pucker after washing due to a different 'shrink-rate'.

Loose mattress covers can be vastly improved by sewing a false seam along each edge (Fig. 110). It's not the pukka piping, (which is very nice but I think

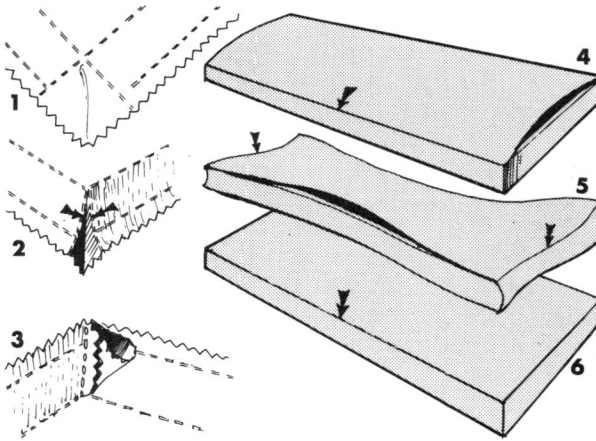

FIG. 110. (1). False seams stitched on right side of material. (2). Bring arrowed edges together for 'box'. Stitch on right side. (3). Cut surplus material from inside. Open out seam and trim surplus off raw edge. (4). Insert foam in cover, ½ inch (12 mm) of raw edge all round. Mark out for joining seam. (5). Remove foam, machine false seams right side. (6). Insert foam and hand-stitch 4th side.

unnecessary, fiddly and time-consuming), but it gives a neat edge forming a boxed look to sides and ends. It also helps to keep the material located on the foam, without it riding around too much and pulling out of shape.

The dinette cushions, being simply rectangular, were easily covered (Photo. 116). First I marked the false seams with tailor's chalk and stitched them on the right side of the material. I sewed three sides, mitred the corners, inserted the foam and then hand-stitched along the remaining seam with big stitches that can easily be unpicked when necessary.

The tapered berth mattresses were more difficult. The material was draped around the foam, smoothed into

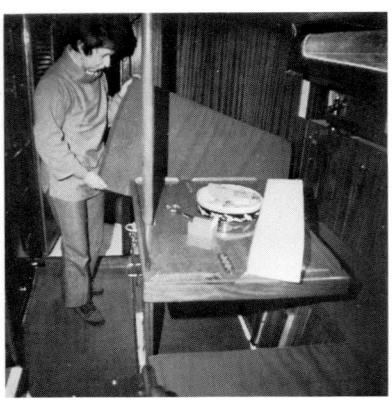

◄ *PHOTO. 116. Once the foam shapes were cut it was a fairly straightforward task to cover them with a suitable upholstery fabric.*

PHOTO. 117. Anne at work in the ► *forepeak hand-sewing the last seam. Note the slatted ceiling and lined deckhead.*

place, and the positions of the false seams were marked all the way around. I needed an extra hand for this, and the mate was dragged back from his boat to help. After machining the long seams I fitted the cover on the foam once again—no easy job for the foam being full of static electricity the material wouldn't move easily over it!

Again I stitched the widest end by hand when the foam was in—sitting on the berth so that the mattress was kept flat and the material did not drag (Photo. 117).

Dralon can be machine-, or hand-washed, in hand-hot water using soap or detergent. After washing a light press with a cool iron should smooth out any wrinkles. Alternatively it may be dry-cleaned—but take care to tell the cleaner that it is an Acrylic material—otherwise it may go through a very hot process which will distort and damage the material.

Engines—some considerations

One of the biggest jobs—or rather series of small jobs—that you will meet with during a complete fit-out concerns the engine installation. Your supplier of mouldings may include the engine as some sort of 'package deal'—alternatively he may supply the engine beds fitted for some particular engine—the one he fits as standard. This may or may not agree with your plans, and if it does not then you are really on your own.

When scouting around for engines you will find that the larger makers are geared up to answer your questions. Their sales literature is good, and they will also be prepared to provide you with scale drawings of the outline of the engine commensurate to the scale of the boat drawings supplied with your mouldings. This is a great help for it enables you to marry the two sets of lines up and decide if the engine in question will fit in with you plans.

But first there are some other considerations to take

into account—apart from size, price and availability.

The easiest place to site the engine is on the centreline well aft and with a straight drive to the propeller which is ideally sited in a moulded aperture. Such an arrangement is advantageous because: (1) The engine may be 'lost' under the cockpit and bridgedeck. (2) Cockpit controls are easily arranged and may even be 'direct'—dispensing with the need for complicated, and expensive, systems. (3) Shafting is kept to the minimum length with no need for intermediate bearings to restrain 'whirl'—the tendency for a long length of shaft to rotate in an out-of-balance state. (4) The engine is effectively isolated from the accommodation.

Conversely the boat tends to narrow hereabouts and it is often hard to get the engine low enough—particularly with those wide horizontally-opposed units. Engine makers recognize this fact, and to ease the installation of some of the larger units, and some of the not so large they have the final output drive shaft from the gearbox around 2 inches (50 mm) lower than the input shaft. Once again the detailed brochures should make the point clear. With the engine sited right aft accessibility is often bad, and you will have to think about how you are going to get around the engine for routine maintenance. On *Solitaire* for instance there is a complete side panel which when removed lets me work on the waterpump, fuel lift pump and exhaust system from the relative comfort of the WC compartment. Other possible arrangements are watertight hatches let into the cockpit sole, or removeable panels down the sides of the quarter berths and lockers, for example.

Good access is important, for if the engine goes wrong it will invariably be out at sea, in bad conditions. Working over a hot unit is then difficult enough without having to hang head down in a locker grasping a pencil torch in your teeth!

Together with access it is also important to come to a decision on sound-proofing at an early stage. Now you may have thought that this aspect could safely be left until the engine is installed but sadly such an approach is doomed to failure, or else lots of additional work and expense.

Engine noise can be reduced by four basic methods; isolation, insulation, absorption and damping (Fig. 111). Each of these calls for a slightly different approach which may, or may not be possible with the engine you have on your short list.

Isolation in the truest sense is not really practical in the case of an auxiliary yacht for it is a method of stopping engine vibrations exciting other parts of the boat by installing the engine on a massive base. To achieve that you need a heavily constructed craft along the lines of a commercial, or fishing boat. Although with an encapsulated fin keel yacht it would be feasible to install the engine directly on the keel mass and so use that to deaden any engine vibrations. This procedure would naturally raise many other complications apart from the attachment of the engine to the keel; length of shafting, controls, exhaust—and how to disguise the fact that the engine was under the cabin table.

A far more practical approach, provided you are not trying to take advantage of some rating rule, is to isolate the engine from the rest of the boat by using suitable flexible mounts (Fig. 112) and either a flexible shaft-log (Fig. 113), or a flexible coupling between the engine and the propeller shaft. This method is perhaps the most widely adopted and most engine makers specify the types of mounts and couplings to use. It also means however, that all fuel-pipes, water pipes and exhaust systems must be able to accommodate engine movement. This may be simply arranged by fitting short lengths of suitable flexible pipes into the systems.

Insulation of the engine compartment, allied to isolation can give an extremely quiet installation. Insulation starts by building the engine box from materials such as plywood, or resinglass laminate, or even aluminium or steel. All these materials have the characteristics of high-density coupled with relatively low stiffness. Plywood is obviously the easiest to use and a minimum thickness of $\frac{1}{2}$ inch (12 mm) should be considered. The plywood should be faced on the inside

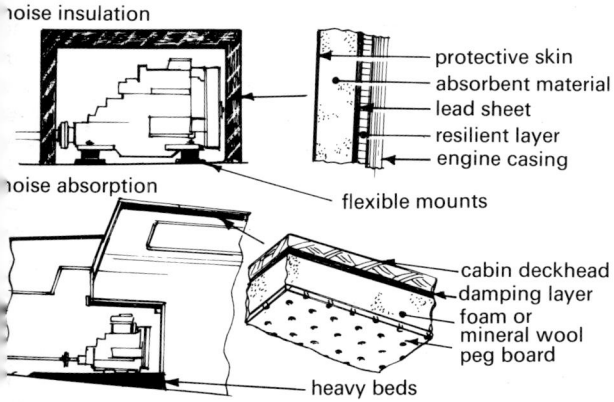

noise insulation

protective skin
absorbent material
lead sheet
resilient layer
engine casing

flexible mounts

noise absorption

cabin deckhead
damping layer
foam or mineral wool peg board

heavy beds

FIG. 111. *Noise insulation and absorption call for slightly different approaches—although both may be used together if need be.*

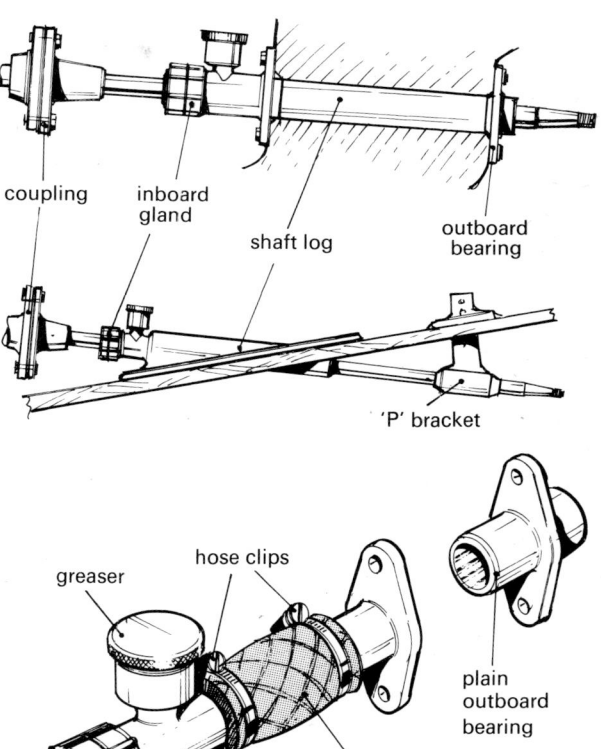

coupling   inboard gland   shaft log   outboard bearing

'P' bracket

greaser   hose clips

reinforced hose

plain outboard bearing

flexible inboard-gland bearing

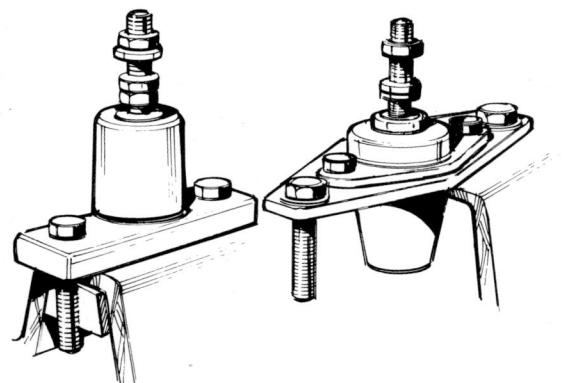

FIG. 112. *Depending upon the type of flexible mounts supplied (or recommended) the engine beds must be designed to suit. Note that flush bases are easier to accommodate.*

FIG. 113. *Some typical stern-gear components. Shaft and bearings should be ordered to a compatible system—Imperial and Metric do not mix!*

with either a proprietary barrier material, or one of your own make-up. Bought materials usually comprise foam-lead-foam, or foam-plastic-sheet-foam, sandwiches. A possible alternative is a thin protective layer of plastic sheeting, pvc for example with an inch or two of felt or glassfibre mat behind it. Then comes a layer of some resilient material—sheet rubber, or better still lead sheet and rubber next to the inner wall of the engine box.

I do not think it wise to use a perforated sheet zinc, or aluminium mesh material for the outer protective skin. Oil and grease will pass through this type of barrier and collect in the backing material and pose a possible fire risk.

So far then we have found two methods which can drastically affect the engine installation. Flexible couplings and amounts will need beds designed to accept them, and the engine will have to be sited so as to accommodate the extra length required by the former. In addition the fact that insulation materials require at least one inch (25 mm) of extra wall thickness means that the engine box will need to be that much bigger all round too.

Damping, to get back to methods of reducing engine noise, is applicable to those instances when engine vibration causes some other part of the boat to pick up the mood and vibrate by induced resonance. This may happen if your engine box is relatively thin steel or aluminium—it can also occur with some structural bulkheads which just happen to vibrate in 'sympathy' with the higher engine vibes. Engine boxes can be 'de-tuned' as it were by increasing their mass by the use of some flexible material which could be of the paint-on bituminious type, possibly containing a loose scrim material for stability. A bulkhead which vibrates is much more of a problem. Perhaps the addition of a shelf containing lots of books may be sufficient to increase its mass and so move the structure out of the 'resonance' range.

Absorption is necessary where sound waves are being reflected off some hard surface—like the deckhead of the cabin, or even the un-insulated surfaces of the engine box. Normal domestic materials may be used under the cabin head-liner, though glassfibre mat could be fitted, so could acoustic tiles, thick underfelt (sold in carpet shops) or polyurethane, or polyethylene foam. These would need fitting behind a decorative 'peg-board' or similarly perforated material for good results.

An engine box which has been insulated must also have some baffled arrangement whereby fresh air can enter and engine cooling air exit (Fig. 114). 'Cooling air?'

Well even if the engine is water-cooled—as most will be—items such as the alternator, or dynamo need to be kept relatively cool for a long working life. And in

FIG. 114. *Petrol and diesel engines both need a good supply of fresh air to operate properly. The inlet for a diesel need only go down to about mid-engine level.*

addition a very hot engine compartment effectively 'de-rates' the engine. In other words its becomes less powerful. Baffles are very easy to make—and if you cannot see through them then noise does not have a straightline path through which to escape. But sound will bounce from the baffles if they are not faced with an absorbent material. More advice on engine ventilation will be given later on.

Other possible noise sources, but ones which will not immediately affect the design of the beds and compartment, are those from the propeller and its shaft, together with water passing the hull. A propeller working in too-small an aperture is likely to be inefficient—especially if the edges of the aperture are abrupt thus producing a turbulent water-flow. And if the clearance between the bottom of the hull and the tip of the propeller is much less than 2 inches (50 mm) it is likely that the propeller will cause the hull to vibrate. A tip clearance of under one inch (25 mm) will produce vibrations which at certain revolutions can be excessive. The propeller shaft bearings need to be well fixed in to help prevent vibrations being transmitted into the hull. This means that a massive cross-floor is needed—not just the minimum thickness web that is so often seen. Also the diameter of the shaft, its length and the position of any support bearings should be scaled so that there is no chance of shaft flexure near the propeller. Once again this will result in vibrations which may be construed as 'noise'. Similarly with a two-bladed propeller working behind a vertical post, or deadwood there is every chance that it will be a 'noisy' arrangement. A three-bladed propeller will reduce the vibrations but increase drag. Ideally what one is searching for is the biggest diameter propeller working at the lowest possible speed with a tip clearance of more than 15 per cent of its diameter, working in a clean waterflow. Once again your selection will be a series of compromises, aided I hope by the foregoing and a helpful salesman!

Before we leave the subject of noise and how its mitigation affects the design of the installation, let me mention two other areas; induction and exhaust. Induction noise is not really a great trouble in the horsepower range we are considering—that is up to about 40 hp (30 kw). If you arrange to point the air intake on the inlet filter away from the cabin, or wheelhouse, that is really as much as you can do. Some makers do have available special induction air-cleaner silencers, and will advise if need be.

The exhaust system with engines up to 40 hp (30 kw) will invariably be water-cooled (see later for more details) and as such it is not really essential to incorporate a silencer in the system. Small two-stroke petrol engines seem to be much noisier than comparable diesels in this respect and even when water-injected exhaust systems are fitted an additional silencer may be required to reduce their constant 'pop-popping'.

Having mentally resolved such matters as engine mounts, the length of the engine with a flexible coupling fitted, and the extra size of its compartment, much work can be done initially with the aid of drawings. You will need a set of lines drawings for the hull, and a side view and plan of the boat construction drawings. Then, armed with the relevant engine brochures containing, side and front elevations *to a compatible* scale you can start to see how they might be installed.

As you start looking at the drawings you will find that there is often an automatic starting point; for instance on my Atlanta 8.5 Viking there is a skeg in which is moulded the propeller aperture. The centre of this combined with maximum installation angle for the engine gives a datum, or shaft line, somewhere along which the engine must be fitted.

The recommended maximum installation angle takes into account the engine maker's knowledge that boats do not run with their waterlines level with the horizon. Under power a hull tends to squat down by the stern; when motor-sailing modern beamy hulls go along well-heeled and with their bows down. Then again fore-and-aft pitching introduces further elements and might lead you to suppose that the nearer an engine may be installed to the horizontal the better.

That would be so if it were not for a point that is often missed. If you observe a sailing boat under power you will notice a marked tendency for her stern to drop or 'squat'. This is due to a basic hydrodynamic law which limits speed. At near-maximum displacement speed the hull is trying to climb up the face of a wave and thus is working against gravity. However, by installing the engine shaft line at around 15 degrees to the horizontal the propeller will be giving a small but positive lift component to the stern. 'Propping it up on the prop' so to speak. Below 15 degrees this effect drops off rapidly as

the propeller shaft approaches the horizontal. Above 15 degrees on the other hand, so much of the propeller's effort is going towards lifting the stern that forward speed may suffer. Thus with an engine installation which gives a horizontal shaft-line there is no lift component at all, while if one is tempted to fit an engine 'nose down' there is every chance that it will suffer from air-locks in the after-end of the water-cooling jacket. In any case you will in all probability *have* to tilt your engine by 10–15 degrees, possibly up to the maximum recommended, just to get it in.

So having decided, put the installation angle on the lines drawing from the centre of the prop' aperture. It will be seen when you lay down a tracing (to an identical scale) that the really critical area is likely to be around the shaft coupling. Aft of that the hull is squeezing in rapidly, while forward of that point the hull expands at roughly the same rate as the engine shape.

Making due allowance for the stuffing box, extra inboard bearing, etc, one then has a tentative position which must be checked with the construction drawings to make certain that the proposed engine will fit neatly under the cockpit and/or bridgedeck. Check too that there are no cross webs or floors which may get in the way of the engine sump and remember too that the lines drawings are to the *outside* of the hull. Interpreting drawings comes more naturally to some than to others, but given care and the co-operation of the engine supplier you should be able to draw up a satisfactory plan.

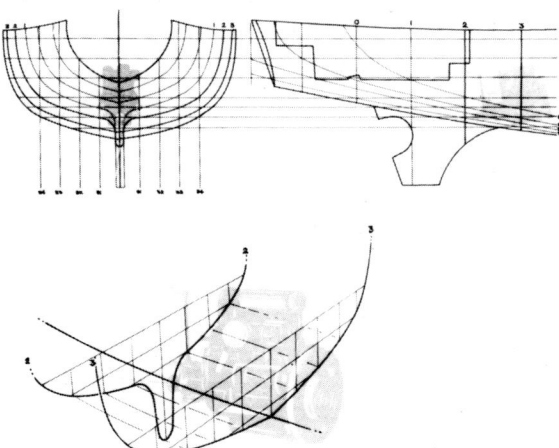

FIG. 115. *You need to consider the lines drawings about a limited area. Turn them round in perspective and the engine installation starts to look like this. Very difficult to picture with the mind's eye. Far easier (and safer) for most of us to work in three dimensions using as much detailed information as possible. Note how tipping the engine up increases its overall dimensions.*

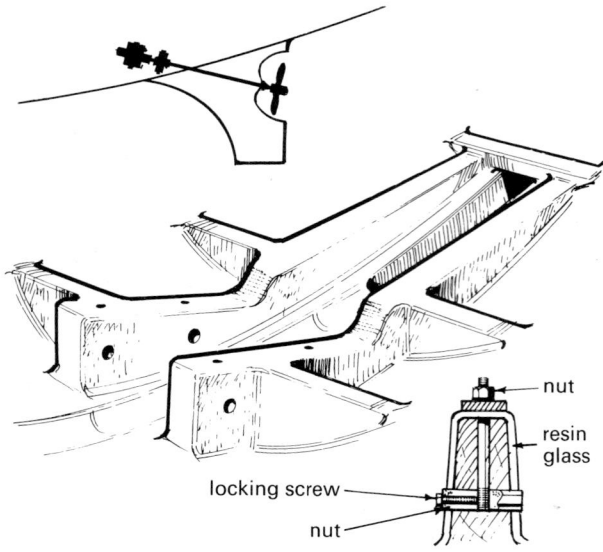

nut

resin glass

locking screw

nut

FIG. 116. This is how Solitaire's engine beds look. Ideally they need to be twice as long as the engine and well-braced into the hull with large webs. Note detail showing holding down bolts.

When it comes to the lines drawing you will soon see that you are only considering a section of the hull around about two station lines—in my case Nos. 2 and 3 (Fig. 115). These show the hull to be fairly flat and relatively full, due no doubt, to the skeg being faired in around this area. Try not to work to very fine limits since there is no guarantee that the hull, even a resinglass one, will conform absolutely to the drawings. (Fig. 116 shows the beds which I fitted to *Solitaire*—note the substantial webs).

Having opted for a nominal engine position you are now able to start looking at engine beds. These need to be robust enough to spread the engine loads, with side webs to absorb engine torque and weight when the boat is heeled, and in the case of a relatively heavy engine, to prevent high beds from 'spreading'. The beds need to be run as far forward and aft as possible. At the same time consider how the engine is to be held down— conventional bolts, flexible mounts, tapped steel inserts etc. The answers to these considerations may give another set of data which may mean moving the engine a little—if so check with the drawings that the new position is viable.

By now the engine position is nearly finalized—or is it? Does the engine profile drawing include the hand-starting mechanism and the alternator? Is it intended to fit a swan-neck in the exhaust close to the engine because there is insufficient room at the transom? Back to the drawings and check again.

Some aspects of engine beds

Some people call them bearers, others beds, I fall into the second group and so will stick to it throughout this section. When it comes to designing engine beds the prime consideration should be adequate strength. Apart from the fact that your boat may (God forbid) find herself completely upside down—and imagine the chaos if the engine broke free—the engine beds must be able to keep the propeller-shaft alignment constant. They may also have to accommodate the propeller thrust—both ahead and reverse—and withstand both torque and vibration from the engine. Add to that the increased loads caused by the boat going up and down in rough seas— 'acceleration forces'—and you see that it is almost impossible to build them too stoutly.

The engine beds need to be braced into the hull structure with side webs and cross-members so as to spread the loads. Since you will be bonding them with resin and glass fibre materials you must allow a large area of contact with which to 'stick' them in. It is essential that the engine itself is not used to brace the beds.

Flexible engine mounts must be throughbolted to the bearers using nuts-and-slots, or alternatively, and perhaps better, a threaded (tapped) steel insert. Note that if this method is adopted then the thickness of the steel embedded in the beds should be slightly greater than the diameter of the securing bolts. This will give sufficient thread depth to prevent the stripping which could take place with sections smaller than the root-diameter of the thread-form selected.

If timber is incorporated in the beds it will need to be rot-proofed to prevent a possible source of trouble at a later date. (See under *Materials* for a suitable treatment.)

Figures 117–120 show some possible arrangements for engine beds and in all cases the lay-up resin and glass will need to be at least $\frac{1}{4}$ inch (6 mm) thick. Note that one layer of $1\frac{1}{2}$ oz (450 g/m²) CSM with a resin: glass ratio of 3:1 gives a laminate thickness of 40 thou (1 mm). Thus six layers well rolled and consolidated will give that $\frac{1}{4}$ inch minimum. Apply three or four layers and allow them to set—otherwise the exotherm could damage the hull.

In all cases the hull area will need to be scrupulously prepared—abraded and degreased—if a satisfactory job is to be made of this vital installation. Similarly, whether you choose to use solid wood, plywood, foam or simply resinglass flanges, a layer or two of CSM will be needed underneath them to improve total adhesion.

Of the four methods shown figure 117 is really suited only to very small lightweight engines. Perhaps figure 119 is the one to aim for; it is a great aid to lining the engine up if the steel angle is slotted to allow it to be

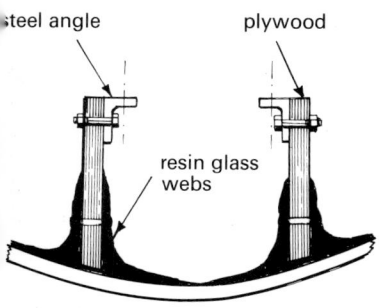

FIG. 117. Suitable for a small lightweight engine—the 7 hp VIRE petrol unit—for example.

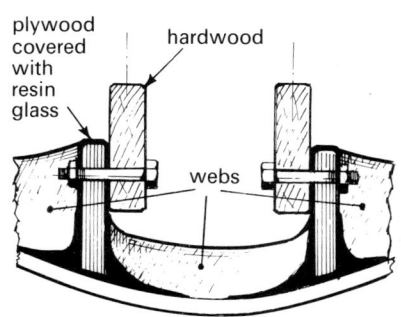

FIG. 118. Hardwood beds may be trimmed (or built up) when it's time to line up the engine. Once 'solid' resinglass beds have been glassed in it is difficult to modify them.

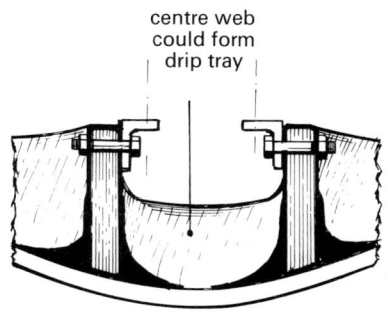

FIG. 119. Angle irons are an attractive alternative to the hardwood beds in figure 118. They may be slotted for initial adjustment—and finally drilled when the engine is lined up.

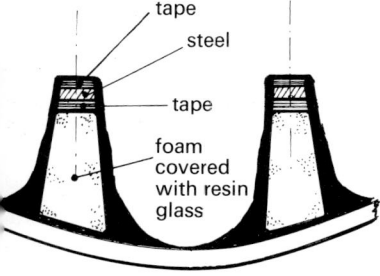

FIG. 120. Unidirectional tapes incorporated in 'top-hat' beds will provide extra stiffness. Note the steel inserts which will be drilled and tapped to take the mounting bolts.

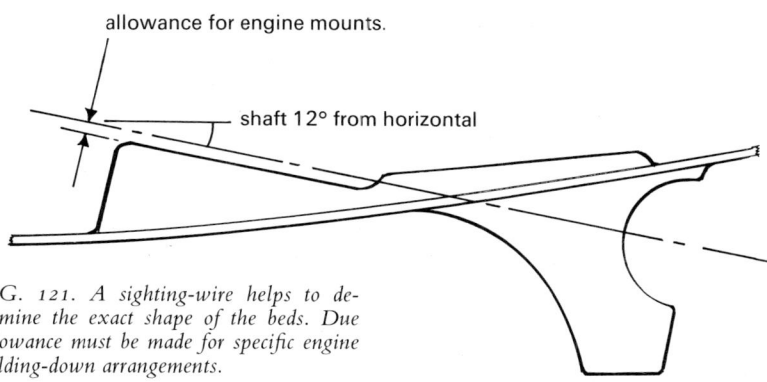

FIG. 121. A sighting-wire helps to determine the exact shape of the beds. Due allowance must be made for specific engine holding-down arrangements.

raised or lowered—final securing bolts may be drilled after the engine is accurately installed. Figure 118 is suited to non-flexible or flexible installations.

Should you adopt the foamed-core method (Figure 120) then select a high density foam and note that the girder of resinglass needs to be really substantial. It would also be a good idea to use a couple of layers of unidirectional tape in the top faces to increase longitudinal stiffness. Note too that the inclusion of steel inserts provides a potential weakness unless special care is taken—lots of through holes with roving threaded through them, for example. Once again this calls for careful planning since if the bonding holes are drilled in a random manner you may put one exactly in the tapped wall of the hole needed for one of the holding down bolts. I would recommend that you use at least $\frac{1}{4}$ inch (6 mm) of resinglass over and under the mild steel inserts which need not run the full length of the beds—instead short sections could be positioned directly under the engine mounts. The length of these local inserts would need to be about twice the span of the mounting's fasteners. When I came to fit the engine beds to *Solitaire* they were designed to take a SABB 2HSP traditional-

style diesel engine from Norway. I designed the beds as previously outlined and cut them out of softwood which had been generously soaked with preservative. Working from drawings is one thing, but when it came to actually installing the beds in the boat there were other conditions to take care of. For example: how were they to be accurately positioned relative to the skeg and hull? I could make a series of measurements to assist, and I also drilled through the skeg and inserted the propeller shaft. This may not appeal to you and an alternative would be to drill a small pilot hole through a similar skeg and use it to run a tight thin line representing the centre of the propeller shaft up into the body of the boat (Fig. 121). Now, assuming that you had levelled the boat accurately to her waterline, you would be in a position to align the string at the required number of degrees to the horizontal. A ready way of determining the shaft angle is to measure the difference in height along one metre of the centreline. The angle is then found from the following:

DEGREES	5	6	7	8	9	10	11	12	13	14	15	16
Centimetres	9	10	12	14	16	18	19	21	23	25	27	29

Alternatively a spirit level and protractor could be used.

◄ *PHOTO. 118. This wooden shape represents a Sabb diesel engine—the positions of the holding down bolts, and the sizes of the flywheel and coupling are represented by wooden blocks.*

PHOTO. 119. The beds were set on CSM ► *and glassed into place with layer upon layer of mat. A good job is absolutely essential for the entire weight of the engine is, in the final analysis, 'glued' to the hull moulding.*

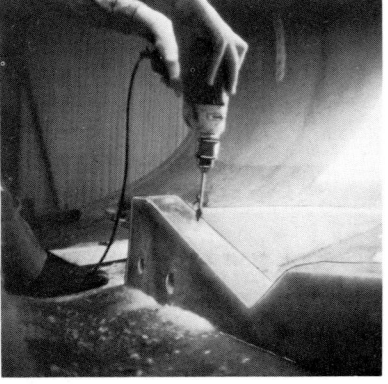

PHOTOS. 120, 121. The locations of the holding-down bolt holes and 'nuts' were easily seen through the 'green' resinglass lay-up and were marked for subsequent drilling.

PHOTO. 122. If you bend a piece of CSM into a hoop and fibres spring out from it surface then you are looking at the side which should be laid into wet resin. The other face will remain relatively smooth and so your resin-brush, or roller, will not pick up a mess of fibres. Its worth checking on.

Having installed the shaft to give the angle and then centred it in the boat, I was able to lay the beds down in their approximate position. To check that all was so far correct I made a simplistic model of the engine using plywood for the flat plan and with blocks representing the coupling at one end and the flywheel at the other (Photo. 118).

The beds were then fitted fairly closely to the hull and the surrounding surface thoroughly prepared to receive them *after* their final position had been accurately scribed into the hull surface. Bonding in (Photo. 119) then followed along the procedures described elsewhere.

Holes for the engine holding-down bolts were drilled from the wooden model and instead of nuts, or flat threaded (tapped) plates let into slots or tenons, I had decided to make 'nuts' from short lengths of $1\frac{1}{8}$ inch diameter (0.28 mm) stock. These 'nuts' are long enough to pass completely through the resinglass/wood/resinglass sandwich thus spreading the loads over a wide

area. In addition, being round, they are self-aligning (Fig. 116).

Before glassing commenced I plugged these pre-drilled holes with candle stumps so as to be able to drill them out easily once the laminate had cured (Photos. 120, 121). The larger through-holes for the 'nuts' I left alone, taking care to well-dimple the CSM into them leaving a depression as a guide for drilling them out later with a hole-saw.

I had taken reasonable care fitting the beds to the hull and the timber—2 inches (50 mm) wide was bedded down on two layers of CSM the first $2\frac{1}{2}$ inches (62 mm) wide, the second 4 inches (100 mm) to give a chance for the irregularities in the fit to be absorbed and high-spots eliminated. (Narrower beds would have needed another mat, or two, under them).

But before that could be done the CSM had been cut to predetermined sizes and rolled up the *rightway round* This important point is very often over-looked. If you take a piece of CSM and bend it into a hoop and glass fibres spring out from the surface you have it the wrong way round. If on bending the fibres remain flat then this is the outer (i.e upper) face upon which you will be working with brush and roller (Photo. 122). A small thing perhaps but lay a piece of CSM upside down and chances are you'll end up with a brush full of fibres. My cut rolls of CSM were held and marked with masking-tape on which their positions were noted: '*Bearer front end*' being typical. In the heat of the moment one is likely to be confronted with a variety of bits of mat all looking roughly the same.

When glassing anything into the hull it is essential to work from narrow strips, gradually increasing in size so that each successive piece gives a further one-inch (25 mm) minimum overlap. Were you to lay down just one wide piece of CSM to cover the area then you would be relying solely upon the bond between it and the hull. Doing it in progressive steps reduces the chance of total failure.

You will, of course, need to mask up the area to prevent a mess developing and have everything you need to hand. Come out of the hull for a breather while awaiting the first layers to cure—prolonged exposure to styrene will give you a hang-over! (See also *Working with Resin and Glass*).

As ever, when working in such items as engine beds it is worth considering whether you may be able to use parts of them for other purposes. For instance I designed the webs on the port side to form the basis of the floors in the WC compartment. Similarly the webs on the starboard side were used to take the structure for the dinette-end and also the head of the quarter-berth. Thinking ahead and planning carefully can make fitting-out that much easier and faster.

I had decided from the outset to mount *Solitaire's* engine down rigidly for a number of reasons—space being the prime consideration. However the use of flexible engine-mounts (Fig. 112) offers many advantages, for apart from the previously discussed noise and vibration isolating benefits these mounts often have means of adjusting the height of the engine vertically. An important consideration if you have adopted steel inserts in your beds since you cannot readily shave off small amounts to assist in lining up. Of course shims may be added or subtracted as desired but the screw adjustment in flexible mounts means that they are infinitely variable over a short height.

Then again flexible mounts used with larger, heavier engines, will help prevent shock loads being transmitted to the hull with the possibility of damage to the laminate.

Usually four mounts are needed for the range of engines discussed here and the engine supplier will advise on a suitable specification of engine mount. This selection is critical, for if the rubber-type components are too soft then the engine will 'dance' especially at its lower critical revolutions; too hard and a higher proportion of vibrations will be transmitted to the hull. As previously noted the use of flexible engine mounts means that all pipes, exhaust runs etc, must be arranged to tolerate engine movement. A suitable flexible coupling, or a flexible shaft log is also necessary.

Propeller shafts and couplings

Once again the engine-maker will be in the position to offer advice on the actual size of propeller and shaft needed together with a recommended installation scheme. He may supply direct, or via an agent who carries the stock needed.

The position of the engine relative to the propeller shaft will also have a bearing upon your selection for, although so far we have been dealing with directly coupled engines and shafts, it is worth remembering that the engine could in fact be installed above, or to the side of the propeller-shaft. You would then need to use a system of stepped, or multi-vee belts to carry the drive across. Indeed this system will even allow you to run the engine 'back-to-front' if it fits more conveniently that way round. Use of a belt-drive system also allows you to vary the reduction of engine to propeller revs precisely to suit your specific installation. This area is well outside the bounds of this fitting-out book, but if need be your engine supplier should be able to provide helpful advice.

The more commonly-fitted types of sterngear in small auxiliary sailing yachts are (1) a rigid stern tube (2) a flexible shaft log and 'P' bracket. (Fig. 113).

The former arrangement uses a threaded metal tube with a plain bore which is inserted through the 'deadwood' or in our case the moulded skeg cavity. On the outboard end of this tube is fitted a bearing which may be a plain one requiring some form of lubrication, or more probably a fluted-rubber bush which is water-lubricated. Take care to provide means for the water to actually enter the bearing—often via a scoop external to the boat, or occasionally by tapping the discharge cooling water via a pipe.

The inboard end of the shaft log, as the tube through which the prop-shaft runs is called, then has either a solid gland-bearing, or a flexible gland-bearing complete with either 'O' ring type seals to prevent water entering the boat, or a packing material and lock-nut arrangement.

If the engine is on flexible mounts and the rigid shaft log is used then a flexible coupling must also be

PHOTO. 123. *This P-bracket contains a rubber bearing. There needs to be water flowing into the bearing—and in this case the forward area is completely unobstructed. The propeller is a special folding type which cuts drag under sail.*

PHOTO. 124. *Solitaire's variable pitch propeller which has had one-half of its casing removed to show the internal thrust bearings which transmit the propeller thrust straight into the hull.*

PHOTO. 125. *This is one of the engine holding-down bolts specially fabricated for an easy engine installation. Four such bolts were needed—plus a spare.*

introduced to allow the engine to 'float'.

A flexible shaft log with 'P'-bracket installation also has a metal tube running through the skeg and the floating inboard bearing will eliminate the need for a flexible coupling on many craft *providing* that the dimension of the shaft and shaft log have been correctly chosen. A more generous clearance on the log is needed to allow the engine to move about slightly on its mounts.

There is no outer-bearing fitted to a flexible shaft log, instead the propeller-shaft is supported by a special bracket fixed to the hull. This bracket contains a

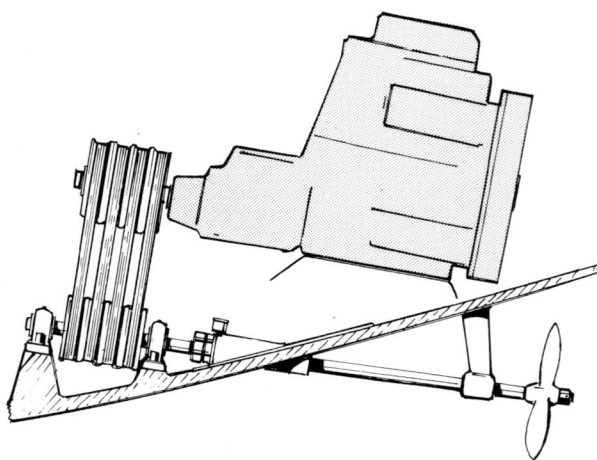

FIG. 122. *Stepped-belts, chains, or V-belts could be used to give a compact engine installation. Thrust bearings will be necessary to allow the hull to absorb the propeller's drive (thrust) in both ahead and astern.*

bearing—again usually of the fluted-rubber water-lubricated type, known as 'Goodrich' or 'Cutless' (Photo. 123).

A third, special, case is the type of installation I have fitted to *Solitaire* (Photo. 124). This uses a rigid stern tube but incorporates a variable pitch propeller—or my 'feathered friend'. For it is indeed a friend once you get used to it, and I will describe it more fully later on. Apart from its other advantages this arrangement uses an outer bearing to take the thrust from the propeller both in ahead and astern. With the two arrangements previously described provision must be made to tolerate the slight amount of axial movement which will occur when ahead and astern drives are engaged. Usually marine type gearboxes can absorb end thrust, but note that any thrust which is put into the engine is ultimately applied to its mounting bolts. If you have decided to use a belt-drive system instead of the more normal direct drive then a thrust bearing will need to be fitted to the propeller shaft (Fig. 122).

If the engine centreline and the centreline of the propeller shaft cannot be made to coincide then universal couplings will have to be considered. These must always be used in pairs and great care should be taken to fit a well-engineered system for this type of shafting is prone to troubles. A single universal joint cannot be fitted to accommodate even a slight angular displacement. The lining up of the shafts is still critical—there is a tendency to fit a pair of universals to an intermediate shaft and think that gross misalignments can be tolerated. This is not the case for the joint angles at each end of the intermediate shaft must be within half a degree of each other for satisfactory operation. Mostly the maximum operating angle of a universal jointed system should not exceed 15 degrees at the joint angle. Should compound angles be encountered, that is angles in more than one plane, then it will be necessary to seek the makers advice on this type of application.

Note that the yokes on the intermediate shaft must be accurately assembled with perfect alignment if you are to get constant velocity. Slight fitting errors here will cause the shaft to 'wind up', and ultimately fail due to torsional loadings.

When fitting a needle-roller type of universal joint it is essential that a small displacement angle—not less than one-degree be arrived at. This deliberate misalignment will cause the needles to rotate slightly as they turn and thus prevent the loads occurring on the same contact area each time. A needle-roller race fitted without this slight angle will fail due to 'brinelling'; a condition in which the roller 'beds' into the bearing.

The need to accommodate end-thrust must be considered and generally speaking it is best to assume that a system using universal joints should have provisions to absorb the thrust separately. Note that a single patent universal joint known as the 'Brightshaft' is available. This will take angular misalignment up to 15 degrees and accept propeller thrust in both directions. Tested under Lloyds A1 conditions further detailed information on this device is available from Yacht Chandlers of Great Britain Ltd, Newton Abbot, Devon, England.

Flexible couplings are recommended when the engine is on flexible mounts with a rigid sterntube and gland. This coupling is fitted directly to the output flange of the gearbox and provided that the shaft distance from the gearbox flange to the stern gland bearing is more than 2 feet (600 mm) a single flexible coupling will suffice. But if the length of shaft is shorter, the amount of flexibility inherent in it will be reduced thus introducing the necessity for another flexible coupling close to the stern gland bearing.

The size and type of flexible coupling needed will vary from engine to engine and in all cases the engine maker should be consulted.

Novel nuts to spread the load

The 'nuts' I fitted to *Solitaire's* engine beds were, as previously mentioned, made up from lengths of $1\frac{1}{8}$ inch (28 mm) round mild steel bar (Photo. 125). I chose these since they would be self-aligning and spread the loads over a wide area. And because I would simply be drilling holes they would be easier to fit than slots, which would need chopping out.

The engine holding-down bolts were in fact lengths of steel studding threaded at each end. I used $\frac{5}{8}$ inch (16 mm) steel rod and a Whitworth thread was run on each end or for about $1\frac{1}{2}$ inches (37 mm). Cutting the thread was easy enough—just tedious. Care must be taken that the die starts off square in all planes and liberal amounts of engine-oil cut 50/50 with paraffin will both lubricate and cool the die.

Before starting it is worth spending time to form a decent bevel all round the top face, and if it is not sawn square to dress it with a file until it is; otherwise the die will not want to start cutting square and the thread will run out on one part of the bar and dig deeply into the opposite face. This fault also means that the nut will not screw down evenly.

When cutting the thread do not be tempted to turn the die over and clean the last little bit of the thread out sharp. It is far better to let the thread run out gradually, thus avoiding a sharp corner, or notch, at which, as any good engineer knows, there will be a weakness.

Thread gauges, if you have them, are a help when cutting the threads—but a selection of new nuts tried on with fingers alone will tell you if the thread is correct. Remember that it is possible to cut a near-perfect thread on stock that is undersized to start off with—but be wise—check the diameter first!

When it came to drilling the holes which were to be tapped to take the studs a little more care was called for. To start with the holes have to be started off on a round surface. A generous size centre-punch mark followed by a small diameter drill is a help. So too is a set of V-blocks or a good machine vice. The final through-hole was drilled $\frac{1}{2}$ inch (13.5 mm) diameter and once again lots of oily paraffin was used to assist the cutting. It is easier to work with a long length of stock and part it off when all the operations are done.

Having drilled the holes I filed flats at the top to let the tap enter evenly and the four inch (100 mm) lengths were cut off with a hacksaw (Photos. 126–134).

Now although there are several good thread-locking glues on the market I decided to lock the bottom threads mechanically. Some readers might think that excessive but better safe than the other thing. I drilled down the centreline of each 'nut' and counterbored it before tapping it with a $\frac{1}{4}$ inch Whitworth thread to take the locking bolts.

While on this metal-working theme did you know that there is a right and a wrong way of hacksawing? If you are righthanded then always saw with the work poking out from the righthand side of the vice. Then if the blade breaks you won't punch the vice with your hand. And while on this safety theme never wear gloves when drilling with a power tool. The swarf might drag your hand into the drill. Instead of gloves invest in a good barrier cream and lots of hand cleaner!

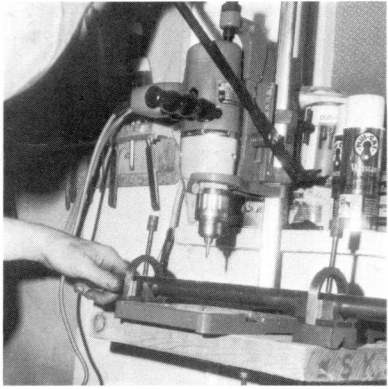

PHOTO. 126. *It obviously helps if you have the right gear . . . here a centre-drill is being used to start the holes.*

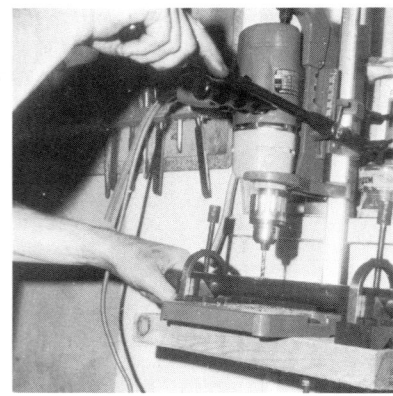

PHOTO. 127. *Alternatively the holes can be started by filing a flat surface on the round stock. A pilot hole is drilled all the way through to ease drilling loads.*

PHOTO. 128. *When drilling metal lots of coolant is needed to keep the drill cutting. The work needs to be firmly clamped to prevent accidents.*

PHOTO. 129. *Running a thread into the holes, or tapping them, is fairly easy if you start the tap off square and use lots of tallow. Back off occasionally to let the metal chips fall through.*

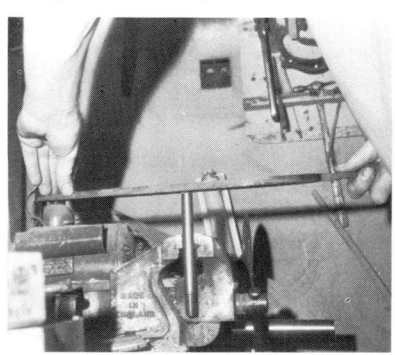

PHOTO. 130. *If the stock and die starts off square then you have every chance of running a parallel thread down it. A generous bevel helps the die get started.*

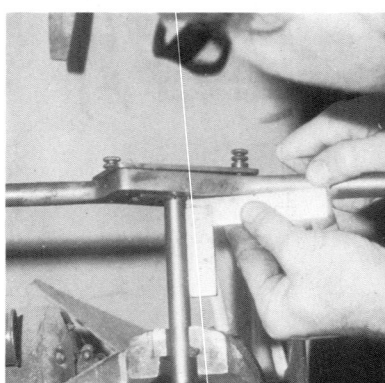

PHOTO. 131. *An early check with a square in two places 90 degrees apart tells that the die is cutting correctly.*

PHOTO. 132. *Lots of oil, or tallow is needed to prevent excessive wear and heat build-up. It also makes the operation less-tiring. . . .*

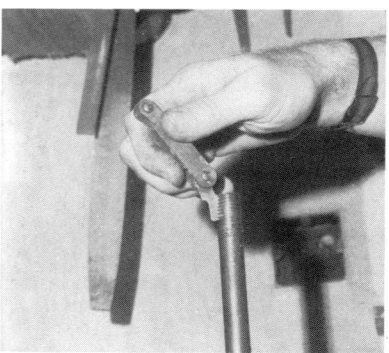

PHOTO. 133. *If you have them, or can borrow them, then thread gauges help you check on the progress of the die.*

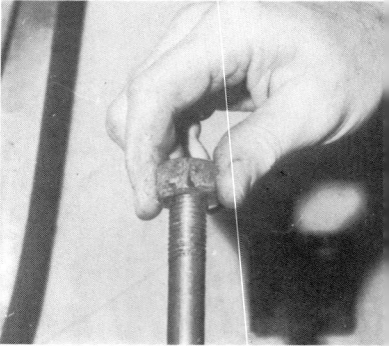

PHOTO. 134. *Otherwise you will have to rely on a steady supply of new nuts and try to get them running down the cut thread with finger pressure.*

My feathered friend

Let me tell you about my particular engine arrangements and then we'll take a look at some of the general requirements for a successful installation.

The engine in question is a 16 hp SABB diesel (Photo. 135). with a variable pitch propeller. I knew the previous owner, and I also knew that the only reason he was having it replaced with a similar engine with a conventional gearbox was mainly because his wife had difficulty operating it. All it required was a modest 'breathing' on, clean up and a new clutch disc to make it ready again for many years of hard work. Most boat engines 'die' not from hard work—rather they expire from neglect and corrosion. This particular marque of engine is made in Norway and marketed there as a fishing boat engine. It is a true marine unit, not a marinised automotive engine, and as such is by comparison 'over engineered'. Everything is on a massive scale—the over-large crankshaft, good-sized bearings, generously proportioned castings—all add up to a very long working life. But that is paid for by a hefty weight penalty compared to lightweight marinised industrial engines!

Lifting the engine in to the boat—it weighed 420 lb (145 kg) was relatively straightforward once the 'crane' had been made (Photo. 136). I already owned the equivalent of one length of scaffold pipe (destined to make the tubular bowsprit) and this together with other lengths borrowed from friends, and a sprinkling of scaffold clips, plus some lengths of timber formed the crane shown in figure 123.

Once the engine was resting in a suitably padded cockpit, the crane was rearranged to make a 'rocking gantry' which was used to lower it onto the prepared beds. Holes for the engine holding-down bolts had already been drilled to a plywood pattern made up from the engine installation drawings. In fact the engine sat on its beds surprisingly well—once I had cut away some of the front end of the beds to allow clearance for the flywheel! (See photo. 137).

That apart, all that remained was to cut the propeller shaft to length, glass into the skeg a large support for the front bearing, and when the stern-tube assembly was in place fill the skeg cavity with a two-part polyurethane

PHOTO. 135. *The engine fitted and final adjustments being carried out. Valve clearance is critical with a diesel engine for not only does it need a good supply of air, but it relies upon compression for ignition.*

PHOTO. 136. *Minus its flywheel, starter-motor, alternator and other easily removed items, the engine was hoisted up into the cockpit by the 'crane' shown here.*

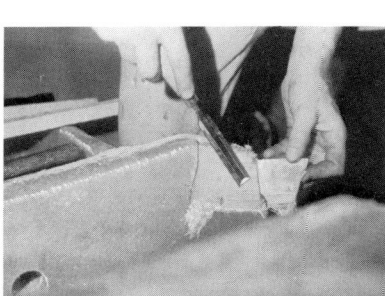

PHOTO. 137. *And that's when I discovered that flywheels are round! Clearance had to be cut from the front of the engine beds—and I was surprised by just how tough they were!*

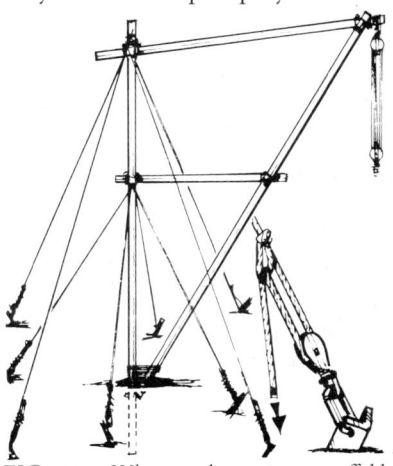

FIG. 123. *When needs must . . . scaffold pipe, clips, wood, rope and blocks enabled me to hoist Solitaire's engine into her cockpit.*

PHOTOS. *138, 139. Two-part poly-*
urethane foam can be used to fill cavities such
at this skeg. It needs applying in small batches
and remember that the fumes are decidedly
dangerous. So get well clear.

PHOTO. *140. These 1½ inch BSP galvan*
ised pipe fittings and nipples are entirel
commensurate with 1¾ inch bore diesel hose
A suitable gate valve could be fitted to give
positive shut-off and prevent water entering

foam. Once this had stopped foaming it could be cut off
and faired down and then sealed off with a couple of
layers of CSM (Photos. 138, 139).

One word of caution: the foaming process produces a
toxic gas (isocyanate) so get out of the boat as soon as
possible and allow at least an hour for the hull to
ventilate.

The fuel tank I fitted was the standard Sabb 9 gallon
(40 litre) unit. It was secured to the engine beds in a
cradle well-upholstered to prevent damage, and fastened
down with long aluminium straps. The tank sits exactly
under the bridgedeck and is filled via the usual deck-
filler through the very centre of the bridgedeck. Any
spillage goes straight in to the cockpit drains aided by a
bucket of water. The fuel tank is separated from the
engine compartment by a plywood bulkhead with a
chute-type door through it giving access to the tank's
shut-off cock.

Fitting the tank immediately behind the engine has
kept pipe runs to an absolute minimum and although

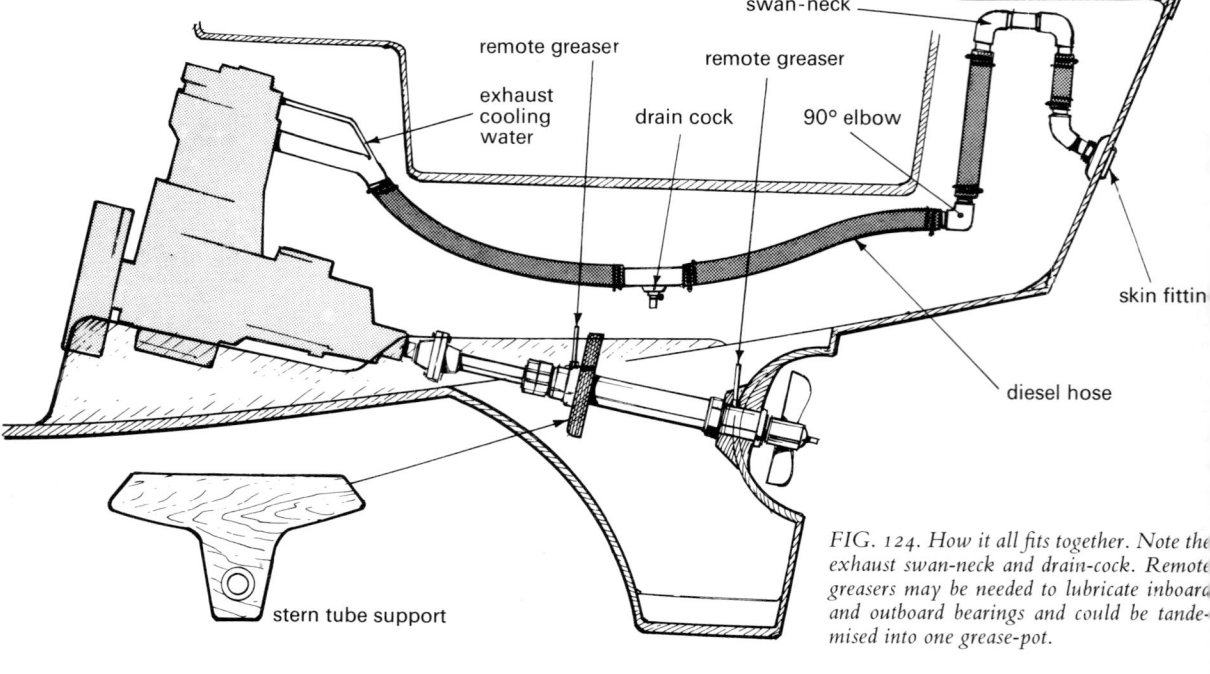

FIG. *124. How it all fits together. Note the*
exhaust swan-neck and drain-cock. Remote
greasers may be needed to lubricate inboard
and outboard bearings and could be tande-
mised into one grease-pot.

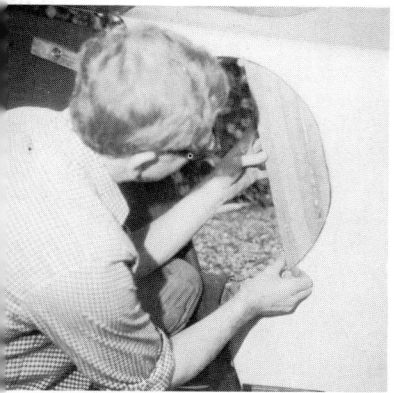

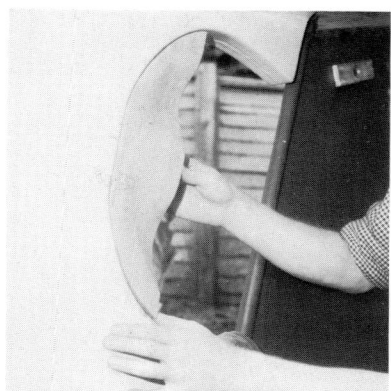
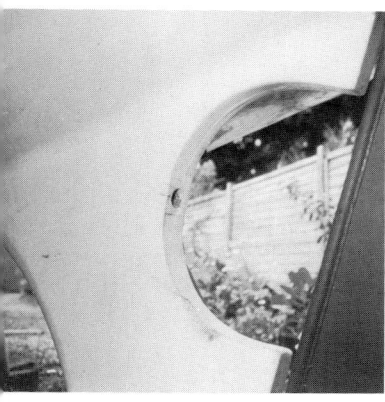

PHOTOS. 141, 142, 143, 144. A wooden block was used to position the propeller in its aperture and also give a smooth flow of water. The original square end to the skeg would have caused a large amount of turbulence and would have reduced operating efficiency—probably 10 per cent or more.

PHOTO. 145. The final installation ▶ showing the propeller blades feathered. They can be lined up behind the skeg by means of a lock in the clutch unit.

low in the boat there is still sufficient head to give a slight gravity feed to the fuel lift pump. I also fitted a Lucas-CAV water separator/sedimentor close to the tank. No other fuel filter is fitted although, of course, there is a screen filter in the fuel pump and the usual final filter before the injector pump.

Sorting out the watercooling circuit and electrics presented no problems—it was simply a case of following the maker's handbook. The exhaust is water-cooled after a water injection chamber which lowers the exhaust pressure—and hence its temperature. I fitted 1¾ inch (45 mm) bore diesel hose making use of standard 1½ inch BSP waterpipe nipples and right-angle elbows (Photo. 140) to help form a swan neck which carries the exhaust line high up above the waterline before discharging through the transom (Fig. 124). The pipe is clipped at 18 inch (350 mm) intervals with padded straps screwed to blocks glassed to the hull. A generous pad was fitted behind the exhaust skin-fitting and although the rubber exhaust pipe cut its own thread on to the nipples aided by liquid detergent, I also used double-hose clips to be absolutely certain that nothing would come adrift. Similarly the exhaust pipe is run through a separate compartment not used for any stowage whatsoever—thus removing the risk of accidental

damage which could seriously affect the safe running of the boat.

The Sabb variable-pitch propeller is actuated by a cranked handle reminiscent of that used by a tram-driver. I extended this up into the companion way where, despite initial misgivings, it does not get in the way. One Plummer block (with plain bearing) was used to locate and support the extension tube into which the tram-handle was welded.

The propeller itself had to be moved into the centre of the moulded skeg aperture on a batten, or block. This was carefully shaped to provide a clean flow of water into the propeller. The skeg moulding is about 2½ inches (60 mm) across, and being square-ended would have caused a nasty amount of turbulence which might have dropped the propeller efficiency by at least 10 per cent (Photos. 141–144).

The batten is fastened to the skeg by four long silicon-bronze bolts, two of which also secure the special propeller thrust bearing which incorporates the ahead-neutral-astern-feathered mechanism (Photo. 145). A grease pipe for the bearing was also fitted and led into a stern cockpit locker to its pressure grease-pot.

The VP propeller system works perfectly, giving infinitely variable pitch in ahead and astern up to its maximum coarseness. Control is via the tram-handle and, with the engine ticking over, coming alongside and other manoeuvres are performed with good control. The propeller blades feather and may be locked in the vertical position behind the skeg thus reducing drag still further. As a concession to the crew I fitted an indicator on the tram-handle so that a peep over the companionway tells immediately what the propeller is set at—a very useful feature.

That then is a brief description of the engine installation on *Solitaire*. Let's leave the particular and return once more to the general with a look at a typical fuel system.

Fuel tanks

Fuel tanks may be part of the boat—integral—or separate. Separate was my choice. Moulded integral fuel tanks for diesel are possible in a resinglass hull provided that certain considerations are taken into account.

If the resin is not of the fire-retardant type then it must be externally treated with a suitable fire-retardent material—an intumescent paint for example. The only fillers which can be used with the resin should be fire-retardant or thixotropic and the proportion of filler to resin must be less than 5 per cent. The resin in contact with the fuel is especially important and must be backed with a fine mat—less than 300 gm/m²—to form a barrier to prevent the laminate absorbing the fuel by capillary action. Whatever type of lay-up is selected the final laminate thickness should be at least 0.20 inch (5 mm) for tanks up to 40 gallons (200 litres) and 0.25 inch (6.5 mm) for tanks from 40 to 80 gallons (200–400 litres).

Boat tanks with a rectangular section should have a good radius of about 2 inches (50 mm) in all corners at their sides and bottoms. If the tank measures more than 30 inches (750 mm) or more in length, or width, then it must be fitted with baffles—which need to be as thick as the tank laminate. Baffles need to be strongly bonded to the tank and provision should be made to fit a hand-hole to give access to the inside of the tank. The hand-hole cover may be fastened with bolts using a steel tapping insert moulded into the top of the tank, or with throughbolts passing through a moulded flange. Lids may be resinglass, steel or aluminium.

Connections for filling and other pipes which are not secured by an inner nut should pass through an area of laminate which has been increased to double thickness. Any hole drilled into the tank must be sealed around the cut edge to prevent fuel entering the laminate. Naturally such tanks should be well away from possible sources of heat and well isolated from the accommodation. If you use the keel cavity for a fuel tank then the interior moulding will need special treatment to prevent the hull laminate from absorbing fuel. Note that in the U.K. integral tanks are not permissible for use with petrol.

Where an integral fuel tank is positioned close to an integral water tank then a moulded raised flange or web-type coffer-dam should be arranged to prevent the possibility of contamination through leakage.

All-in-all, although an integral tank seems to have some advantages I would much prefer to fit separate tanks for water, and fuel. Water tanks moulded into the hull need special treatment, particularly in the final layer of resin which is in contact with the water if it is not to be grossly fouled by resin products. While I would have no hesitation in making use of a 'rubber' bag tank for water—indeed *Solitaire* has just such a tank, I would hesitate about their use for fuel—even diesel.

Metal tanks should be plain steel, lead-coated steel, stainless or Monel metal. Never use copper or galvanised steel tanks for diesel, for these materials react catalytically with the fuel and cause sludging. Petrol tanks may be made from copper (tin-coated internally) hot-dip galvanized mild steel, lead-coated steel, brass Monel or stainless. As with any stainless fabrication care should be taken that it is of a suitable grade, or pinholing from the inside may develop. Construction should be welded, brazed, riveted and soldered, or rolled-seamed and soldered, and must not rely solely upon crimped seams for integrity. Soft solder should never be used.

The tank must be well secured to withstand shock loadings and the securing bands used must be padded with non-absorbent material to prevent damage to the tank. A well ventilated position is recommended, and if the tank has a flat bottom it should be supported to prevent it sagging under load (Figure 125 shows a typical twin-tank system suitable for a diesel engine).

The tank filler plate should be watertight, and well away from ventilators leading into the body of the boat. Ideally any spillage should immediately run overboard. The filler-pipe itself needs to be as direct as possible without a bend over the first foot or so for that might prevent the proper insertion of a filler nozzle. The material for the filler-pipe needs to be fire-resistant and not less than $1\frac{1}{2}$ inch (37 mm) bore. The fuel tank and the deck filler plate should be electrically bonded to earth any electrostatic charges which may develop. Flexible fuel pipe sections need bridging to give continuity right back to the engine. If a flexible tank filler pipe is fitted then it should be non-kinking and resistant to hydrocarbons—armoured neoprene is a suitable material—and double hose-clipped for safety.

Tank ventilating pipes need to be $\frac{1}{2}$ inch diameter (12 mm) and carried from the highest part of the tank

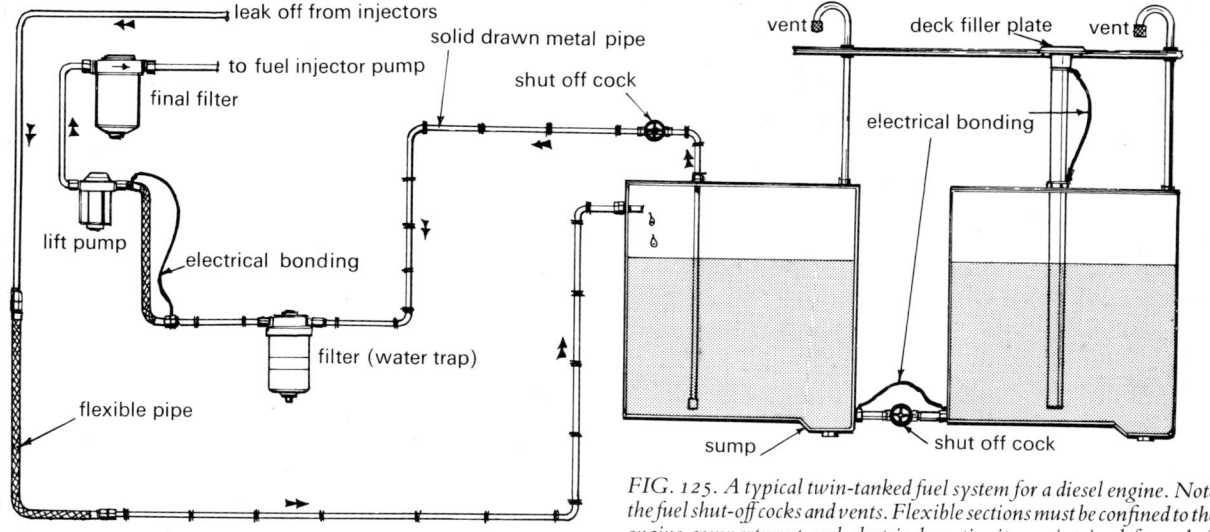

FIG. 125. A typical twin-tanked fuel system for a diesel engine. Note the fuel shut-off cocks and vents. Flexible sections must be confined to the engine compartment and electrical continuity maintained from deck filler plate right back to engine block.

extending to atmosphere and terminating in a suitable flame arresting arrangement—usually a screen of 30 × 30 mesh. The pipe needs to be of fire resistant material and it should be so arranged that there is no possibility of water entering the tank especially when the boat is sailing. Where two or more tanks are incorporated they should be linked by a connecting pipe so that they may be filled from one position. A shut-off cock should be fitted to enable the tanks to be isolated and you could arrange dual fuel supplies, filters and separators, to the engine. Balancing pipes should not be fitted to petrol installations for safety.

Gravity feed to an engine is not recommended and fuel should be drawn from the centre of the tank top via a pipe which terminates just clear of the tank bottom. This will prevent it sucking up water and sludge. Fuel lines must be softened seamless copper, seamless Monel, stainless steel, or for diesels only, mild steel. They should be run at an even height to the engine and not pass through areas which make inspection impossible. Connections should be well-made and as few as possible and must be metal-to metal joints, or brazed—never use soft-solder for it may be 'dissolved' by the fuel, or crack under vibration. Pipes must be well clipped to prevent movement and the possibility of chafe, and protected where they pass through bulkheads. A spacing for fixing clips of 4 inches (100 mm) is recommended.

The use of short lengths of flexible fuel pipe should be confined to the engine compartment and it should be of flame-resistant type with well-made connections.

The reason why a gravity-fed tank is not recommended is that should a leak occur in the fuel pipe the entire contents of the tank(s) will empty into the boat.

Similarly, care should be taken with a system using a section of flexible pipe that should the pipe be cut its free end cannot drop down and start the tank syphoning.

Stop cocks must be accessible and ideally secured to their tanks, and it is a wise arrangement to have them capable of remote shut-off so that in the event of a fire in the engine compartment the fuel supply can be quickly cut off.

Most engines arrive complete with their fuel lift pump but if you are doing your own thing note that fuel pumps, electrically or mechanically-operated, should be put at the engine-end of the fuel line. Electric pumps must be wired through the start switch so that they are only energised when the engine is turning. Pressurised tank systems are not considered to be suitable for inboard engine installations.

All the foregoing may seem a little daunting at first reading but the fuel system is vitally important to the continuous operation of a diesel engine, and where the fuel is petrol greater care needs to be taken for it is a much more dangerous fuel than diesel oil.

Exhaust systems, some considerations

Two types of exhaust system may be used; wet or dry. Dry exhaust systems are difficult to arrange in the cramped confines of a boat and if used they must be well-lagged with at least $\frac{1}{2}$ inch (12 mm) asbestos fibre tape. Should they be routed through accommodation areas there is risk of fire and increased noise. A proper installation needs flexible joints, resilient supports and some means of draining off condensates. If steel pipe is used then it should be appreciated that some means of accommodating thermal expansion may be necessary. (Steel expands at the rate of 7 thou. per foot per 100°F temperature rise). All this means that within the context of this book dry exhausts are really suitable only for small engines with horsepowers around 3–4 hp (2.5–3 kw) or for workboats. An exception may be found with keel-cooled installations—but even then it may be preferable to fit a separate water pump to allow a watercooled exhaust system to be used.

With a direct or heat-exchanger system using a wet exhaust raw cooling water is taken from the engine outlet and discharged into the exhaust pipe thus cooling the gases and also the system itself. With most small engines all the cooling water is put into the exhaust pipe although some installations split the flow to give a separate discharge overboard to act as a 'tell-tale'.

The exhaust pipe material may be iron or galvanized steel with either wet or dry diesel systems. Copper and brass tubing may be used for petrol engines, but must not be used for diesel exhausts for the gases cause rapid corrosion.

Diesel exhaust hose must be suitably reinforced to prevent kinking at bends. Its use is limited to wet systems, where it must never be used closer to the engine than that point where the water is injected. The engine maker will recommend the minimum bore required and specify the maximum length suitable for that size of pipe. A long run of pipe, especially with fittings which reduce the bore locally, causes back-pressure which prevents the engine reaching its maximum output. So too will abrupt bends. Ideally lengths of exhaust pipe should terminate at each end with a flange coupling so that they may be removed without disturbing the engine, or skin fitting.

When selecting the bore of the wet exhaust pipe note that with some arrangements, particularly where the pipe is run low in the boat, it may be necessary to accommodate the water introduced into the system while trying to start the engine. This will prevent the possibility of the water getting back into the engine.

The final outlet of the exhaust should be at least six inches (150 mm) above the loaded waterline, and if there is a chance of water flowing back through the system into the engine, a high swan-neck should be incorporated. If it is not possible to arrange a swan-neck then a full-way valve could be fitted—in fact most installations even with a swan-neck would be improved by some positive means of shutting off the exhaust system in severe weather conditions. Similarly it is good practice to fit some form of drain to the lowest part of the exhaust—a ¼ inch BSP plug is the minimum. A drain plug such as this is certainly worth the trouble involved

in fitting it for when it comes to laying up the engine for the winter the exhaust line can be quickly drained. Otherwise it may involve dropping the engine end of the exhaust off its coupling flange. Should you not take this precaution then even though the outboard exhaust fitting is plugged there will still be a chance of moisture getting into the cylinders during those months when the engine is idle and rusting the pistons into their bores.

By-and-large, water-cooled diesel engines with water-injected diesel hose exhaust systems do not require any additional silencing. The use of a synthetic rubber silencer may be advised by the engine maker whose advice should be sought.

Should you end up with an engine which has its exhaust manifold below the waterline, and if it is impossible to use a raised mixing/expansion chamber with its section of dry exhaust pipe, then a water-lock exhaust system could be used. Like a wet exhaust this arrangement has the advantage of a minimum length of dry exhaust pipe with an obvious reduction of heat dissipation and lagging requirements.

As figure 126 shows, the system is essentially simple; the raw engine cooling-water is fed into the exhaust pipe immediately after the manifold. The mix of water and exhaust gases then pass into the water-lock chamber where water builds up to a level after which surplus amounts are forced out into the outlet pipe with the exhaust gases and thence overboard. When sizing the chamber it is necessary to ensure that its capacity should be ample to contain the water draining into it from the inlet and outlet pipes. The water injection pipe must be taken up above the waterline by at least 12 inches (300 mm) and provision must be made at the highest point of this loop to prevent syphoning. This could be

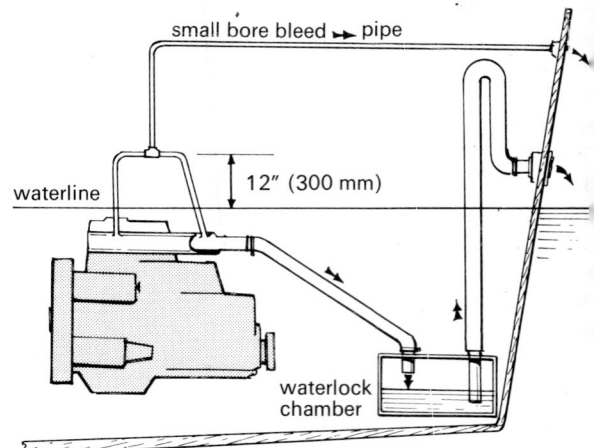

FIG. 126. *A waterlock in the exhaust may be used when the engine is installed with its exhaust manifold below the waterline. Its capacity must be sufficient to contain residual water draining into it from inlet and outlet exhaust sections.*

either a special vacuum relief valve, or more simply a small-bore bleed pipe which while discharging overboard provides a 'tell-tale' that the system is functioning.

A swan-neck in the outlet pipe should be provided to prevent water entering the outlet skin-fitting flooding the system, and once again a full-way valve would be a valuable heavy-weather safeguard. That apart, the usual care should be taken that under conditions of heel, roll or pitch, water in the system cannot enter the engine: if it does considerable damage will result.

Engine compartment ventilation

It is essential that the engine compartment is adequately ventilated, both to allow the engine to reach its maximum operating efficiency, and also to prevent the build-up of potentially dangerous vapours. Good ventilation will also let the engine work at a satisfactory temperature level—an important factor for high temperatures effectively de-rate the engine and can lead to a disappointing performance.

Good ventilation is fairly easy to achieve and need not be fan-assisted—but if a fan is used it must be of the non-parking type and approved for the task. If possible it should be fitted outside the engine compartment. Where deep cross-webs have been fitted in the engine compartment then care should be taken to site the extract ducts to prevent a build-up of heavy gases (and that includes petrol vapour) in these 'troughs'.

Fans should be installed as high as possible with their ducts led down to just above the level at which bilge water might normally rise. In most installations it will be found satisfactory to have the inlet duct terminate just below the carburettor intake of a petrol engine, or about mid-engine level for a diesel unit. Normally compartments would have their outlet ducts start just above engine height. Cowls should be fitted and sited so that there is no chance of water entering the engine space. Air flow quantities around 3.5 ft³ per horsepower per minute are desirable for good performance. One change of air every five minutes should also be aimed at. Diesel engines need more air then petrol units and a rule of thumb is that they need a compartment which has total ventilation five times greater than the air they consume.

The switch operating the fans should be sited next to, or wired into the starter switch and operated for a minimum time of two minutes before the engine starter is engaged. In addition to the fan-assisted system provision must also be made for natural ventilation when the boat is under way and the fans not working. Fans which are not rated for continuous use must not be wired through the ignition switch.

The minimum duct opening for an engine compartment volume of 40–100 ft³ (1.1–2.8 m³) would be around 30 in²(0.02 m²). The same amount of natural ventilation would also be necessary for enclosed fuel tank compartments.

Note that the boat's motion through the air may be used to provide a beneficial 'ram' effect if the inlet duct cowl faces forward and the extract aft. Care should be taken with the siting of all inlet and extract cowls to prevent extracted vapours being drawn back into the engine compartment.

Cooling systems

Most small marine engines are raw-water cooled and the temperature of the water must be kept below 135°F (57°C) to prevent salt being laid up within the water-cooling jacket. Although this type of system is the simplest to arrange, the limit imposed on performance by that low temperature may lead the engine manufacturer to choose a heat-exchanger. With this, raw sea water is circulated through a chamber containing a stack of small-bore pipes through which freshwater is pumped. The seawater then goes overboard via the exhaust while the cooled freshwater is pumped once more around the engine cooling system. The circulation of the freshwater is thermostatically controlled and since it is running in a self-contained system it can be pressurized to allow the temperature to be raised to over the boiling point of salt water at 212°F (100°C). An additional advantage of this system is that it enables an antifreeze to be introduced for winter running.

Other possible cooling arrangements include skin tank cooling and also keel cooling. The sizes and arrangements needed are beyond the scope of this book and the engine maker's recommendations should be sought.

With all water-cooling systems the preferred pipe material is copper with short lengths of reinforced synthetic rubber hose introduced to accommodate engine movement. Stainless steel hose clips—in pairs for extra security—should be used. A very long run of rubber hose is not desirable—especially on the raw water pump inlet, for it could suck flat and cause the engine to overheat. Pipe-runs should be well clipped, and sited to prevent damage from badly stowed items of gear.

The inlet seacock should have a coarse screen filter, or 'rose' fitted over it outside the hull and inside it should incorporate a removeable strainer. Note that the size of the seacock should match the raw water pump, and the minimum open area of the strainer screen should be four times greater than the bore of the seacock.

S-drives for simpler installations

One of the more exciting engine arrangements to arrive on the boating scene over the past few years is that of the S-Drive; an assembly designed to go through the bottom of the hull. This system is very attractive to the home-completer since it is relatively simple to fit. The unit comes with a ready-moulded resinglass bed which you cut to fit the hull and then carefully laminate in position (Photo. 146). Thus there are no engine beds in the traditional sense to worry about, nor are there a stern tube and bearings to line up. The drawback is perhaps the size of the hole which must be cut through the bottom of the hull to allow the leg of the S-Drive to pass through. True the hole is sealed with a synthetic rubber diaphragm which if correctly designed and fitted will produce a watertight seal. One maker, the Danish Bukh uses a double-layer diaphragm with a sensing device in the 'sandwich' which warns if water should enter between the layers.

Apart from being simpler to install, the S-Drive type of installation offers quietness and smoothness and since one is not constrained by the shaft angle there is much more freedom to choose the engine location.

Another 'plus' factor is that the engine may be located in front of, or behind, the actual through-hull leg.

Use of a rubber diaphragm to seal the hole together with rubber engine mounts means that all rotating parts are isolated from the hull. Were I fitting this type of drive I would, if possible, install it in a watertight box carried as high above the waterline as possible—a needless complication some might think but you will need to separate the engine from the accommodation and the rest of the boat to keep smells and fumes and noise at bay. Such a high box means that in the event of seal failure the only thing to suffer would be the engine!

One other varaition on the S-Drive theme is made by the Dutch company Jurjens. This comes in the usual sub-frame but instead of a gear-box it has a variable-pitch propeller. The propeller blade arrangement is altered to give ahead-neutral-astern (just like my Sabb) and it can also be feathered to reduce drag when sailing. With the Jurjens the propeller thrust is imposed upon the hull through a bearing in the propeller drive housing—and not, as is commonly used with S-Drives through the shaft to the engine. S-Drives are available to cover engine sizes from $7\frac{1}{2}$ hp (5.6 kw) to over 50 hp (37 kw).

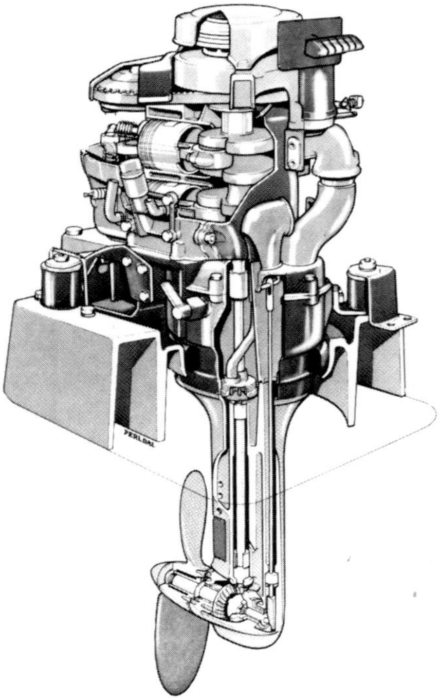

PHOTO. 146. This cutaway shows the compact Volvo Penta Sail Boat Drive—or S-Drive. Note the moulded 'bed' which is cut to fit the hull and then glassed in. Instead of a strong diaphragm this model uses a thick 'o'-ring seal to prevent water entering the boat.

8

Electrolytic corrosion

Electrolytic corrosion occurs when dissimilar metals are immersed in seawater (or grossly polluted freshwater) and are also connected together electrically outside the electrolyte. This causes a small current to flow and one of the metals corrodes. In effect a galvanic cell is set up (Fig. 127) and the electrical current passes from the metal with the least potential (the anode) to the higher potential (cathode) resulting in metal 'dissolving' away from the anode (Photo. 147).

All metals have a potential voltage rating, and the values for a selection of metals you may be working with are given in the table. Corrosion becomes severe when the two metals in contact electrically have a difference in potential greater than 0.25 volts. Where such mixtures cannot be avoided a sacrificial anode may be 'wired' in. This uses metals of a low potential such as zinc or magnesium which corrode away preferentially and thus protect metals to which they are electrically bonded. The anodes may be replaced periodically—usually annually—as required.

Since this corrosion is caused by an electric current it will also be appreciated that current leakages from onboard equipment can set up a galvanic cell even though a sacrificial anode system is in use. Should the leakage of current be excessive it may even cause previously cathodic (protected) metal to become anodic with resultant corrosion ensuing. For this reason insulated earth return systems are recommended for the

boat's electrical installation. Where the engine starter motor incorporates an earth to the engine block great care should be taken to prevent a build-up of oil and dirt which in a damp atmosphere could result in leakage. It is good practice to isolate the battery by a switch when not in use. Most engine makers supply detailed information on electrolytic corrosion, if not there are several specialist firms with engineers versed in the subject.

Low potential (least 'noble') anodic

(Corroded end)

Magnesium	-1.65v
Zinc	-1.10v
Galvanised steel	-1.10v
Aluminium alloys	$-0.73-0.75$v
Mild steel	-0.60v
Cast iron	-0.61v
Stainless steel (18/8) (Active)	-0.53v
Copper	-0.36v
Aluminium Brass	-0.32v
Naval Brass	-0.29v
Manganese bronze	-0.27v
Gun metal	-0.25v
Silicon bronze	-0.18v
Stainless steel (18/14/Mo) (Active)	0.18v
Monel metal	-0.075v
Stainless steel (18/10/2/Mo) (Passive)	-0.050v

(Protected end)

Cathodic (most 'noble')

From the above it will be seen that zinc and magnesium are among the least 'noble' metals and when arranged with any of the others in the table will corrode preferentially.

Note that although stainless steel is grouped among the more 'noble' metals (with the exception of 18/8 grade) it should not be used below the waterline for it is susceptible to rapid corrosion under certain circumstances—some of which are unpredictable (Photo. 148).

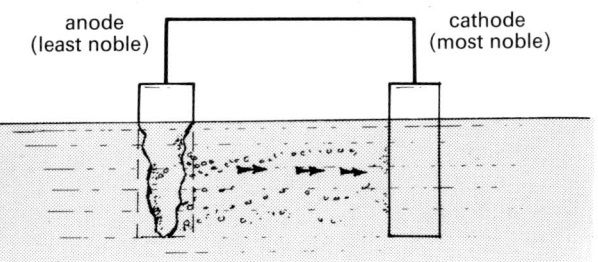

FIG. 127. A galvanic cell actually produces electricity, and in doing so removes metal from the least noble (anode) component. Common brass, being an alloy of copper and zinc, is very prone to this form of attack.

PHOTO. 148. *The behaviour of even marine-grade stainless steel fastenings below the waterline is unpredictable. This bolt looks sound enough at either end where the metal is exposed to air in the waterflow. The shank of the bolt has been subjected to rapid corrosion simply because it was surrounded by airless, stagnant, water. Silicon bronze is a safer alternative. . . .*

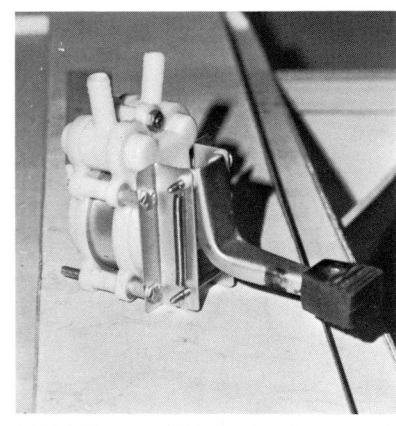

PHOTO. 149. *This Jupiter foot-pump is available in salt, or freshwater, models. It is a double-acting diaphragm and my only real criticism is that the foot lever is under-engineered and only electro-plated.*

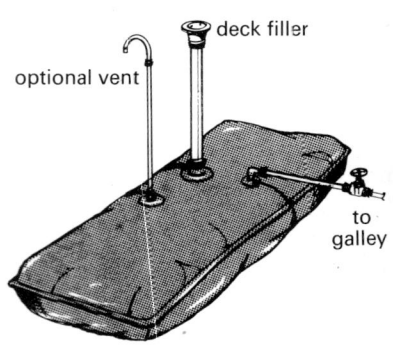

Fig. 128. *Flexible, or bag-tanks, are suitable for water and may be arranged with a vent pipe—although strictly this is not really necessary. The pump feed pipe may be tee-d to provide a sight gauge for the tank contents.*

PHOTO. 147. *Zinc anodes such as this may be used to protect underwater metal fittings. If severe corrosion takes place then a specialist should be consulted.*

Plumbing for perfection

As with integral fuel tanks, so for fresh water there may be a temptation to use ready-made structures in the boat which look ideal for use as tanks—the keel cavity for instance. Having sailed a large number of boats and made a point of tasting their water I am of the opinion that those with moulded tanks have the worst taste. So on *Solitaire* I fitted a 'bag-tank' which, made of food-grade material, does not taint the water (Fig. 128). The temptation with a flexible tank is to stuff it into any likely looking locker and call the job done. That is a mistake, for the space will need lining to prevent the tank from fretting on pinnacles of resinglass. All sharp corners on surrounding woodwork should be eased and provision made to strap the tank down to limit movement. That apart this form of tank makes an easy installation for it needs only one inlet from the deck filler and one outlet to the galley sink(s). A further take-off

could be used to provide a sight-tube to determine the tank contents and provided this is taken high up into the deckhead there should be no chance of water pouring out when the boat is heeled. You might find though that the end of the sight-tube will need reducing to a pin-hole to prevent the galley pump drawing air and malfunctioning.

A good water system starts with good hoses—use only food-grade hoses and if your source of supply is doubtful fill the hose with water and let it stand for an hour. Should it taste of 'plastic' then chances are that you have the wrong grade. Generally it is easy to recognise suitable hose: it should be crystal clear, but if it has a purple sheen you are looking at the plasticiser which will leach into the water, and even years later it will taste peculiar.

A suitable alternative to flexible tanks would be blow-moulded foodgrade polyethylene tanks, stainless steel, or galvanized tanks. Tinned copper and aluminium tanks are also sometimes used. Metal tanks should be well-supported and secured against movement and their size is very much dependent upon your needs and plans. Generally coastwise cruising seems to get through about one-gallon per head per day. Deep sea sailormen make do with perhaps half a gallon (4.5 litres and 2 litres respectively).

Foot pumps at the galley offer the advantage of both hands free—one for you the other for the kettle—and footpumps suitable for salt or fresh water are available (Photo. 149). Alternatively you may decide on a more traditional galley pump and if so remember to fit it on the right side of the galley.

Flexible tanks do not need venting—rigid tanks do. Be sure to run the vent pipes high into the boat to prevent fouling and if possible arrange them completely inside—if they overspill into the galley sink so much the better, that is far better than getting salt water into the tank.

Both rigid and flexible tanks may be arranged in multiples to increase capacity as desired. It is best if the tanks can be sited low in the boat so that the weight of water acts as ballast—a 30 gallon (136 litre) tank will weigh 300 lb (136 kg) and need not measure more than 2 ft × 1 ft × 2 ft 6 inches (600 mm × 300 mm × 760 mm). Dual tanks can be filled via a common deck filler but it is best if they are isolated from each other so that contamination of one does not ruin all your drinking water. This is easy to arrange using ordinary domestic copper water pipe and brass fittings. I would opt for compression fittings for they seem to last longer than soldered ones. Since flexible tanks are harder to strap down securely than their rigid counterparts it will be necessary to plumb them using plastic hose, and if you wish to fit say a brass full-way valve in the supply line then it will be necessary to use short lengths of copper pipe and hose-clips. Where such gate-valves are used it will also be necessary to clamp them against some convenient part of the structure. Once again how much water you carry and where you position the tanks is up to you but in my opinion it is best to keep such weights out of the bow and site them as near possible amidships.

And the WC

Plumbing-in the WC, once you have decided upon its position, is relatively simple. The actual connections will vary from make to make, but generally the inlet will be $\frac{3}{4}$ inch (20 mm) bore hose and the outlet $1\frac{1}{2}$ inch (37 mm).

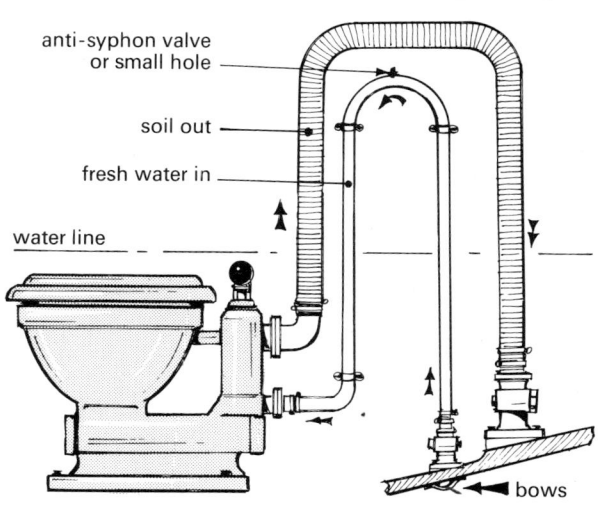

FIG. 129. If the W.C. bowl is low in the boat then on one tack it will probably be below the waterline. That means that inlet and outlet pipes should be run high up to prevent flooding. A small hole must be bored into the apex of the inlet pipe to prevent syphoning. A hot needle will melt a suitable hole which is very difficult to drill cleanly in plastic pipe.

No matter what the make the hoses should be well secured and of the reinforced plastics type for the inlet could suck flat under the strong pump action. It is not unknown for a blocked discharge pipe to rupture under too-enthusiastic pumping with annoyingly foul results. When warming these pipes to get them on to the necessary fitting I find that hot engine oil—carefully heated in a double pot of boiling water—seems to warm the plastic more evenly, and it also lubricates the pipe end.

With any make of toilet it is a good idea to run the pipes as high in the boat as convenient—and this becomes essential if the WC is fitted lower than the waterline

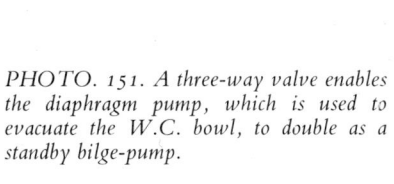

PHOTO. 150. The actual proportions of a W.C. compartment need not be large; in fact a 'snug' one offers definite advantages since it allows the users to wedge themselves in.

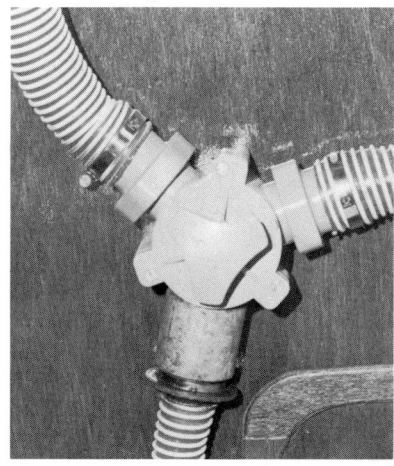

PHOTO. 151. A three-way valve enables the diaphragm pump, which is used to evacuate the W.C. bowl, to double as a standby bilge-pump.

(Photo. 149). 'Think-heeled' once again, for what is above the waterline on an even keel, may dip below when heeled. Use two hose clips (stainless—they are well worth the extra initial expense) for security and remember that if the WC is below the waterline then the inlet pipe will need a small air-bleed hole (or valve) at its apex to prevent syphoning (Fig. 129).

On *Solitaire* I fitted a Lavac WC which uses a Henderson-type bilge pump to evacuate the bowl and draw flushing water and soil through the system (Photo. 150, 151). By incorporating a Y-cock, or more properly a 'three-way cock' in the system I am able to use this pump as a stand-by emergency bilge-pump. The pump moves about a litre a stroke—so five pump actions pass one-gallon. Being a diaphragm pump it dislikes intensely sharp objects such as matchsticks which could pierce its synthetic rubber diaphragm. Thus a fine filter—or strum-box is fitted to the end of the pipe run from the pump to the bilge.

Note that some boating locations require holding tanks and pump-out facilities. The majority of WC makers are familiar both with the requirements and also the arrangements needed to meet specific requirements.

The door into the WC on *Solitaire* closes on to a step—arranged as part of a long-term plan to install a shower in there—should I ever get enough time off to go 'walkabout'. The compartment currently lacks the shower and also a nice teak grid on which to stand. Meantime it *does* drain into the bilge and this means that it can be given an occasional scrub with large amounts of water to keep it 'sweet'. When I get around to fitting the shower in there I will also have to use a plastic 'roller-blind' to prevent water splashing through the louvred door . . . how one thing leads to another!

Electrics afloat

The electric installation you fit may be as simple or as complex as you desire—but it must be a 'two-wire' system: no earth return. The first thing to do is decide upon how many fittings you want and for how long you are likely to want them on in a 24 hour period. Armed with the wattage you may then work out the total load and with the knowledge that you are working on a 12 or 24 v supply, you can discover the amperage. Add time and you can decide on battery capacity.

Very easy to write like that and in fact it is fairly easy to work out as the example shows:

Six lights at 20 watts	= 120 watts
Navigation and compass	= 50 watts
Vent fans (two) × 48 watts	= 96 watts

Sundries—echo sounder, log, searchlight, etc	= 114 watts
	= 480 watts

With a 12 volt supply 480 watts = 40 amperes

You then need to determine the average requirements imposed on the system by a 24 hour period at sea;

4 lights at 20 watts for 5 hours	= 400 watt-hours
navigation and compass lights for 8 hours	= 400 watt-hours
sundry loads 20 watts for 3 hours	= 60 watt-hours
	= 860 watt-hours

860 watt-hours = approximately 70 ampere-hours

A battery with a capacity of around 140 ampere-hours would be sufficient for this load, and I would add another one for the engine start. The reason for advocating what may seem an excessive capacity is that it will enable you to go for longer than 24 hours before re-charging is necessary—and also in time you will doubtless add other items of equipment which will increase the load. Buying two large (identical) batteries and fitting them into the boat at this stage will save much aggravation later on when the battery compartment is too small for your needs!

There is currently taking place a transition from the old amp-hour capacity rating to one used by the automotive industry. This uses 'cold cranking amperage' and the 'reserve capacity' and to get back into something resembling amp-hours you take the reserve capacity in hours and multiply it by 35.

Most engines come with a standard generator—usually an alternator, although very small engines may use a dynamo-starter system—the Finnish Vire two-stroke petrol engine for instance. The alternators fitted usually have a capacity ample for your ordinary needs and the best thing about an alternator—apart from its physical size, or rather lack of it, is that it delivers a healthy rate of charge at fairly low engine revs. Alternators also operate over a higher range of revs than the old type dynamo and also use solid-state devices (diodes) to rectify the AC current into a usable DC suitable for your battery supply. The use of these sophisticated electronic devices means that you have to exercise special care when installing them. For example never run the alternator without having the battery connected—by the same token you must never switch the battery off while the alternator is running. Should you do so you may destroy its control equipment.

That control equipment is also polarity sensitive—so

you could wreck it if you connect the battery up the wrong way round! Should you be doing any welding on the engine I would advise removing the alternator and its control equipment to protect it from the high currents flowing.

A pair of batteries may be wired-up in several ways—I used a mechanical switch to select one battery or the other of the pair of 120 AH batteries fitted to *Solitaire*. This switch (Fig. 130) (Photo. 152) is in the engine box so that it cannot be accidently used while the engine is running. Battery No. 1, or battery No. 2 may be used separately, or in parallel, or isolated completely as need be. To my way of thinking this type of arrangement is to be preferred to one using blocking diodes (more solid state devices). These automatically separate two batteries in the same supply circuit and allow one to be used solely for the engine while the other one is retained for domestic services. When the engine is running the greater amount of charge is automatically sent into the battery with the lowest charge state. Perhaps I am 'old fashioned' but I have heard so many bad reports of these devices that I will stick to my switch until otherwise persuaded. (See also figure 131 for further details of *Solitaire's* wiring system).

Yet another possible alternative is to use a heavy duty relay. This is operated by the engine start switch to make a connection between the two batteries so that both are charged together while the engine is running. When the engine is stopped the relay goes out of circuit and separates the batteries once again. The main disadvantage to this arrangement—and it also applies to my changeover switch—is that a very low domestic services battery may 'pull down' the engine start battery and so make starting difficult. But even that can be rectified if the relay is operated by using an oil-pressure switch which will only operate the relay once the engine is running. Your engine supplier, or a good electrical engineer will advise on a suitable arrangement.

Something you can easily sort out yourself is the size of wire you need for various on-board circuits. Boat wires need to be of the 'there and back' type for unlike a motorcar you cannot use the fabric of the hull as the return. Wires need to be of the multi-strand variety—solid conductors will crack under vibration and are also difficult to make into neat looms. PVC covered with

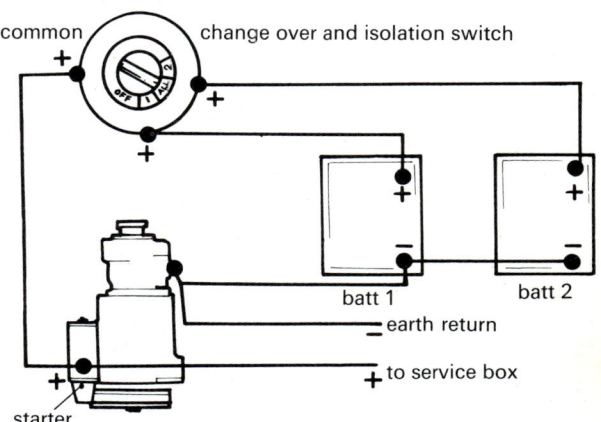

FIG. 130. *Two batteries with a mechanical changeover switch. Most cheap units break-before-make and should not be activated when the engine is running. To do so runs the risk of damaging the alternator control equipment.*

PHOTO. 152. *The main switch in Solitaire's engine box is used to bring either Battery 1, or Battery 2, into circuit. Alternatively both batteries may be connected in parallel, or completely isolated when the boat is left unattended.*

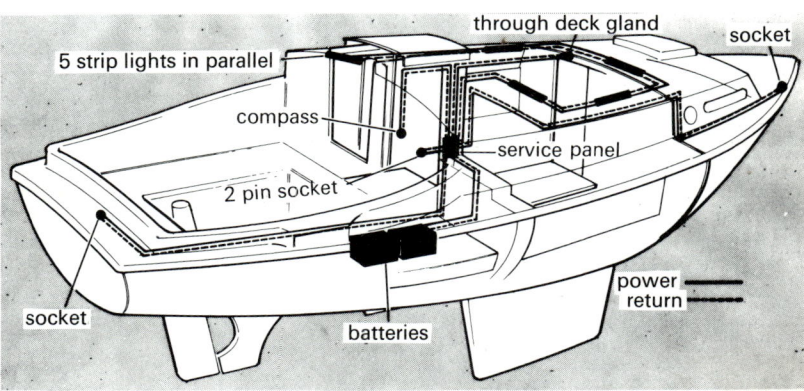

FIG. 131. *Two wire (there-and-back) circuits should be used on boats, no matter what they are made from. I kept things as simple as possible on Solitaire. Some fluorescent lights cause large amounts of interference to radio reception, and to other delicate electronic equipment. One solution is to have dual circuits containing strip lights for harbour and filament bulbs for overnight passages.*

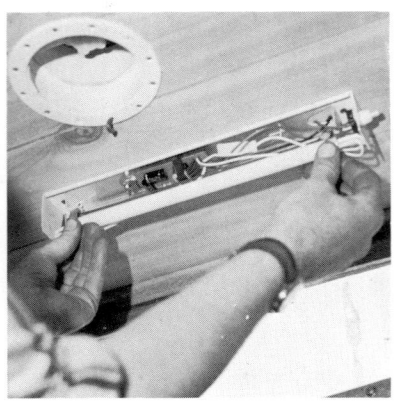

◄ PHOTO. 153. *Strip-lights are very economical on current consumption. They may however, cause interference to radio reception. Note the ventilator and bezel.*

PHOTO. 154. *Where supply wires run* ► *close to compasses and delicate (sensitive) electronic equipment they should be twisted together to prevent an electro-magnetic field being set up. Such a field may cause deviation in the compass. Here the internal lighting wires of a Suunto bulkhead mounted compass are getting the treatment.*

PCP—or if you prefer '*polyvinylchloride covered with polychloroprene*'—are recommended for PVC alone deteriorates at temperatures above 120°F (50°C). Wires should be run as high as possible in the boat and with a DC supply a ring main is not advised, even for lighting. You see, it will set up an electro-magnetic field which will play havoc with your radio equipment (Photos. 153, 154).

It is wise to run the electrical cables through ducts or pipes, and this means that before the headlining is fitted—and possibly even before much of the interior furniture is completed—you should have an idea where your electrical equipment is going to be installed. This will enable you to bond in suitable lengths of plastics pipes through which the cables can be led.

Where cables do not run through ducts they need cleating at 12 inch (300 mm) intervals to protect them and, where they pass through such items as bulkheads, rubber grommets or special glands should be used to prevent them chafing through.

Selecting the size you need calls for another little mathematics session; take my navigation lantern for example. This has a 25 W bulb which at 12 volts consumes $25/12 = 2$ Amps. There is a formula which states that $E = I \times R$, where E is the voltage drop, I is the amperage consumed, and R the resistance in ohms along the length of wire. (i.e. the resistance per foot × the length of wire). For a satisfactory 12 volt system the voltage drop should not exceed 0.5 volt. For my lantern I chose a wire (from the table given right) of 40/.0076 with a resistance per foot of 0.00428 ohms. For a 40 ft run of cable $E = 2A \times 40 \text{ ft} \times 0.00428 \text{ ohms} = 0.34 \text{ V}$, well below the 0.5 V maximum drop for a 12 volt system—1 V max for 24 volt circuits. The same type of calculation is done for all the other circuits and the wire sizes chosen. Note that the main cable from the master switch to the distribution board must be capable of carrying the total load of all the circuits through the boat.

All the circuits must be run separately and isolated by means of fuses or circuit-breakers to provide short-circuit protection.

No. & Dia. of strands	Approximate cross-sectional area		Max. cont. rating (twin core)	Resistance per foot (Ohms)
	in²	mm²		
40/.076	0.002	1.3	9 amps	0.00428
70/.0076	0.003	1.94	11 amps	0.00275
110/.0076	0.0045	2.9	16 amps	0.00183
Flexible cable with general-purpose pvc insulation				

Battery connections must be very well made and all battery wires should be kept as short as possible. Heavy starter cable—something like 61/.044—should be used and note that it is not good practice to site the batteries immediately inside the engine compartment. They give off explosive vapour during their charge/discharge cycle and as such pose a hazard. Also battery performance drops off if they become overheated.

When installing your circuits make certain that the wires are joined by mechanical connections—never by twisting them together—always use a connector block, or waterproof junction box. Do not use ordinary metal staples to secure wiring to a batten—use corrosion-resistant metal straps, plastic cleats, or cable ties. When running cables through the bilge (best avoided) protect them by routing them through plastic piping brought well up at its ends to prevent water entering. Make certain that you leave enough slack on all wires so that they can be pulled out for repairs or inspection. Leave some spare capacity in the distribution board to take care of any intended additions to the system. Figure 132 shows how I assembled a distribution board for *Solitaire* using ex-War Department switches and other basic ingredients. Note that the inside of the box should be

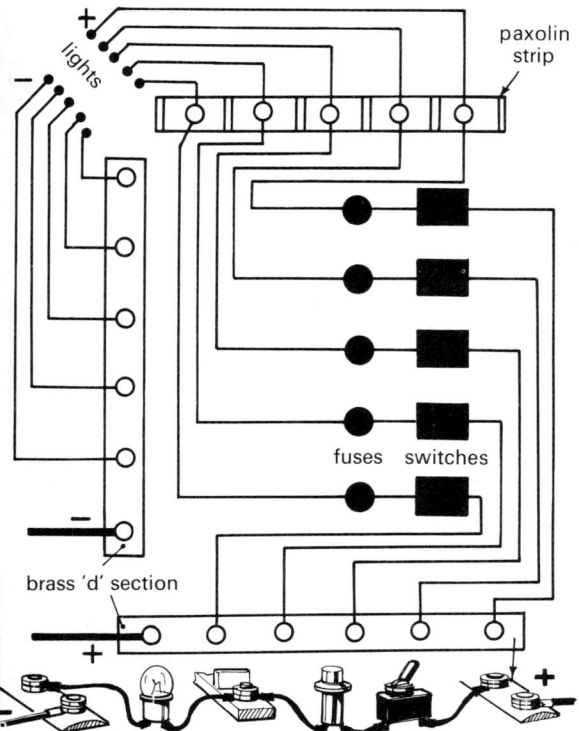

FIG. 132. Once you understand how a distribution board works then you could easily assemble one without too much difficulty. Radio and television repair shops are a good source of suitable components— fuses and the like.

metal-lined to prevent fire-spread in the event of an extreme malfunction. (See also Photo. 155).

Do not use micro-gap domestic switches for marine applications for DC loads will burn them out very quickly. Do not run cables close to hot exhaust systems, or through gas lockers! Keep any wiring running through the engine compartment to a minimum and as you install all wiring circuits keep an up to date drawing of the system. Code all wires and make certain that they cannot be wrongly connected—remember you may be attempting repairs at sea in adverse conditions so a good job now is essential.

Finally give a thought to the integrity of the system. It should be protected against water, easy to check, maintain and replace should the need arise. All batteries need to be well strapped down and should be of marine quality. Those sold for motorcars are not usually able to cope with the large amounts of vibration that they will meet afloat. Fit them where you can get at them and where they will not be flooded with seawater. Protect their external strappings from accidental short-circuits and put them in a 'drip-tray' which could be lead-lined, or more simply a moulded resinglass box.

PHOTO. 155. If you buy a distribution board it will obviously look very neat. You could assemble something which would function just as well for a fraction of the cost.

9

A sail plan for *Solitaire*

Having had a successful cutter-rig on our previous boat we decided to fit one to *Solitaire*. Sold as an Atlanta Viking 8.5, she is sloop rigged and using the maker's sail-plan—and having sailed the sloop-rigged demonstration boat—I set to work to design a sail-plan which would give us what we wanted. With our previous boat there were two sets of sheets to handle each time we tacked and I decided to use a boomed staysail to cut down on our work (Photo. 156). The second priority was a high-cut, large-size jib running down to the end of the tubular bowsprit. I had had the chain plates fitted when the builders put on the rubbing-strake and the mast position was thus already defined. In addition I had built the internal reinforcements on the assumption that the mast would sit on its moulded plinth.

Without wishing to get bogged down with Centres of Effort and Centres of Lateral Resistance I did nonetheless spend a few hours drawing out my proposed sail-plan to make certain that it coincided closely to the C.E.'s of the standard sail-plan. Basing a new one on a proven one is established practice—how do you think designers go about it?

When it came to drawing in the jib I soon discovered that the sheet lead limited the amount that it could be high-cut (Fig. 133). The angle of the sheet lead wants to be slightly steeper than the angle made by a line through the clew of the sail to meet the forestay at a right angle. The most that I could have hoped for was to lead the sheet to a turning block at the stern; from there the sheet would go forward to the winch and cleat. The disadvantage of this arrangement, as any one sailing with a spinnaker knows, is that most hulls pinch in at the stern and consequently sail-setting suffers. As ever it was a compromise and I settled for a sheet leading down to a point about level with the front of the cockpit. Why have a high cut jib? Well apart from visibility under—which I regard as a sensible seamanlike thing to have—a sail so cut does not fill with water each time the bows crunch into a wave. Such loads are not only bad for the sail—but they also strain the forestay and its attachments.

PHOTO. 156. *Solitaire's cutter-rig in action. The jib is fairly high-cut to prevent it filling with water at the foot when the bows 'crunch' into a head-sea.*

As a result of all this pencil work our sail plan gave us a jib of just over 200 square feet (18.6 m²) and a staysail of nearly 100 ft² (9.3 m²).

As I have said, the staysail was to have a boomed foot, so I researched the subject and found that such sails went out of favour with the introduction of high aspect ratio rigs—two sails with large overlaps. That seemed to me to be a great pity for a boomed staysail looks after itself just like the mainsail. One frequently sees the gooseneck of a boomed staysail made up about the stay. That, in my opinion looks very neat, but means that when the sail is squared-off a relatively flat sail is presented to the wind. Also unfair loads may be imposed on the wire stay.

If the boom ends short of the stay, with its gooseneck fitted to 'a short deck-mounted pedestal, then as the boom is squared-off the flatness needed in a reaching sail

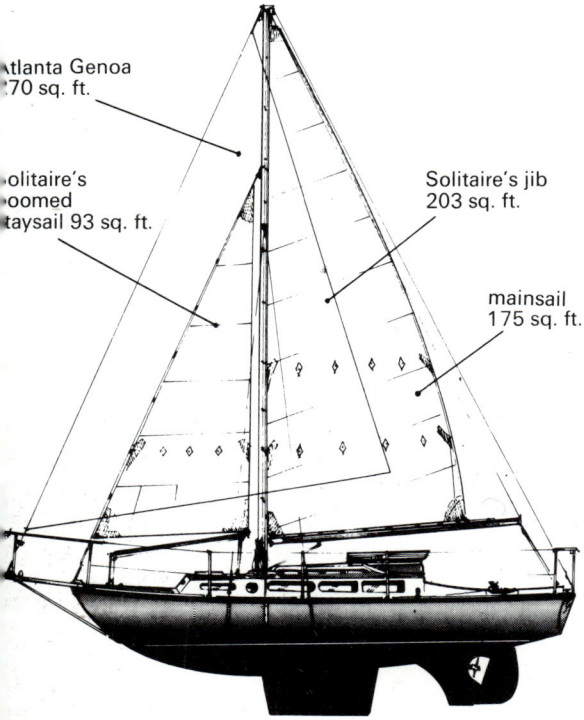

Atlanta Genoa
270 sq. ft.

Solitaire's
boomed
staysail 93 sq. ft.

Solitaire's jib
203 sq. ft.

mainsail
175 sq. ft.

total sailplan—Atlanta=445 sq. ft.   Solitaire's=471 sq. ft.

FIG. 133. This is Solitaire's sail-plan. The boomed staysail seems to be creeping back into fashion and is even to be found on some 'hot' racers—Mega for example.

PHOTO. 157. The staysail is controlled by a boom which finishes short of the inner forestay. The pedestal is free to turn in a threaded fitment in the bitts, and thus the end of the boom needs only to move up and down in the vertical plane to provide the movement normally allowed by a gooseneck.

automatically gives way to a nice rounded running sail. The actual position of the pedestal seems to be about 15 per cent of the foot length of the sail back from the stay (Photo. 157). The best position is variable, and really only trial and error will find the ideal spot. Alternatively one could draw it out in three-dimensions such that the end of the boom does not (1) foul on the front of the mast, (2) hit the forward lowers, and (3) bear on the pulpit or rail.

Naturally, a boomed-staysail cannot have an overlap on the mainsail, but the loss does not worry me, even though it apparently deprives the boat of the benefits of something termed the 'slot effect'. In any case I have no faith in this phenomenon for although aeroplane theory works fine for 'planes it also starts to work at air speeds I would much rather not be out in! A more serious drawback to a boomed staysail is that an accidental gybe could injure someone working on the foredeck—but a set of light sheets could be used to prevent that eventuality and also to allow one to heave-to if so desired. A minor disadvantage is that when the sail is lowered down the stay, the clew of the sail needs to move forward. If it cannot do so, then the sail hanks will jam. This movement can be achieved by a quick-release outhaul, or a pin in the gooseneck which allows the boom to be unshipped.

On the other hand the plus factors are considerable! No sheet handling when tacking. Full control over the sail from the cockpit, and no bearing-out spar (it already has one). I have also gained what amounts to another sail for I had the sailmaker put in extra luff and leach cringles together with reefing points, so that the area of the staysail can be cut down to 65 ft² (6 m²) to serve as a storm jib. Reefing is by a continuous lacing—unlike the mainsail which uses 'jiffy', or shock-cord reefing.

That last sentence, so easy to write, takes me back to the many hours of winter-work making up the booms. Round, or eliptical boom sections were easy to obtain, but I wanted a rectangular one since this is the best type on which to fit the large number of cleats, lacing hooks, fairleads, possibly snubbing winches, bee-blocks, etc, that are needed for this system.

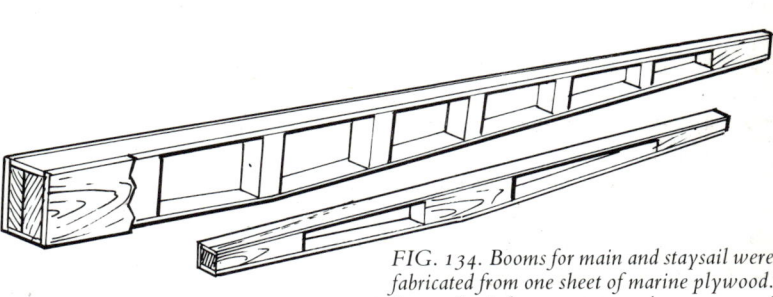

FIG. 134. Booms for main and staysail were fabricated from one sheet of marine plywood. Internal reinforcements may be re-arranged to coincide with external fittings.

PHOTO. 158. The basic structure of the boom is shown here. Plywood side panels are glued and nailed to a wooden 'skeleton'. Note the end-piece, and one of the dividing webs that were planned to coincide with fittings.

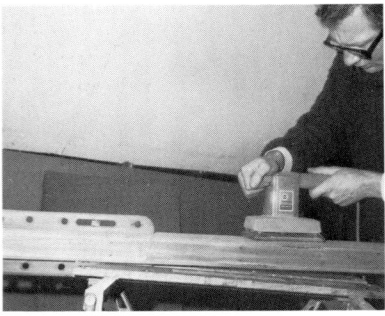

PHOTO. 159. Once all the fittings had been positioned the boom could be sanded down and given many coats of varnish. Once again the orbital sander took the 'sting' out of the filling and sanding operation.

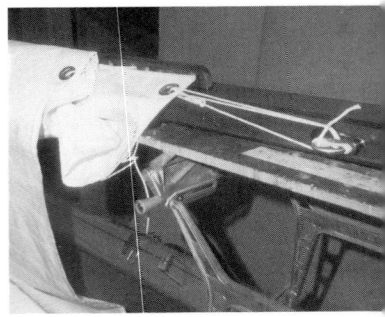

PHOTO. 160. One of the advantages of having the sails at hand . . . here the mainsail outhaul and reefing bee-blocks are being checked.

PHOTO. 161. The main has 'jiffy' slab reefing and the gooseneck has hooks welded into it to take the luff cringles. Note the boom downhaul.

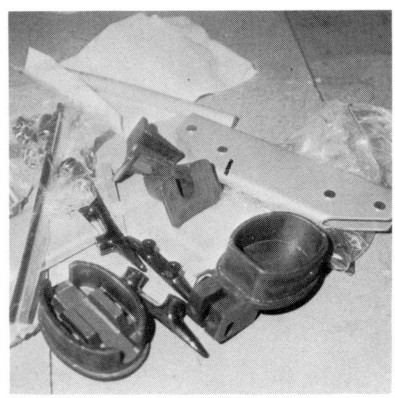

PHOTO. 162. Nearly all you need to custom-make a mast. The basis was a kit and the spreader root fittings, top and bottom castings and cleats are shown here.

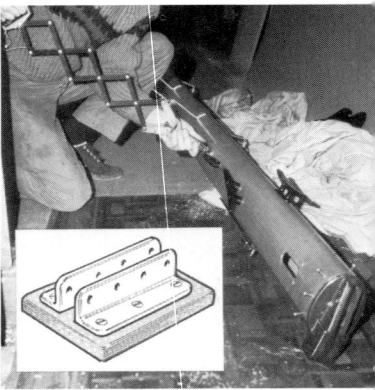

PHOTO. 163. The heel fitting sits about a pair of anodized aluminium angles bolted to the deck pad (inset). here the lazy-tongs are being used to pull the $\frac{3}{16}$ inch Monel hollow rivets used to fasten the steps in place.

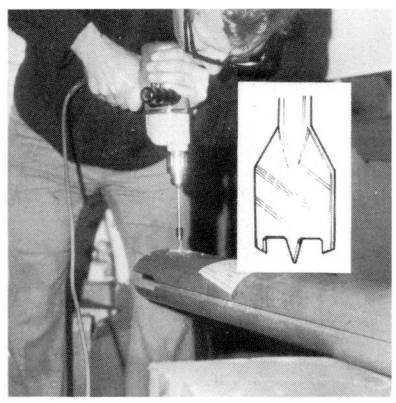

PHOTO. 164. It is important that any slots cut in the mast section have generously rounded ends. A spade-drill, sharpened as the inset drawing, is being used to form the exit sheave slots. Sharp corners are an invitation for the mast to crack from the 'notch'.

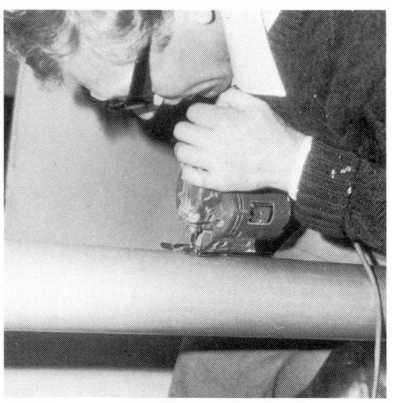

PHOTO. 165. With a suitable metal-cutting blade the jig-saw made light work of the mast. As it cuts on the up-stroke care should be taken to protect the eyes.

PHOTO. 166. Extra tangs were fitted at the top of the mast to enable a pair of additional sheaves to be incorporated. One takes the topping lift, the other is spare. The Tufnol sheaves are run on a stainless steel 'axle' which also holds the tops of the wire that support the outboard ends of the steps.

A dip into *Skene's Elements of Yacht Design* suggested that any section of boom I cared to make using sensible sizes of marine plywood, mahogany strips, spacer-blocks, glue and nails, would be strong enough to take the 175 ft² (16.3 m²) of mainsail.

Construction was very basic—but successful. A large amount of detailed consideration went into the positions of the actual components and I was fortunate in having the sails at home to assist.

Both main and staysail booms (Fig. 134) came out of one sheet of 8 ft × 4 ft (2.4 × 1.2 m) marine plywood, and since the main boom is 13 foot (4 m) long, two carefully made (and staggered) scarf joints were needed. Spacers were put in at one-foot (300 mm) intervals and solid blocks were fitted at either end to take the gooseneck and sheet fittings (Photos. 158–160).

The staysail boom being under 8 ft (2.4 m) was easier to make—blocks each end like the mainsail boom, and just one substantial spacer in the middle.

The main-boom (Photo. 161) and staysail-boom goosenecks had to be fabricated—for no-one sells such items! The pedestal was incorporated into the main bitts using a welded-in threaded pipe-connector to take a stub of pipe flattened at its top end. Thus the stub can turn on the threads—but not pull out (Photo. 157). Since the post can rotate the end-fitting on the boom had only to give vertical movement and rotate through 180 degrees. All these mild steel items were hot-dip galvanised and painted for extra protection as previously described.

A mast from a kit

Many mast makers are prepared to sell lengths of their aluminium extrusions and if you can also get from them the heel and cap castings there is no reason why you should not be able to fabricate the other fittings from stainless steel strip. Flat fabrications should be well within the ability of the handyman and there is no need to get involved with welding—in fact welded stainless fittings are, in my opinion, always suspect. Time and time again one learns of seemingly well-made fittings from quite reputable companies falling apart from 'weld decay'. Provided that flat steel is used in sensible sizes and that holes for rivets are not drilled too close together—say at least ¾ inch (20 mm) apart and not closer to the edge than 3 or 4 times the diameter of the rivet—then you should experience no problems.

Large holes for the attachment of clevis pins should come no nearer the edge than 1½–2 times the pin diameter. Shroud and stay attachments can be made-up using material about ⅛ inch (3 mm) thick × around 1½ inches (37 mm) wide. Laminated fabric sheaves may be

incorporated and the crosstrees may either be purpose-bought fabrications to take aluminium tube type spreaders, or more simply flat plates bent at rightangles and riveted to the mast in pairs to hold wooden crosstrees. If you dislike stainless steel, and admittedly it is not the easiest of materials to work, then there is no reason why you should not use ordinary mild-steel. This is far easier (and safer) to weld and after galvanizing and painting it will put in a considerable amount of sea-time before it starts rusting. In fact I had some unpainted mast and boom fittings which were over ten years old and good for many more.

The sizes and sections of the main and standing rigging should be available from the moulder—in fact they should be shown on your sail-plan drawing. Armed with this information and the knowledge that the chainplates must accommodate a certain size of rigging link or bottle-screw—which should be compatible with the safe working loads quoted for the rigging wire—you can start assembling the components together. A considerable saving may be made building up the spars from scratch like this—if you have the time!

I hadn't; so I went half way and bought a kit mast which showed a considerable cash saving over a complete mast and took about 12 hours to assemble. The kit consisted of a silver anodised aluminium 5840 section (5.8 being its fore-and-aft dimensions in inches—4.0 its depth), internal sheaves, masthead fittings, spreaders and root attachments, halliard exit fittings, heel casting, gooseneck slide, etc, plus all the fastenings required to stick it together as outlined in a comprehensive set of instructions (Photo. 162). I already owned a set of Lazy-tongs, used for pulling the hollow, or pop-rivets (Photo. 163).

Fitting the various components called for reasonably accurate working, sharp tools (for aluminium, though soft, soon dulls drills) and a powerdrill. I also saved myself a lot of effort by using large-size flat spade-drills re-sharpened to trepan, and my ever-willing jigsaw fitted with fine-toothed metal-cutting blades (Photos. 164 & 165).

Although I started off with a standard kit I had to add extra fittings to suit the cutter rig. In addition I had to rearrange its geometry slightly to take care of the loads which would be introduced into the spar in different places, and amounts, compared with a masthead rig. Mast sheaves were let in to take the staysail halliard, and a stainless steel fitting fabricated to take the inner-forestay. This had to also provide attachment points for runners should they prove necessary. The only small criticism I had about the kit I bought was that the sheave for the topping-lift was commensurate with that intended for a small dinghy—or perhaps a burgee halliard. This was overcome by incorporating Tufnol

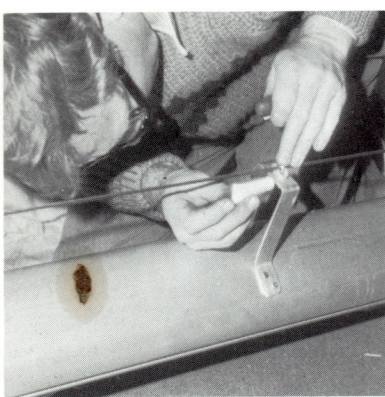

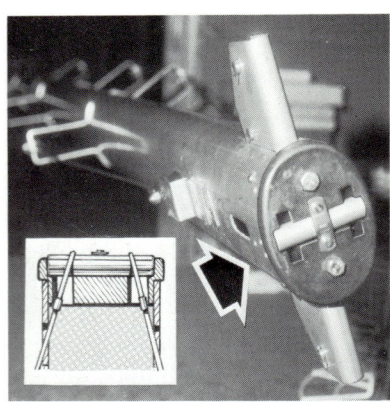

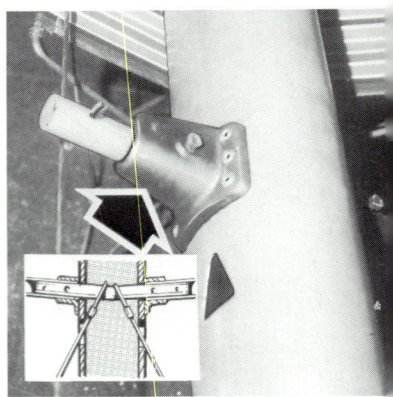

PHOTO. 167. *The steps are fastened to the support wires by bull-dog grips. Instead of locknuts a thread-locking adhesive was used.*

PHOTO. 168. *An aluminium rectangular section carries the masthead sheaves, forestay and backstay clevis pins. The cap shrouds have soft eyes which fit over the one-inch diameter (25 mm) aluminium rod held captive in the truck casting as the inset shows.*

PHOTO. 169. *The spreaders are aluminium tubes which sleeve over the one-inch rod (25 mm) and over which the soft eyes for the lower shrouds are passed. The spreaders also go into aluminium root fittings. Note the triangular slot with rounded corners through which the shrouds pass.*

sheaves into the tangs fitted to take the Talurit eyes of the side-support wires used for the steps (Photo. 166). These steps by the way are not part of the kit, and as photograph 167 shows are simple flat aluminium 'bendings' riveted to the mast and bull-dog gripped to the outside 4 mm wires.

The provision of a substantial topping-lift is important for it doubles as a spare main, or jib halliard, and in fact although only one is rove, with steps up the mast it is possible to reave another one as required—an important safety factor with internal halliards.

While I was putting the mast together I also fitted a masthead light together with a steaming and deck light. Electrical cables should be thick enough to carry the current without excessive voltage drop (see under *Electrics*) and it is essential to protect them with rubber grommets where they enter and leave the mast. I used brass cable-glands with compression seals to take the cables through the deck. Once behind the headlining they are connected into their circuits with block-connectors well Vaselined to prevent corrosion. Cable glands are, I feel, more suitable than 'weatherproof' plugs and sockets—certainly they are cheaper and since the connections are made inside the boat there is less chance of failure through corrosion.

Having made an accurate drawing of the rig I was able to make up all the halliards prior to the launch. I bought a 200 metre reel of 1¼ inch (30 mm) pre-stretched Terylene and used this for all the halliards and sheets and there was some left for a couple of springs. Buying '*on the reel*' shows obvious economies and I extended this philosophy to the standing rigging. By standardizing on

6 mm, 1 × 19 stainless steel wire I was able to get the fore- and backstays, upper and lower shrouds and lower guard rail wire, all from a 200 metre reel.

Having opted to use one size of rigging wire I was also able to standardize on toggles and rigging-screws—which in turn means that one of each in my spares box enables me to have the whole rigging system covered.

The upper and lower shrouds have large soft eyes Talurited in them so that they can be assembled over one-inch (25 mm) diameter aluminium rods as the drawing and photographs 168–169 show. The inlet holes in the mast needed to allow the wires to enter were cut very carefully indeed, taking equal care to leave a good radius in the corners of the cut out. This is to prevent a stress point forming from which cracks could propagate and ultimately lead to a lost mast.

The extra expense (or rather some of the savings I made with the mast kit) of toggles all round the boat is a desirable safety factor. One sees too many boats without toggles, not even in the forestay where a hanked-on sail banging about puts unfair bending loads into the rigging screw and forestay attachment which are primarily designed for tension. A toggle introduced at this point allows the end of the stay universal movement and hence there is far less likelihood of failure through bending, or fatigue.

The mast was finally dressed and stepped at the boatyard where *Solitaire* was launched (Photo. 170) and the saving I made with a kit against the total cost of a standard mast—and mine was far from standard—was approximately two-thirds!

Safe heating and cooking

When it came to choosing a cabin heater for *Solitaire* I was already of the opinion that solid-fuel stoves were out; they are nice—but messy! The choice was between gas, paraffin, or diesel. The balanced-flue type of gas heater together with the catalytic variety were assessed and discarded on the grounds of (1) cost for the former (2) lack of heat from the latter. By that I do not mean that catalytic heaters run 'cool', it is simply that I wanted around 2 kW to comfortably heat both cabins of my 28 footer. An additional drawback to (1) was that for best results the ducting should have been run through the boat at the initial fitting out stages, and to attempt an installation with the boat nearly complete would have been foolhardy—forward planning once again! So paraffin and diesel came to the top of the list and with a diesel engine already fitted it seemed sensible to rationalize on the fuels carried. So I opted for a Danish-made Refleks 66M drip-fed diesel burning stove.

Apart from being readily available the fuel is also inherently safer than gas. So too is storage—I have fitted a separate tank for the heater fuel but had the engine tank been larger it could have been tapped directly to supply the heater.

Once the cabin heater is alight it will burn continuously without further attention for there is no need to pressurize the fuel tank. There is no mess—apart from the fact that is, that the burner chamber and the flue needs to be cleaned out once a season. The output of the Refleks is variable up to around 2 kW via a neatly

PHOTO. 170. *The mast was assembled completely at the boatyard and everything fitted perfectly—much to my relief!*

PHOTOS. 171, 172, 173. *The drip-feed diesel heater has a 'carburettor-type' control which contains a fusible link. Heat is variable up to 2 kw. Note how the deckhead lining has been cut away from the flue pipe. The outer deck flange sits on a neoprene seal and also embodies a deep flange which determines the diameter of the deck cut-out.*

designed control device which looks—and works—rather like a carburettor. The heater can be turned off quickly as required, and the use of a flue to take the products of combustion outside the boat means the stove can be used with the boat fairly well snugged down without danger of carbon monoxide poisoning. There is a fuzible safety link in the carb' so that in the event of a drastic on-board fire the link melts and the diesel fuel is automatically shut off before it can add to the conflagration.

Installing the heater was fairly simple—once I had deciphered the quaint Danish/English used for the instructions! We had decided to put the heater as low as possible in the boat adjacent to the galley bulkhead and as near to the companionway as we could work it. Thus with the airstream from aft-to-forward (see *Ventilation*) the whole boat would be warmed through. The heater was put on a slightly raised plinth covered with ceramic tiles glued in place (Photos. 171–173). They then had to be carefully drilled with a tungsten-carbide drill to take the fastening down bolts for the heater. I chose to use nuts and bolts for they are more reliable than a few woodscrews and I did not want the stove working adrift in any rough weather. The use of tiles is both decorative and functional for should diesel oil soak into the plinth it would smell the cabin out for days afterwards. In fact once the fire has been lit there is no smell at all of diesel fuel—and I might tell you I have a pretty sharp nose for such things.

The deckhead was cut to take the special through-deck flange, below which a metre of stainless steel flue pipe was fitted to the heater. Needless to say the height of the plinth had been carefully determined to allow such a neat fit. The fluepipe has an inner diameter of $2\frac{3}{4}$ inches (70 mm), rather larger than might be used with other types of heaters. it is rolled and mechanically seamed, and lengths are a push fit into each other, and also into the through-deck flange-fitting and cowl—or 'Charlie Noble'. I bought an extra length of fluepipe so that the cowl could be raised well clear of the deck and thus be out of turbulance from the boom when at anchor. When not in use there is a custom-made blanking-off cap to prevent rain or spray entering the flue.

The actual heater consists of a combustion chamber with an outer casing to assist convection which is $6\frac{1}{2}$ inches (164 mm) in diameter and $16\frac{1}{2}$ inches (418) high. As installed there is a $5\frac{1}{2}$ inch (140 mm) gap between the heater and the bulkhead which gets hot—but not excessively so. The diesel fuel is led from its tank to the carb' with $\frac{5}{16}$ inch (8 mm) copper pipe with a short length of reinforced plastic pipe to take out any possible fretting from vibration. The pipe is well clipped and secured and protected where it goes through wooden bulkheads.

To light the heater it is first primed with methylated spirit (alcohol) with the carb' control set to 'start'. When fully warmed the control is turned to the required heat setting. I soon discovered that priming with liquid meths was decidedly unsafe—it ran out on to the tiled plinth while still burning, so I switched to solid fuel tablets. Two of these get the heater going with the least possibility of a flare-up. The Refleks will burn for 24 hours on $1\frac{1}{4}$ gallons (5.6 litres) of fuel going at maximum setting. It will run while the boat is sailing—although we tend to run it down low, and keep the boat nice and warm—just right for those early spring or late autumn sails when the weather is so nice and settled—but cold!

Taking care of gas

Provided that an installation is well made initially and subsequently sensibly used, then gas poses no unacceptable safety risks for small boat users. I have used gas afloat for well over 10 years and get increasingly distressed with tales of 'flare-ups' from people cooking with paraffin.

A safe gas installation starts with the bottle-stowage. this must be arranged so that any (heavier than air) gas leakage flows directly overboard and not into the body of the boat. Where bottles are fitted in enclosed lockers they must be provided with at least a $\frac{1}{2}$ inch (12 mm) pipe fitted to the bottom of the locker—and where the hole cannot be blocked by a shifting gas cylinder. Only metal or armoured flexible tubing of an approved type should be used, and care should be taken that the pipe is well secured where it passes out through the hull.

Containers for the gas cylinders may be fire-retardant resinglass laminates, or brazed or welded sheet metal with a wall thickness of at least 20 swg (0.5 mm). Top access only should be used and lockers must be deep enough to take the cylinder and its regulator valve. The cylinders must be firmly strapped down and the lid of the locker should have a positive catch. Note that cylinders must be stored and used UPRIGHT, and not sited next to any cooking appliance, nor adjacent to a heater, nor inside a fuel or engine compartment.

Pipe runs from the cylinder to the appliance must be of drawn seamless copper tube, or stainless steel, used with compression fittings. Run the pipes as high as possible in the boat and never through fuel tank spaces, electrical or engine compartments. Pipes must be clipped to the structure at intervals of around 18 inches (450 mm) and as few joints as possible used in the run. Where they are used they should have easy access for inspection, and a pipe clip should be fitted close on either side of such connections.

PHOTO. 174. It is not very difficult to marinize a caravan gas stove—in fact the finish is adequate for a life afloat and any work is confined to making up adequate fiddles, and fastening down the burner grids.

PHOTOS. 175, 176. The lid of the gas-bottle locker seals down on a soft neoprene gasket. Access is through a watertight inspection hatch. Should a serious leak develop (and all leaks are serious) the actual pressure build-up in the container is minimal for it is vented low down through a skin-fitting. Half-an-inch (12 mm) is minimum.

Flexible sections of pipe should be minimal and with screwed-end connectors—not hose-clips. All flexible pipe must conform to British Standard or some similar appropriate authority and if the control valve is not readily accessible from the galley—and most are not—then a control tap should be fitted close to the cooker to enable the gas to be turned on and off locally as required. Naturally such a tap must be designed for use with the on-board gas for natural rubber seals used in some gas taps are not resistant to liquified petroleum gases such as butane. In addition the gas in the supply is running at a higher pressure than normal town gas.

Should you fit a small gas cooker, or heater, which uses containers that screw directly into the appliance then spare containers should be stored in a vented locker as previously described.

When it came to fitting a cooker in *Solitaire's* galley we used a 'marinized' caravan twin burner cooker with grill and oven (Photo. 174). It is bolted down rigidly with no provision for swinging. This allowed me to use the maximum possible amount of copper pipe to plumb the supply up to it. The pipe is run along underneath the side-decking and not through any lockers where it could perhaps be damaged by heavy objects thrown against it. The pipe passes through bulkheads and similar dividers and these are thickened up locally to one-inch (25 mm) to prevent the pipe fretting on a relatively sharp edge. Where the pipe changes from the horizontal to the vertical adjacent to the cooker, I introduced a 5 inch (127 mm) diameter loop into it to allow for expansion

and contraction. The connections I used are all compression types and a special gas-tight sealing compound was put on the threads when making them.

The gas bottle—a 9 lb (4 kg) one is fitted into a stainless steel water tank originally used in a lifeboat. This was modified to leave a large flange around its top face to which a lid could be fastened with a foam-neoprene seal to give a fairly gas-tight closure. With the tank vented overboard the actual need for a high-pressure seal is eliminated. There is a water-tight inspection hatch let into the lid and it is through this that the control valve is reached (Photos. 175, 176).

LPG gases are not in themselves poisonous—you could 'drown' with a large leakage, and of course concentrations of gas and air are very explosive. 'Odour' is added to the gas to make it discernible by all but the most corrupt nose, and provided that one has taken care with the initial installation, and that checks are made periodically, I reckon that cooking with gas is safer than crossing the road.

Points to remember are that when gas is burned so is the oxygen in the air—so keep ventilators open to prevent the formation of deadly carbon monoxide in oxygen-starved air.

Never place a cylinder on its side.

Keep the gas turned off at the cylinder until it is wanted.

Take care when changing the cylinder and with those bottles which require a sealing washer make sure it is in perfect condition.

Use a spanner to tighten the connection at the cylinder. Hand-tight is just too loose!

Never tamper with the regulator and replace it about every three years—just to be safe.

Check connections with soapy water and suspect even the smallest bubbling.

Extinguish all flames when changing cylinders and turn off all taps.

Equipped with a cabin heater and a cooker the possibility of cold-weather sailing opens up. However, butane, which is the normally used LPG has a boiling point of 20°F (–6°C) and heat is required at the rate of around 160 BThU's per pound (96 kcal/kg) to convert liquid butane stored in the cylinder into gas. This heat is drawn from the atmosphere. Add to that the fact that the cylinder is pressurised to be used at a normal temperature of around 60°F (16°C) and pressure drops with temperature, and you can see why you cannot use butane on a very cold day. If you fancy winter boating then propane with its much lower boiling point should be used.

Around the cockpit

Just as you spend a lot of time sitting around below decks so another large amount of time is spent in the cockpit. This means that you can better both the comfort and the efficiency of your crew by taking a few simple precautions. Weathercloths added to the cockpit lifelines are obvious improvements which cost very little. Sew in a few pockets and you can use them to stow sail-tiers, lifebuoys etc. Paint the boat's name on the outside and you have a strong recognition feature. Coastguards like letters at least 10 inches (250 mm) high.

I fitted such weathercloths to *Solitaire* and also, as previously mentioned, improved her stark resinglass coamings with a hardwood trim. This extends over the top of the coaming by about half an inch (12 mm) and when she is heeled it provides somewhere for the hand to grip—unlike the original slippery moulding.

Strongpoints must be built in for attaching safety harnesses. They need to be substantial for your life may one day depend on them. Always use bolts in these stressed areas for they are, size-for-size, almost twice as strong as machine-screws. Backing pads need to be robust and it is wise to have several attachment points around the cockpit—one at least on the centreline, the others arranged port and starboard. Then when clipped on you will be able to use a short length of line and, if thrown about, you will not travel very far before the harness line checks your progress. It is dangerous, in my opinion, to rely solely upon the lifelines running around

the boat as harness clip-on points. In many boating mishaps stanchions and rails are damaged, sometimes with the result that the crew member who put his trust in this form of attachment is lost overboard. Should two, or three crew members clip on to the lines then their combined weight—especially if it is accelerating— will be more than enough to burst the wires, or their end fittings.

As a further aid to safety and creature comfort the cockpit drains should be as large as possible and at least four in number. Usually $1\frac{3}{4}$ inch diameter outlets are used and if they incorporate a grid to prevent debris entering then their effective cross-section may be reduced by as much as 25 per cent. Add to that the fact that water dislikes flowing over a sharp edge and you have reduced their capacity by another 10 per cent or so—for I have yet so see the boat where the drains are fitted as a smooth continuation of a nicely rounded hole. Should the cockpit ever fill with water then the weight of it, something like 3 tons for a 6 ft × 2 ft 6 inch × 7 foot area (1.8 m × 0.76 m × 2.1 m) will obviously weight the stern down. Thus while you may have the cockpit sole 10 inches (250 mm) above the waterlevel at rest, with that great mass of water filling it the actual 'head' and hence the pressure through gravity, driving the water out is greatly reduced. Far better to think about reducing the volume of a very large cockpit by building in perhaps special gas-bottle lockers, than adding extra drains. Even with four × $1\frac{3}{4}$ inch it would take our hypothetical cockpit something well over 20 minutes to empty all its contents back to where it belongs.

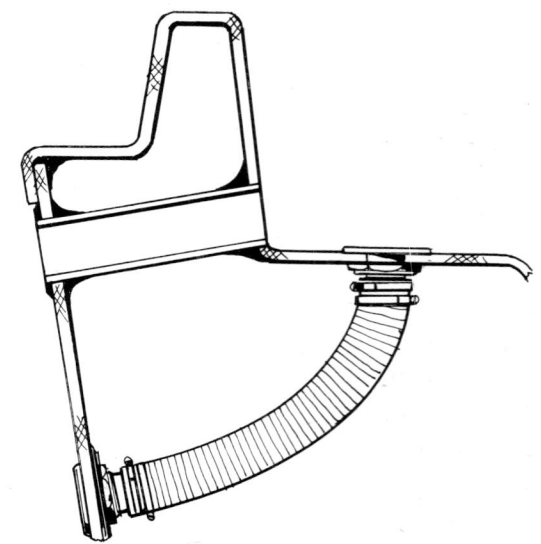

FIG. 135. *Large bore pipes could be used to augment normal cockpit drains. A flexible section may be needed to prevent damage to the pipe should the cockpit distort under the weight of a great mass of water.*

All this means that you should treat the cockpit drains as being suitable only for getting rid of spray and rain. You *could* improve the rate of draining considerably by bonding in a large bore pipe, possibly with a flexible section in it, say from the centre of the cockpit stern seat, out through the transom. If such a pipe were 4 inches (100 mm) in diameter, then in the event of a 'pooping' a great amount of water would quickly flow out of the cockpit. Such a pipe could be a pvc drain pipe—but I would use that as the centre of a strong resinglass lay-up of about 6 layers of 1½ oz (450 gm/m²) CSM. A coarse grid or wire mesh would need to be fitted over the inside pipe opening to prevent small items being lost overboard (Fig. 135).

Cockpit seating can be greatly improved by the addition of teak slats screwed and bedded down. These not only cheer up stark areas of resinglass visually but also help to make it non-slip—and hence safer for the crew. On *Solitaire* I made flat slatted seats of hardwood raised an inch (25 mm) above the locker lids (Photo. 177). Not only does this approach make the seats both warmer and more comfortable it also stops you from sitting in a puddle. Specially contoured slatted seats for greater comfort could easily be made and fitted (Fig. 136).

Now I am aware of the fact that drain pipes can be fitted to cockpit seats to make them self-draining, and also that some thoughtful designers use deep moulded notches around the openings for lockers to take the water away, but *Solitaire* had neither. Drainage tubes (Fig. 137) can easily be glassed in to eliminate seat

PHOTO. 177. *Slatted seats make a cockpit far more comfortable and lift the occupants away from the coldness of resinglass. The after slatted area is not hinged; instead it lifts out to give access to the after-locker.*

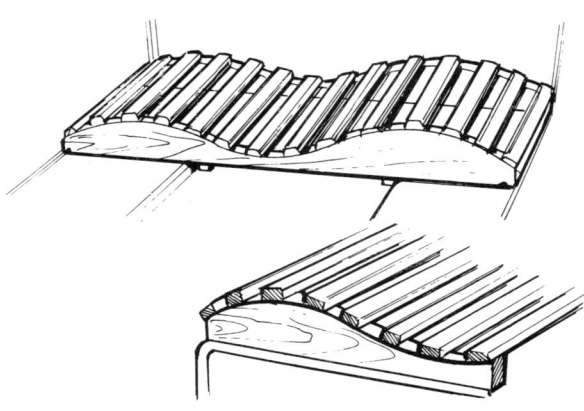

FIG. 136. *There's no fun in sitting for hours in a puddle! Slatted seats are warmer and may be shaped for greater comfort.*

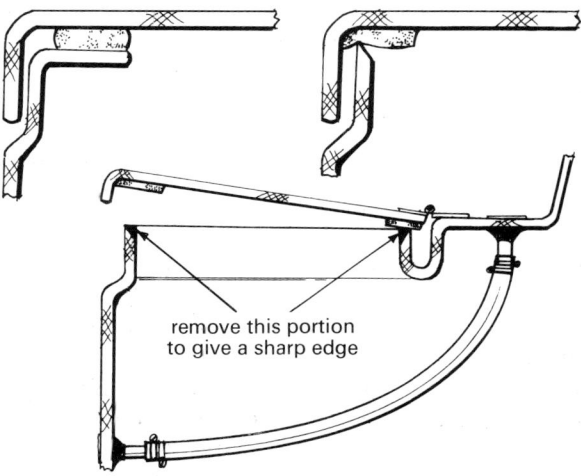

remove this portion to give a sharp edge

FIG. 137. *Cockpit locker lids need to have some form of positive seal to make them watertight. Considerable pressure is needed to distort a wide flat seal. A sharp edge penetrates the sealing strip very easily and is the one to aim for. A plastic tube may be glassed-in to drain the water that always seems to collect during a boisterous sail.*

'puddles' but as the angle of the boat alters from running, to beating, to reaching, so too does the collection point for spray. More than one drainage pipe is therefore needed and just where you site them is a matter for conjecture—at the very least you will need them at the extreme ends of the cockpit seats.

Cockpit lockers should be capable of being locked for security, and positively clamped shut when underway. Hinges need to be stout with some provision made for clipping the locker lids open while you rummage in their contents. Lockers which jam down hard on soft foamed neoprene seals to provide a near-watertight closure are an ideal at which to aim. Note that a fairly sharp edge forced into a soft gasket gives the best type of seal (Fig. 137). Putting such an arrangement around the front and sides of the locker lids is fairly easy—a good closure along the hinge-line may not be so simple to arrange.

While on the subject of making things watertight remember that the companionway door, or washboards, may need careful attention. If the boat has a modest bridgedeck then it may be more satisfactory to seal-in the lower washboard portion to make a permanent closure. Doors, if fitted, need to be really substantial and with this in mind we have equipped *Solitaire* with washboards for offshore security, and a pair of half-doors for use in harbour or at moorings. A needless complication you may think, but passing in and out through doors on a wet and windy day is to be preferred to hassling with three boards. Our half-doors are arranged with lift-off hinges and we also fitted a couple of clear acrylic 'windows' into them to lighten the end of the cabin and also to let us see out into the cockpit. The top washboard also has a small window in it—and so oddly enough does the very front of the cabin moulding. Thus when I sit up in my bunk I can check what is going on forward of the boat, as well as to P & S.

Companionways and hatches

Safe and easy access in and out of the accommodation is obviously a desirable feature—especially when the going gets rough. While you may have personal preferences regarding the size and shape of companionways very often you are limited by mouldings themselves, or by the moulder trimming the resinglass lay-up back to some suitable upstand. He may also have done the same for the forehatch. But if he has made no provision for the forehatch, and you want to fit one, then the following sizes are about right: 23 inches × 15 inches (580 mm × 380 mm), or, if you fancy a circular one then 18 inches diameter (460 mm) will do. Having some means of entry from either end of the boat is an obvious safety feature and, even if the boat is considered to be too small for a 'proper' forehatch, then a safety-hatch may be fitted. A safety-hatch is strictly an 'escape hatch' and as such is not really suited for constant use, and if so used may soon start to develop annoying leaks.

If the boat has a self-draining cockpit then a bridgedeck is needed to prevent water entering the accommodation from the footwell. A bridge deck may already be incorporated in the moulding, or else you may have to form a 'step-over' equal in height to the top of the cockpit seats. Note that the use of a bridge deck, which is essentially a box-girder, stiffens the structure con-

siderably at about a point where it is weakened by the large cut-outs needed for the companionway. Apart from strengthening the boat the bridge deck helps hide the engine. Alternatively, it may provide the volume needed for a small galley, or even a chart-table and worktop.

Companionway doors are very difficult to make strong enough, the more so when you take into account the need to have them on lift-off hinges, unless, that is you have room to fold them back out of the way against the bulkhead. This proviso is almost always impossible to meet and the sharp corners of the doors poking out into the cockpit could be dangerous. Far better to fit washboards in the companionway, and if you must have doors, use them only in harbour. We have this arrangement on *Solitaire*, and apart from the need to find a stowage place for them, it works very well.

Washboards, or dropboards if you prefer, have the considerable merit of being very easy to fabricate. They are simple to install, and may be used to shut the ship up progressively—by which I mean that one board may be fitted on leaving harbour, another when the sea-state picks up, and the third (or final) one fitted when it gets really rough.

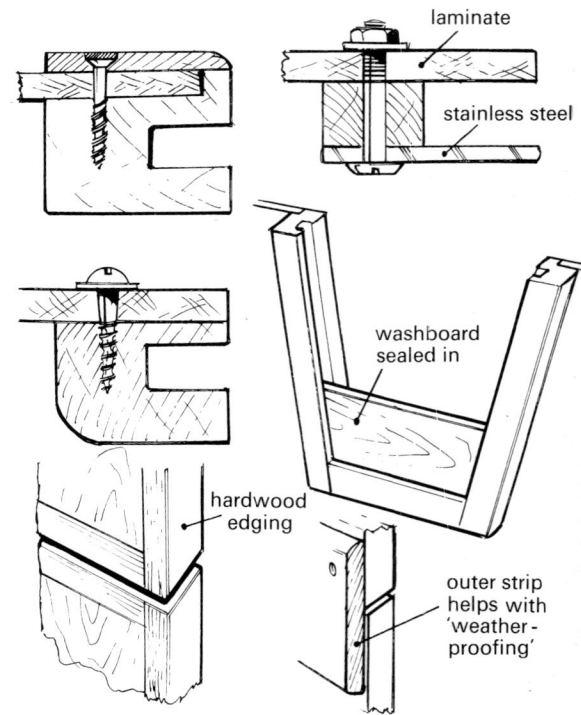

FIG. 138. *The slides for the companionway washboards need to be stoutly sectioned to prevent cracking across the rabbet. Alternatively they could be reinforced with stainless steel strips.*

As stated, the moulder may have trimmed your moulding back to a finished cut-out and the raw edges of the laminate are best concealed behind a hardwood moulding rabbeted as in figure 138. Alternatively, rabbeted lengths of hardwood could be fitted flush with the trimmed laminate—which would then need to be protected with a gel-coat resin to prevent moisture take-up. In both cases screws, or counterbored and plugged throughbolts can be used to secure the wood. Note that in all cases a generous amount of sealant will be needed between the wood and laminate to give a watertight seal. A look at the hardwood slides will highlight the fact that unless very robust sections are used then the rabbet will weaken them considerably. If you are assembling a kit, and if the slideways look a bit 'mean', then one solution would be to reinforce them with stainless steel strips throughbolted to give a very strong assembly. The thickness of the metal would need to be around 10 swg ($\frac{1}{8}$ inch, or 3 mm) and all sharp corners will need removing to prevent a potential danger point being introduced. In fact this philosophy of bearing in mind possible dangers is a wise one to adopt right through the boat.

The washboards are best made from proper marine-grade plywood (1088 and all that). Hardwood strips will prevent the endgrains soaking up moisture, swelling, and perhaps jamming the board in its slide. The tops and bottoms of each board will need cutting on the slope to prevent rainwater draining into the cabin, and, for added security, overlapping strips could be fitted, although these will need to be fairly substantial—$\frac{1}{2}$ inch (12 mm)—to prevent them cracking off. The thickness of the boards is variable, although I would tend to opt for $\frac{1}{2}$ inch (12 mm). You may care to fit a Perspex window into one of them as we have on *Solitaire*, where

it will serve to lighten up an otherwise dark area. Remember that one day you may need to seal up the accommodation against severe weather, and if you are tempted to fit louvres to improve ventilation then you should also make some provision for shutting them off.

While the boards may be finished with a hard-wearing, two-pot polyurethane varnish for preference, the rabbets are best left bare and treated to an occasional rub over with a wax candle. If you varnish all the faces then those touching will very often pick up (spall) and so make sliding very difficult.

The number of washboards you fit is largely a matter of personal choice. Two big ones may prove better than four smaller ones, and you could also hinge the top board so that (with the addition of a suitable stay) it could fold down to make a small cockpit table. Obviously such an arrangement has its limitations—if only in restricting access to the cabin, but if you decide to adopt this scheme then note that the washboard will have to be cut to provide the necessary clearance.

If you are assembling a kit then chances are the companionway sliding hatch will be a moulded one. It may even slide open into a moulded 'garage' and there is no doubt that such an arrangement makes a very neat, and fairly watertight assembly. One aspect of this type of fitting that your moulder may have missed is the possibility of using the garage-moulding (Fig. 139) as a plenum chamber which can be tapped to give water-free ventilation down into the cabin. Of course, for such an arrangement to work, there must be sufficient clearance—and if the system appeals but you haven't a garage moulding, then why not make one. By now your prowess with resin and glass makes this job perfectly feasible, and you have the advantage of trying the mould in place to make certain that (a) you like it (b) you have an

FIG. 139. Hatches which slide into a garage moulding are very popular. All hatches need to have substantial stops to prevent them pulling out, and some means of locking them shut from the inside is essential.

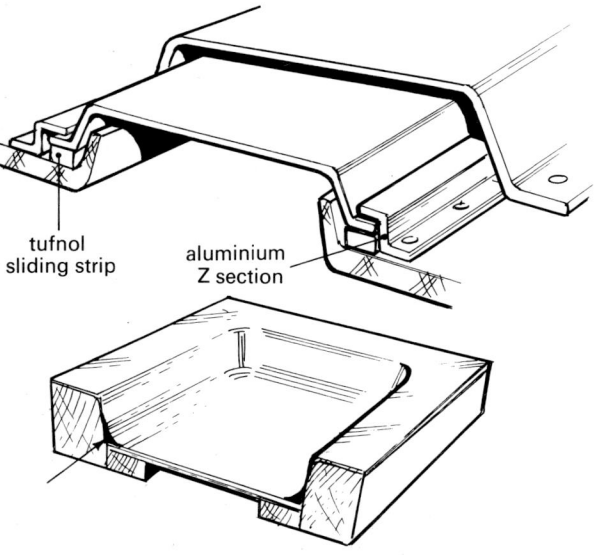

tufnol
sliding strip

aluminium
Z section

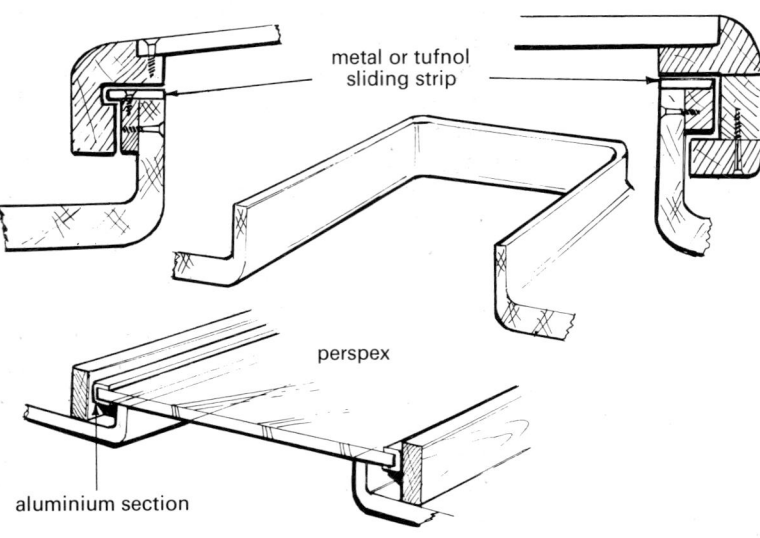

metal or tufnol sliding strip

perspex

aluminium section

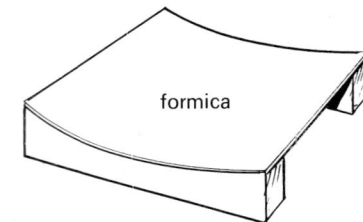

formica

FIG. 140. The upstand left on the deck moulding determines the size and shape of the hatch, and several methods of arranging the slides may be used. Note that all aluminium sections must be of marine grade alloy or rapid corrosion will result from exposure to salt water.

FIG. 141. A simple mould using Formica, or some similar laminate, will produce the desired curved section of translucent laminate. Stiffeners may be incorporated in the moulding if required.

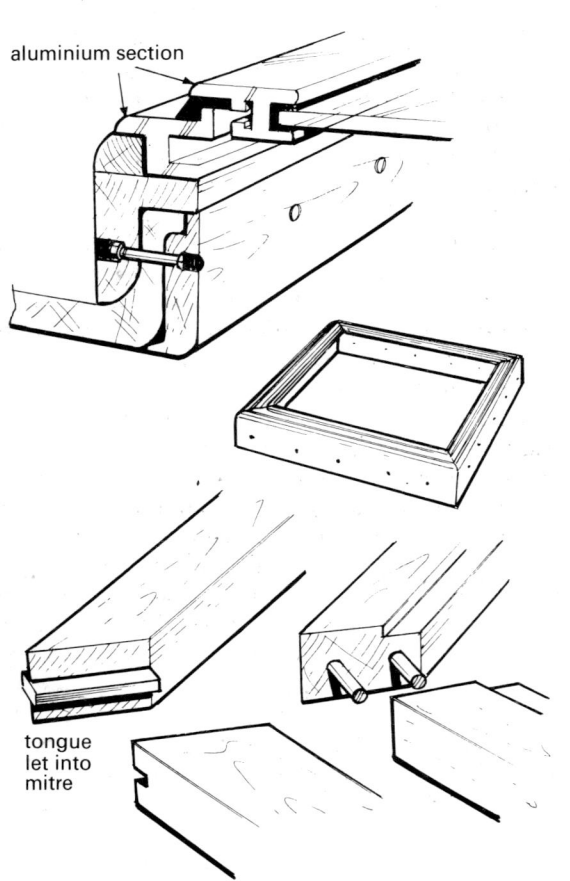

aluminium section

tongue let into mitre

FIG. 142. If you intend to fit a bought hatch then a suitable hardwood surround will have to be constructed to allow it to mate up with the moulding. Some 'lightweight' hatches are strictly escape-hatches and start to leak if they are extensively used.

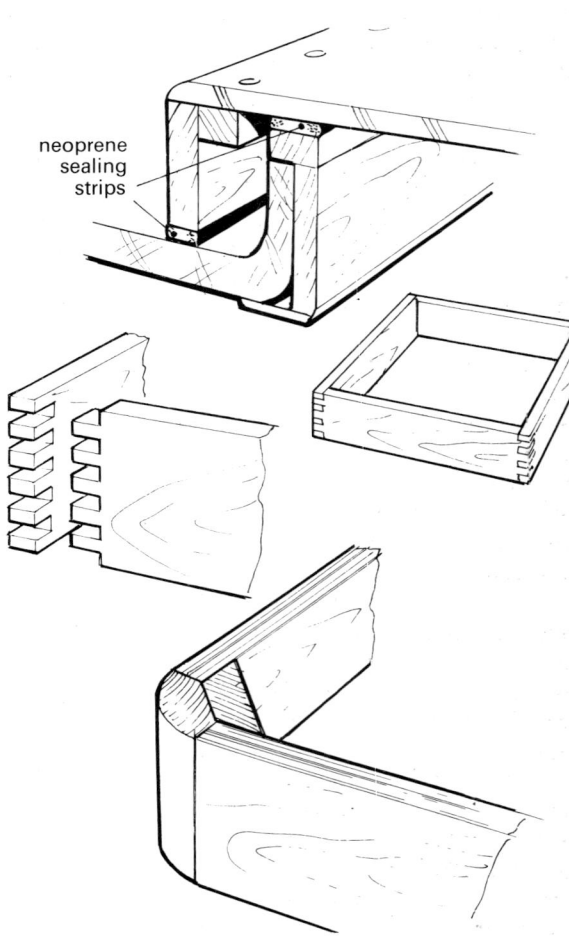

neoprene sealing strips

FIG. 143. A wooden hatch with plywood or Perspex top is fairly easy to construct. Neoprene sealing strips will make it watertight.

acceptable fit, and (c) there is sufficient sliding clearance. With all contact moulding it is wise to have a generous fillet, or radius, in all the corners, and this may be formed from hard wax, plaster, or plasticine. Don't forget the release agent . . .

If the moulder has not supplied you with a sliding hatch then you will have to make your own, for such items cannot be bought over the counter at your favourite chandlery. Figure 140 shows some typical working arrangements and which method you adopt depends largely upon your woodworking skills and materials available. The use of a metal slide (minimum thickness 10 swg, ⅛ inch, 3 mm) gives a very neat assembly and the necessary groove, or rabbet, may be cut with a 'wobble-saw' attachment on a circular saw. Note that once again such an arrangement could introduce danger points unless care is taken to cut and file generous radii.

The other method outlined in figure 140 uses a laminated plastic (Tufnol) wear strip to hide the raw edge of the laminate and top face of the hardwood strip. One easy source for the right section of Tufnol is a sail batten, provided—that is—you buy one thick enough to take the countersink needed for the screws. The rest of the slide is formed by joining hardwood strips of various dimensions. You could also utilize parts of either method to suit your own circumstances, and the choice of a solid plywood top, or a see-through Perspex one, is also optional. Note that should you find that a clear Perspex area lets too much light into the boat then it may be reduced somewhat by scratching up with a medium grit sand-paper. Alternatively a coloured (tinted) Perspex could be used.

The amount of hoop you introduce is again a matter of choice but if you are using Perspex then one inch (25 mm) over a distance of 18 inches (460 mm) is about all you will achieve without heat. Perspex (like all acrylics) softens under gentle radiant heat and once bent it stays in shape with no tendency to spring back. Should you be tempted to experiment then I suggest you try with scrap first.

Yet another way of achieving almost the same translucent arched panel is to laminate it up using glass and resin. The former can be a sheet of formica with its best surface being used to impart the finish to the outer face of the moulding. The necessary mould is very simple as figure 141 shows, and should you adopt this method, then bear in mind that small top-hatch sections could be used to substantially reinforce the moulding. Note that a clear (unpigmented) gelcoat resin will be needed, and the laminating resin must also be unfilled to give maximum light transmission.

The forehatch may be either a bought aluminium confection, a plastics concoction, or a home-built wooden model. If the moulder has provided one as part of the deal then it will invariably be a 'biscuit lid' such as we have on *Solitaire*. Despite being a single-coaming hatch this has never let in so much as a drip of water—thanks to the soft neoprene foam seals we have fitted.

The moulder may have produced an upstand in the foredeck, or coachroof, with some particular hatch in mind, and should therefore be in the position of supplying decent working drawings to enable you to complete the job. Figure 142 illustrates the wooden trim needed to suit an aluminium Houdini hatch.

However, just because the upstand is there it does not mean that you cannot do your own thing. A wooden hatch, perhaps with mock laid-teak strips (which may also be applied to a plywood companionway hatch) can add a certain amount of 'class' to a boat. Wood is also very functional in that it allows you to proportion the hatch so that generously sized hinges and latches can be used. How you go about the actual construction is once again dependent on time, facilities and expertise. Comb, or stopped-dovetail joints for the corners are very nice—but beyond me. Mitres dowelled and glued, or tongued, could be used, or you may care to consider using the hardwood corner posts shown in figure 143.

Whichever method you adopt the essential requirement after size is that the hatch should be as near-watertight as possible. To this end a double-coaming is far better than a single one for before any water can enter the boat, it must first insinuate itself along a labyrinthine route. Drain holes will be needed at the corners of the outer coaming—and I would make them on the small size to make certain that they *drain* and not *fill*! Once again soft neoprene seals can be used and it is best to fit them on faces where they cannot be damaged by anyone passing through the hatch.

Latches for the hatch are again a matter of choice—but ideally one is looking for a latch which may be worked from outside or inside the boat. Oddly, such a latch does not seem to exist. Special stays to hold the hatch open are, however, readily obtainable and these work mostly on the friction principle rather like cabinet stays. As stated, hinges need to be substantial and you may fit them on either the fore, or after side, of the hatch. Once again it is a compromise for, if the hatch opens aft, then it allows you to prop it slightly open to aid ventilation. Arrange it to open the other way around then any wave crashing on the foredeck will tend to close the hatch and not force it open. Very often you have little choice in the matter for some other arrangement gets in the way—a baby-stay for instance, the mast and tabernacle, or the proximity of the hatch to the foredeck which would let it open further than its hinges could tolerate (figure 144). Of course if the hatch is exactly square in plan, then a system of substantial barrel-bolts, or special pins, could be used to give you a multiplicity of hinging arrangements—see figure 145.

Note that when fitting the wooden hatch surrounds there is a temptation to use woodscrews directly through the laminate. While you may get away with dome-headed screws and oversized washers (at least four times the diameter of the screw head) the use of countersinks may seriously weaken the laminate locally and possibly even allow the screw heads to pull through.

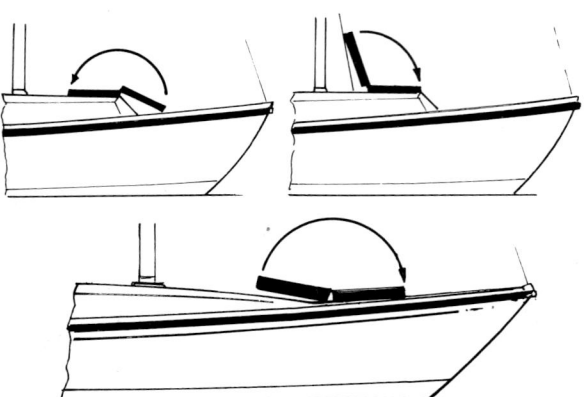

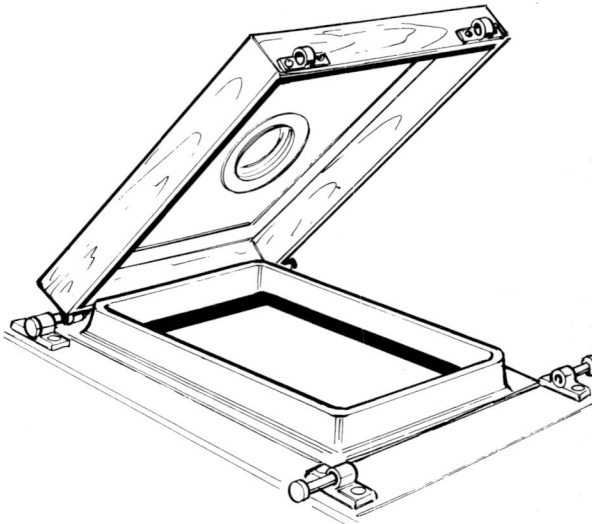

FIG. 144. *Which way the hatch is hinged will often depend upon other factors. Personally I favour the hinge line on the after edge—but it is your boat . . .*

FIG. 145. *If a square forehatch is made then it is perfectly possible t arrange it to open fore, or aft as desired . . . but it is risky when it is able t lift off completely.*

IO

Osmotic blistering

Given that your boat is nearing completion and due to be launched there is one outstanding area that you should consider. Osmotic blistering—or 'boatpox'—causes a large amount of concern both among owners, and to a growing extent among the better moulders. It is not certain that there is one single factor which causes one gel-coat to blister, while the very next boat escapes it (Photo. 178). The latest resin formulations—particularly the use of isophthalic gel-coat used clear below the waterline and pigmented above, appears to offer improved resistance compared with the older (cheaper) orthophthalic resins. With the use of isophthalic resins throughout the lay-up there is the advantage that this type of resin has a shrinkage rate closely related to that of the reinforcement—thus fewer stresses are locked up within the laminate. This type of resin also has a low water-absorption rate and high chemical resistance combined with higher heat distortion factors. Thus this type (isophthalic) of resin is to be recommended for dark hulls destined to be used in tropical climes.

In the UK Tyler Mouldings Ltd use isophthalic resins and are outstanding in that they give Warranty against the effect of osmosis for a minimum period of five years. The same company also use two coats of gel-coat resin with a pigment content of under 10 per cent. The gel-coat is brushed on to the mould in two operations to prevent the problems associated with spraying. The surfacing mat is a powder-bound one and the other reinforcements are all 'E' type low alkali glass and contain a silicon linking agent. The laminates incorporate CSM not exceeding $1\frac{1}{2}$ oz (450 gm/m²) so that they can be easily wetted-out and consolidated to remove entrapped air with disc-rollers.

They also point out that a resinglass laminate may vary in terms of durability, mechanical strength, permeability, etc, in much the same way as does wood. They also add that there are wide variations in quality even when Lloyds is specified.

This means that you have to be just as careful in selecting your mouldings from a good manufacturer as you do in fitting out the boat with an honest assessment of its end-use in mind.

The main causes of osmotic blistering are that of poor material selection, quality control, poor environment, miss-use of materials and equipment—and all the other things over which you, as a customer, have no control. You might consider that leaving this chapter to the end is rather unfair—had you known about it sooner you would have gone in for something like hang-gliding—but relax. No boats have sunk on their mooring through osmotic blistering—though wooden ones go down through rot.

Osmotic blistering starts with a vapour-phase which precedes true 'boatpox'; although in all honesty the trouble started when the very first layer of resin was put in the mould—or even before that.

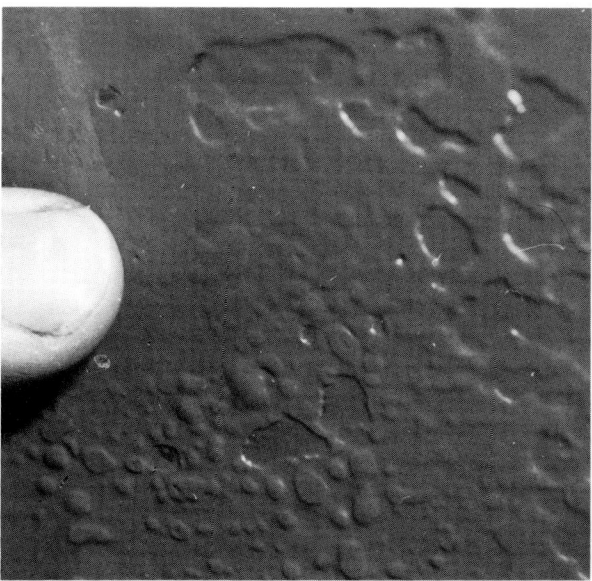

PHOTO. 178. Osmotic blistering may start as patches of scabs which when pierced exhude a foul-smelling liquid. Initially it may appear around zinc-anodes, or skin fittings, but in a year or two the whole hull area below the waterline could be covered.

For instance it may start when the gel-coat resin is being power-mixed and a vortex sucks large amounts of minute bubbles into the material. Or it may be that the operator does not allow enough time for the resin to stand and let entrapped air work its way out. Alternatively some moulders who spray on gel-coat resin blow the catalyst through the gun before the thicker resin reaches the mixing chamber; no harm is done unless the operator sprays neat catalyst over the mould surface. Then again the actual resin formulation must be suitable for spraying—not brush-type thinned down with acetone. When spraying each droplet of resin carries with it a bubble of air which must escape from the surface before that starts to thicken and set.

Perhaps brushing is safer . . . well it may be, but an ideal gel-coat layer is a uniform 15 thou (0.38 mm) thick. Take a section through a brushed gel-coat and it could resemble a ploughed field with hollows as little as 7 thou (0.19 mm) and peaks over 20 thou (0.5 mm). There is a delicate compromise in a gel-coat resin; too thick and it is brittle, too thin and it is permeable. Then again perhaps all the gel-coat conditions were absolutely right and the mould is to blame. It may have been prepared and left uncovered overnight and so became contaminated with airborne debris. Or perhaps the temperature and humidity were wrong and a film of moisture had condensed out on the mould surface. Or the resin had just been wheeled in from a cold store room. But then again it all might be perfect until the moulding was released from the mould and taken out into a cold yard to await your collection. The crux of the matter is that osmotic blistering is caused by a faulty gel-coat and there are so many variables which may be to blame that one cannot hope to control them all. During my researches I was told that this trouble with boatpox could be avoided by:

'*Choosing a reputable builder. . . .*'
'*pick someone with a proven track record*'
'*have a hull moulded in the summer*'
'*never leave the boat afloat all the year round*'
'*never use 'jelly type' anti-fouling—always a hard one*'
'*have a drying mooring, and never go on freshwater*'
'*specify no pigments below the waterline . . . .*'
'*have a black hull*'
'*have a white one . . . but never a green one*'

And so forth!

But the common point was that a painted hull seemed immune!

The current approved repair technique for severe blistering (Photo. 178) is to remove the gel-coat to three or four inches above the waterline, fill any surface voids, and rebuild a new skin of polyurethane or epoxy paint.

With this in mind I argued with myself that if that is the cure, might it not be wiser to apply a couple of coats of polyurethane paint before the hull ever got wet? Not a guarantee of course, but a good bet. It took me about twenty hours of hard labour plus the price of the paint but compared to the bills presented by a yard for a 'cure' my bet still looked good.

Before painting, the hull must be absolutely clean. This means that not only visible dirt must be removed but also those invisible waxes and mould-release materials. You must not use acetone to clean the hull and only a special oil-removing fluid is recommended.

I started off the paint job on *Solitaire* by giving her a thorough wash-down with hot water and detergent. A hot rinse or two was given time to dry and then the hull was examined for wax problems. This is easy since if you wet the hull and the water lies flat over an area then no waxes are present. Conversely if the water stands up proud of the surface in beads then you have trouble. Several applications of Oil-Removing Fluid are then called for, and if they do not do the trick, then suspect silicones. These are the devil to remove and may even force you to rub down the hull area to be painted with medium-grit wet-and-dry abrasive paper and the aforesaid 'ORF'.

When the surface was clean I abraded it all over lightly with an orbital sander both as an aid to total cleanliness and to help provide a key for the paint to hitch on to (Photo. 179). What you really need for a good paint job is good weather and good ingredients. I was fortunate

PHOTO. 179. *After thoroughly degreasing and cleaning the hull it was abraded with an orbital sander containing a medium-coarse grit paper.*

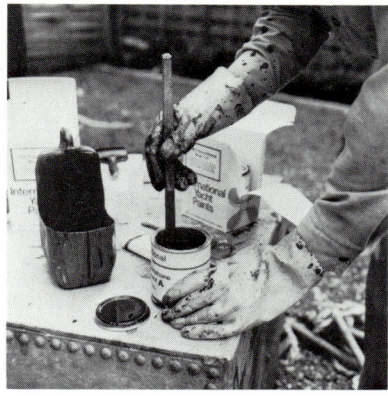

PHOTO. 180. Gloves and goggles were worn when it was time to paint on the etch primer. When using modern materials it is important to apply them as the manufacturers recommend, especially in terms of time.

PHOTOS. 181, 182. A flat stick is best for mixing paint—a power stirrer could suck in large amounts of air and the paint would then need to be 'rested'. Painting in vertical bands keeps a wet-edge going.

that the weekend set aside for painting was a fine one. This is essential, for after the special etch primer is applied (Photo. 180) the first coat of two-pot polyurethane paint must go on before more than six hours and less than 24 hours have elapsed. If that time is exceeded then the hull would have to be rubbed down to remove the primer and work restarted.

I painted alternate coats of green and blue so that coverage could be seen to be complete. As with all painting, technique counts for a lot, and I was putting on the paint with the largest brush I could manage and working in vertical bands to keep a wet-edge going. It took approximately two hours to apply one coat of paint and I used just under a litre of paint each time (Photos. 181, 182). I also used one-litre of primer, one litre of Oil-Removing Fluid, and a litre of thinners to wash out the brush. Apart from rubber gloves I also used an oil-proof barrier cream, goggles (under the hull) and large helpings of resin-removing cream to get paint spots off me!

The anti-fouling—a hard racing copper type—had to be put on before the last coat of poly had fully dried. This enabled the solvents in the AF to soften the underlying paint and hitch on to it for a chemical bond.

So far, four years later, there is no trace of boatpox and it may be that the treatment was efficacious. Or perhaps it was totally unnecessary and Atlanta Viking 8.5's simply do not ever suffer from the scourge. . . . time will tell!

Protection and routine maintenance

Having spent so much time completing your mouldings it would be a great shame if she suffered through lack of basic protection. There is much which may be done to the boat in a prophylactic sense, and at the same time such precautions will save you both time and the subsequent labour of putting things right. Many boats have bonded-in ballast keels but such keels should be fitted with shoes to save gel-coat damage when she runs aground, or dries out. That is important, for although resinglass is virtually waterproof, the laminate will absorb water through wicking, or capillary action, along the reinforcement fibres. Some early production boats were shod as a matter of course; nowadays they are the exception. Metal reinforcements around vulnerable areas are best, although a good lay-up of woven glass fibre tape is better than nothing. Once water enters the laminate your chances of drying it out are remote. Should it collect in pockets due to some fault in the lay-up then freezing may cause the laminate to burst.

A stroll around any boatyard or marina will show you that a great deal of needless damage is caused to the stems of resinglass craft by their mooring chains. It may be feasible to fit a wide brass, stainless or galvanised 'D'-section to the stem to prevent this abrasion damage. Alternatively the mooring strop or chain will need to be padded with a length of plastic tube, and perhaps a special bow fender rigged.

Chafe and abrasion are the main causes of work on a resinglass boat. Scratches caused by sandy fenders are the very devil to polish out of the gel-coat. Chips and gouges made when coming alongside—or when a dinghy

◄ FIG. 146. Protection is better than repairing! By extending the base of a fairlead, chafe, that arch enemy of gel-coats, may be defeated.

FIG. 147. This 'film-and-squeegee' technique may be used to 'repair' a micro-crazed gel-coat area. ►

is sailed carelessly through the moorings—will cause precious sailing time to be spent repairing them. When moored alongside, springs and breast-ropes led across unprotected topsides, or toerail, will fret away at the gel-coat.

If fairleads are inadequate—as most of them are—extend their base area over the gunwale by means of a suitably sized piece of stainless steel (Fig. 146). This same arrangement may be used to protect the edge of cockpit bulkheads on those boats where the halliards are led aft. Mats should be fitted under tumbling blocks, or else use elastic shockcord strops hitched to the guardrail to keep them standing. Cleats and bitts should be bedded on a sheet of thin rubber or neoprene, or a rubber-type mastic gasket as previously outlined. This will prevent localised stress cracks often found where the cleat is bedded down hard, due to the flexibility of the laminate, allowed to tip. Care should be taken when handling the anchor and running out its chain; a few moments carelessness will cause you much work later on.

Above all you should think about the material and be aware of its limitations. In this way you will reduce maintenance with a commensurate increase in the time devoted to pleasure. Having said that there is one chore which cannot be avoided—washing and polishing.

Hulls should be periodically cleaned down and polished with a non-silicone wax to prevent colour-loss from strong sunlight. Modern boat waxes sold by your chandler are formulated to reduce the damage caused by the ultra-violet content of sunlight, and also to help prevent the gel-coat ageing and eventually chalking. It is essential that you never use a car-wax for though cheaper they may contain silicones and subsequent painting or repairs will be made doubly-difficult.

In the end, of course, your hull will need painting, but with care and attention you may delay that day by up to ten years. Prudent owners of new boats may, like me, consider painting the underwater areas of the hull from new with two or three coats of two-part polyurethane, or epoxy paint. As stated this treatment may well delay,

or even prevent, the onset of osmotic blistering which affects some hulls, especially those left afloat the whole year round.

Cosmetic repairs

These repairs are essentially confined to small cavities, chips and scratches. The latter may be burnished out with a mild abrasive cleaner, aided perhaps, with superfine (600 grit) wet-and-dry carborundum paper if the scratches are no more than a few thou' deep. Any deeper and they will have to be filled, for remember that your gel-coat is only 15–20 thou' (0.5 mm) thick and thus

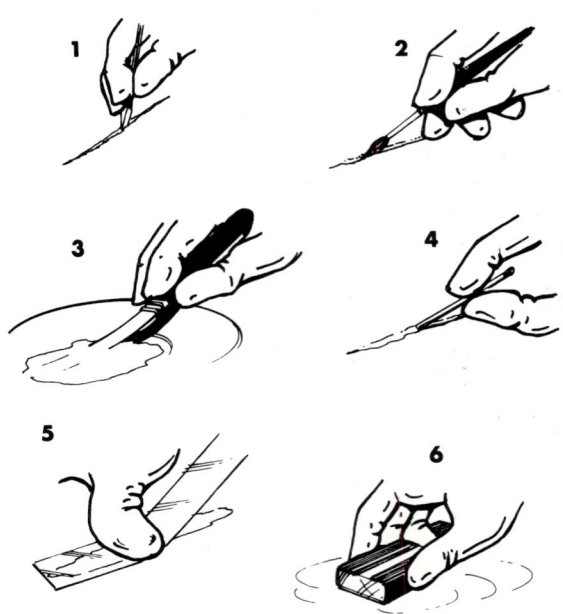

FIG. 148. Deep scratches may need enlarging to a deeper vee (1). Then degrease with acetone (2) mix the gel-coat resin (3) and apply (4). Cover with tape (5) and when cured burnish (6) to match surrounds.

may soon be removed from an area by too-enthusiastic rubbing-down.

Sometimes one is confronted by a mass of tiny scratches, and these may be 'repaired' by cleaning carefully with a cloth damped in acetone, and then painting with either a clear varnish or lacquer. When dry—and that means fully-cured—anything up to one week, remove with 400–600 grit wet-and-dry and, after burnishing, wax to match the rest of the hull.

When you need to repair large areas of micro-crazed gel-coat then you may find the following gives good results: Clean with acetone (used sparingly) and allow to dry. Then tape down along one edge a generously-sized piece of thin plastic film material. Brush on a prepared gel-coat resin, cover with the film and 'squeegee' down with a spatula or shaped piece of firm plastic (Fig. 147). The film will 'suck' down and force the resin into the surface cracks. Wipe away surplus resin as it extrudes from under the film, and remove any air bubbles by re-working over the area with the squeegee.

Long deep scratches, and chipped gel-coat areas, must be thoroughly cleaned with acetone. Apply acetone very carefully as it is harmful to the gel-coat. After drying off, the colour-matching gel-coat is applied to the scratch with a cocktail stick, or matchstick (Fig. 148). Sellotape is then laid down over the gel-coat to hold it in place. The tape also excludes the air and allows the resin to cure off without remaining tacky. There are also proprietory brands of coloured two-part epoxy fillers which will cure without the need for first excluding the air. Alternatively you may use any from a range of primary colours, plus black and white, to mix any colour shade—but it takes a lot of practice to get perfect results.

Occasionally you will need to enlarge the scratch to a deeper vee to provide a better shape for adhesion.

Blisters and cavities in the hull and topsides may sometimes appear months after the boat was launched. This is nearly always caused by the moulder failing to adhere to the resin-maker's recommendations regarding the amount of catalyst to use. Too much catalyst gives a hot mix which causes styrene to be trapped in the laminate. This slowly cures into hard nodules or blisters under the action of UV light. In some instances cracks may develop as a thin lay-up becomes highly stressed internally.

Such cracks should be treated as wide gouges. Clean them back to solid material, chamfer the edges, clean with acetone, and allow to dry. Then fill them with a non-shrink epoxy putty to nearly the top, and when cured, slightly over-fill with a matched gel-coat. This can then be cut back with wet-and-dry; start with 240 grade, through 400, and burnish with 600, used dry before polishing.

Star cracks

Star cracks in point of fact may also look like cobwebs—only rarely do they truly look like stars (Photo. 183). They are caused by impact damage, moulding flaws, or stress. If you take a coin and tap around the area it will 'ring' if the underlying laminate is sound; but a dull note warns that further damage is present. This could be localised delamination caused by the impact, or a dry (no resin) area of laminate. Provided that nothing structural is found, repairs are straightforward.

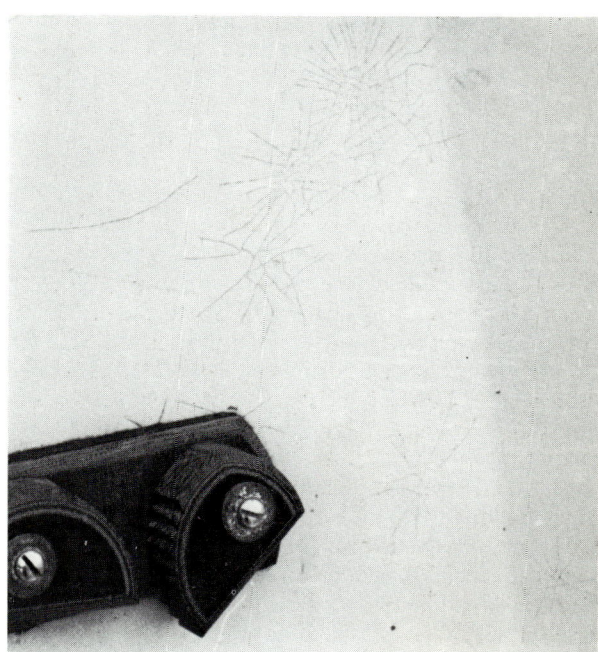

PHOTO. 183. *Star cracks around a stressed area. The jam-cleat is in fact used to take the tail of a barber-hauler. The loads imposed are too great for the laminate. Extra reinforcements are needed. Note the cracking around the base of the jammer. Either the laminate is too flexible or the gel-coat resin is too hard. A soft gasket may have helped.*

Veeing-out is best—but tedious, and the easiest cosmetic repair is once again to wipe sparingly with acetone, wipe in some gel-coat resin and burnish away the surplus with a cloth. When cured polish up as before. Assessing the amount of gel-coat needed is difficult, but generally it is better to be mean—say a teaspoon to a couple of square feet (0.18 m²) of damage. In really severe cases of damage, say when a dinghy has fallen off its trailer, the entire damaged area may have to be ground off back to the underlying laminate and replaced. That is outside the scope of this book.

Star cracks may also be a sign that the area is too flexible and needs stiffening as previously described.

Severe gouges and impact damage

Really deep gouges which enter the laminate must be prepared by first removing the crushed materials back to sound. Edges must be chamfered, dusted and cleaned with acetone. While that is drying, cut small pieces of $1\frac{1}{2}$ oz (450 gm/m²) CSM to size and mask up the area around the repair with tape and polythene sheet. Mix polyester resin (two percent catalyst) and stipple into the cavity with a clean brush. Apply the first piece of mat, and stipple again with more resin until the mat wets out. Apply another patch of CSM and continue to fill the cavity. After four patches have been applied wait until they have cured or the exotherm may locally heat up the laminate and harm it. Similarly if working on near vertical faces too much CSM and resin may 'slump' out under their combined weight (clean the brush).

Continue filling nearly to the top and allow the resin to fully cure—one hour at 68°F (20°C). Finish the repair with a matching gel-coat as previously described.

Where the prepared gouge or crack is narrow and deep a 'putty' of resin and glass fibres may be knifed-in to start the repair. Should the prepared gouge go all the way through the laminate (or nearly all the way through) it must be reinforced on the inside with four or five layers of $1\frac{1}{2}$ oz (450 gm/m²) CSM. The inside face must be cleaned of any paint, thoroughly abraded to provide a key for the resin, dusted and degreased with acetone. The surrounding area should be masked up to prevent unsightly resin-runs. The first layer of CSM should overlap the damaged area by half an inch (12 mm) all round, and each subsequent piece of mat should also overlap its predecessor by never less than the same amount. In addition to stippling with the resin brush the new inside lay-up should be consolidated with a washer-roller to remove any entrapped air.

Punctures

These are holes that go all the way through the laminate. All damaged material must be removed back to sound, and both sides of the laminate must be chamfered to give a Vee front-to-rear (Fig. 149). Thoroughly clean the inside face for at least three inches larger all round, roughen to give a key, dust, degrease and allow to dry. If the hole is a few inches square then a backing of cardboard may be simply taped in place using a barrier of polythene to prevent the resin sticking to the board. Anything large may require fastening mechanically with self-tappers or even nuts and bolts, and in this case a piece of Formica, faced hardboard, or aluminium sheet, may be needed. If the inside shape is heavily concave

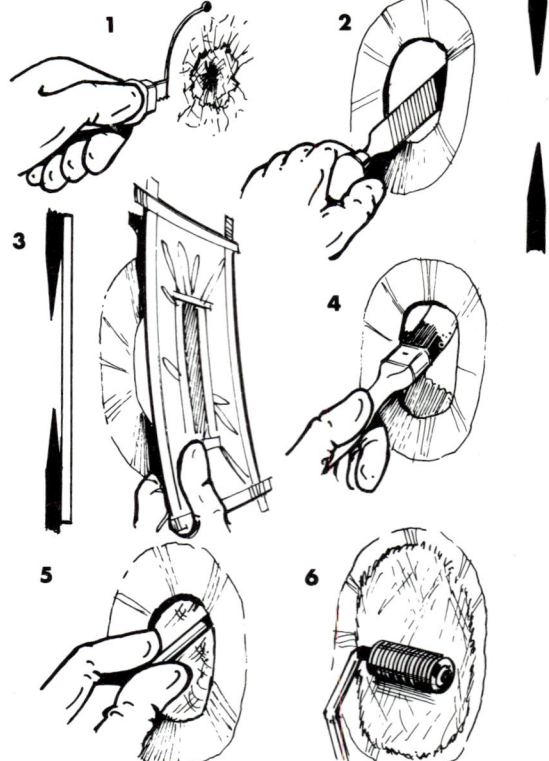

FIG. 149. *Punctures are fairly easy to repair. Cut back to sound laminate (1) then file to give a vee front-to-back (2). Roughen and degrease and tape on backing (3). Apply gel-coat (4) and follow with patches of CSM (5). Consolidate (6) to remove bubbles. Extra layers of matt to half hull thickness should be applied inside the laminate to reinforce it.*

then a shore of timber and wedges across to a convenient point may be used to force the back-up material against the inside face of the hull. Alternatively a soft material such as heavy-gauge pvc may be used—cut perhaps from a bucket. Most materials will need waxing or a non-stick barrier to prevent them sticking to the new lay-up. When the back-up is in place tape all round with masking-tape to prevent resin runs.

Mix the resin as before, and proceed to fill the cavity, taking care to work the first layers of CSM well into the corners between the laminate and the back-up. When cured fill with gel-coat and cut back as before.

Occasionally, it may be better to work from the inside of the hull. In this case the backing piece should be held firmly against the outside surface of the hull and a thin layer of gel-coat resin applied and let dry before the CSM and the repair continues. On removing the back-up a peripheral indentation will invariably be found. This should be treated as for a deep scratch. Once the repair is made the inside of the hull should be reinforced as previously described.

Blind holes

These are holes where access is limited to one side of the laminate. The hole must be prepared as described and a backing pad positioned. This is done by 'posting' through the hole a piece of cardboard through which a length of wire has been bent (Fig. 150). Once inside the cavity the cardboard is manoeuvred by the wire until the hole is covered. A 'bridge' of wood is then arranged to hold the back-up against the laminate. The first piece of CSM is then applied and allowed to cure before the rest of the repair is tackled. When the layup is nearly completed the wires are cut off close to the surface, and the repair finished as before, taking care to match the gel-coat.

There are several variations on this repair. The first is to post through the hole a piece of CSM pre-wetted with resin and suspended on a U of wire which is used to pull the mat back against the inside face of the laminate. Alternatively an oversized piece of CSM may be used in conjunction with the wire-and-cardboard method. It is sometimes possible to stuff the hole with paper or rags to form an internal support for the CSM; possibly a one-, or two-pack polyurethane foam could be used to locally fill the void. Note that all of these repairs lack the additional internal reinforcements and are therefore weaker than the original laminate.

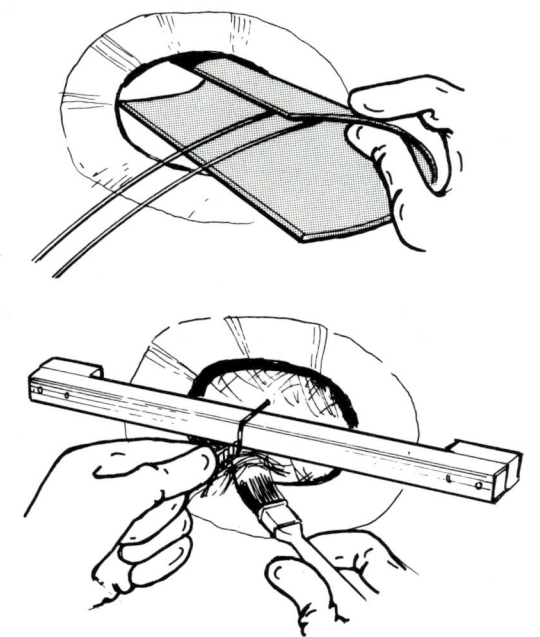

FIG. 150. *Holes into sealed compartments call for a special technique. The wired backing piece must be 'posted' through the prepared hole and held against the back-face with a 'bridge'. The repair then continues as before except the lay-up is left shy of the top surface to take a subsequent gel-coat.*

Some other repairs

Large panels of lightly constructed laminate may need reinforcing to prevent surface cracking due to flexure. The easiest reinforcements are 'top-hat' sections laid up as previously described.

If a bulkhead, or item of furniture, has started away from its moulded angle then rebonding is almost impossible. A grout of epoxy adhesive might do the trick but a far more certain method is to use mechanical fastenings; screws, or nuts and bolts, and then to extend the area of bonding with extra layers of CSM.

Moulded 'Trakmark' type non-slip deck areas may be 'repaired' by filling with polyester putty or gel-coat resin and then reworking with a triangular 'riffler' file.

Emergency repairs

If the boat is in danger of foundering then speed is essential. To this end you should have already formulated a plan of action along the lines of '*what would we do if. . . .*'

Fothering (an ancient method) can be updated by using a polythene sheet. With no way on the boat the plastic sheet will 'suck' on to the wet hull, perhaps allowing a respite in which to plan a more permanent 'temporary repair'. This may be affected by bolting on a plywood patch well-larded with mastic (grease, thick paint etc). Self-tappers and pop-rivets could also be used as could a piece of lead sheet, or a thick piece of polythene cut from a bucket or bowl.

Polyester resin will not adhere to wet surfaces, but one can buy special underwater-curing epoxy putties—which must be applied with sufficient pressure to exclude water from under them.

If possible dry the boat out alongside, or careen her, to affect a quick patch-up with resin and mat, or even polyester putty. Conditions will invariably be far from ideal, and possibly too cold for a good repair. The area of laminate local to the repair could be warmed with a hot-water bottle to speed the curing process. A hotter mix of resin would help too, although fast work is called for with anything above a 3 per cent mix; potlife could be as little as 10 minutes before it starts to gel. Remember that emergency repairs are TEMPORARY, and a proper job must be made as soon as possible. Note too that laminating resin has its own 'shelf-life' and may set in its container in under one year. Thus your repair kit needs to be continuously updated—just like flares, life-jackets, charts, torches etc, etc.

Cleaning resinglass

The pigmented gel-coat resin which gives a moulded boat her smart appearance and protection against a hostile environment is only skin-deep. It is not a NO-maintenance material, but a LOW-maintenance one. A little work goes a long way towards preserving its shine.

Wash her down frequently with plenty of water and detergent—any mild domestic type will do, and if at all possible give her a freshwater rinse. Avoid using harsh scouring powders. Super-mild ones sold for cleaning acrylic baths are suitable—although your chandler will doubtless recommend something more expensive!

Tar spots and stubborn oil stains should be removed as soon as possible with methylated spirits, paraffin, alcohol, turps-subs, polyurethane thinners and acetone—provided that the last named is used very sparingly indeed for it can damage gel-coats. Wash off well with detergent and water before re-waxing.

Avoid using scouring powders, caustic solutions, ammonia and trichlorethylene together with anything else of an 'exotic' chemical nature.

Having cleaned and rinsed the hull and topsides wax them up with a non-silicone polish. This prolongs the gel-coat life and protects if from the chalking which sometimes develops after long exposure to UV light. It also stops stains entering the surface and makes the next clean-up that much easier.

When cleaning the inside of the hull again use only mild detergents or some special proprietory product formulated to remove oils and greases safely. The inside of the laminate may not be protected by a gel-coat, although it may have a resin-rich layer of polyester resin at its surface. It is thus susceptible to strong solvents and cleaners.

Advances in paint and varnish strippers over the past few years have produced products suitable for use on resinglass. Even so it is worth avoiding extra work by applying varnish and paints carefully, and masking-up surrounding areas whenever possible. The same care should be extended to spills and splashes of teak-oils which quickly stain gel-coat surfaces—and so too does sun-tan oil!

development of finishes more waterproof than the original gel-coat; those much-advertised two-part polyurethanes. Whichever paint system is used the hull must be absolutely free from blemishes and scratches which would show through the new paint. A warm, still, dry, day without too much direct sunlight and no chance of an early dew is the ideal—often prayed for but seldom found.

It is always best to paint the hull in vertical bands, working clockwise around the boat if you are righthanded. Keep a wet-edge going and start and finish at the bow or stern—never amidships. Try to use the biggest brush you can sensibly manage, and use it at a convenient height—even if that means erecting some kind of staging first. Note that while polyurethane and epoxy paints may be cut back and burnished up to a mirror-like gloss after they have fully cured (after a week or so), ordinary enamels cannot.

Painting with Yacht enamel, or one-pot polyurethane
After cleaning and degreasing apply one coat of etch-primer, one undercoat, filler if needed, another undercoat and then one or two coats of yacht enamel or one-pot poly' as required.

Painting with two-pot polyurethane
After cleaning and degreasing apply one coat of etching primer, one coat of two-pot poly', filler if needed, 3–4 coats of two-pot poly' rubbed down between coats. Burnish if required after about one week at 68°F (20°).

Painting decks, Recoating
Clean, degrease, make-good surface and apply one coat of finish. New decks may be painted as for hull topsides using one-, or two-pot poly' and the addition of non-slip grit mixed in, or sprinkled on as required.

Anti-foulings, new, conventional
One coat etching primer, one coat underwater undercoat, one coat anti-fouling

Anti-foulings, new, hard types
One coat etching primer, two coats anti-fouling.

Painting

No matter how well a resinglass hull is looked after, sooner or later it will need painting. When the time comes your choice will be whether to use the more traditional yacht enamel, or to avail yourself of the advances in paint manufacture which have led to the

Fire retardant paints

Resinglass as used for boats will burn fiercely. Special fire-retardant resins are available but rarely used except in 'high-class' moulding shops. It is more practical to paint high risk areas such as galleys with intumescent paints—check with your chandler.

Repair kit

Just as the prudent boat-owner carries a sail-repair kit and a set of spares for his engine, so the skipper of a resinglass craft should carry a suitable repair kit for his hull. The list below is by no means comprehensive, and it should be noted that all resins and catalysts need replacing completely at the start of each season. The shelf-life of these products averages under one year. The same might also apply to special sealants—check with your supplier.

Pre-accelerated polyester resin—2 litres
Six tubes of catalyst paste (safer than liquid MEKP).
Two-square yards (2 m²) of 1½ oz (450 gm/m²) chopped strand mat.
One lb (0.5 kg) resin putty with hardener.
Measure for resin, small polythene bucket.
10 paper cups (not polystyrene) and stirrers (ex-lolly sticks).
10 resin brushes, or cheap one-inch (25 mm) paint brushes.
Masking tape, plastic bags, clean rags, wet-and-dry, hand creams.
Acetone, half a pint (0.3 litre) in a sealed metal container.
Pre-accelerated gel-coat resin, topsides colour, or epoxy gel-coat in tubes.
One tube under water-curing polysulphide caulking compound

Tools

Scissors, old chisel, padsaw, coarse file, trimming knife, spatula.

Conversion tables

English to Metric		
Pounds	To Kilos	× 0.454
Tons	To Kilos	× 1016
Lineal Inches	To Millimetres	× 25.4
Lineal Feet	To Millimetres	× 304.8
Lineal Inches	To Metres	× 0.025
Lineal Feet	To Metres	× 0.305
Square Inch	To Square mm.	× 645

$\frac{1}{8}$ of an inch of circumference = 1 mm of diameter
Diameter into circumference, multiply by 3.142

Metric to English		
Kilos	To Pounds	× 2.205
Kilos	To Tons	× 0.001
Millimetres	To Inches	× 0.039
Millimetres	To Feet	× 0.003
Metres	To Inches	× 39.37
Metres	To Feet	× 3.28
Square mm.	To Square Inch	× 0.0016

Diameter in mm ÷ 8 = circumference in inches
Circumference into diameter, multiply by 0.318

Inches to Millimetres

$\frac{1}{16}$	=	1.59	$3\frac{1}{4}$	=	82.55
$\frac{1}{8}$	=	3.18	$3\frac{1}{2}$	=	88.90
$\frac{3}{16}$	=	4.76	$3\frac{3}{4}$	=	95.25
$\frac{1}{4}$	=	6.35	4	=	101.60
$\frac{5}{16}$	=.	7.94	$4\frac{1}{4}$	=	107.95
$\frac{3}{8}$	=	9.53	$4\frac{1}{2}$	=	114.30
$\frac{7}{16}$	=	11.11	$4\frac{3}{4}$	=	120.65
$\frac{1}{2}$	=	12.70	5	=	127.00
$\frac{9}{16}$	=	14.29	$5\frac{1}{4}$	=	133.35
$\frac{5}{8}$	=	15.88	$5\frac{1}{2}$	=	139.70
$\frac{11}{16}$	=	17.46	$5\frac{3}{4}$	=	146.05
$\frac{3}{4}$	=	19.05	6	=	152.40
$\frac{13}{16}$	=	20.64	$6\frac{1}{2}$	=	165.10
$\frac{7}{8}$	=	22.26	7	=	177.80
$\frac{15}{16}$	=	23.81	$7\frac{1}{2}$	=	190.50
1	=	25.40	8	=	203.20
$1\frac{1}{4}$	=	31.75	$8\frac{1}{2}$	=	215.90
$1\frac{1}{2}$	=	38.10	9	=	228.60
$1\frac{3}{4}$	=	44.45	$9\frac{1}{2}$	=	241.30
2	=	50.80	10	=	254.00
$2\frac{1}{4}$	=	57.15	$10\frac{1}{2}$	=	266.70
$2\frac{1}{2}$	=	63.50	11	=	279.40
$2\frac{3}{4}$	=	69.85	$11\frac{1}{2}$	=	292.10
3	=	76.20	12	=	304.80

Feet to Metres

1 (12″) =	0.30
2 (24″) =	0.61
3 (36″) =	0.91
4 (48″) =	1.22
5 (60″) =	1.52
6 (72″) =	1.83
7 (84″) =	2.13
8 (96″) =	2.44
9 =	2.74
10 =	3.05
11 =	3.35
12 =	3.66
13 =	3.96
14 =	4.27
15 =	4.57
16 =	4.88
17 =	5.18
18 =	5.49
19 =	5.79
20 =	6.10
25 =	7.62
50 =	15.24
75 =	22.86
100 =	30.48

Pounds to Kilograms

1	=	0.45
2	=	0.91
3	=	1.36
4	=	1.81
5	=	2.27
6	=	2.72
7	=	3.18
8	=	3.63
9	=	4.08
10	=	4.55
20	=	9.07
30	=	13.61
40	=	18.14
50	=	22.68
60	=	27.21
70	=	31.75
80	=	36.29
90	=	40.82
100	=	45.36
200	=	90.71
300	=	136
400	=	181
500	=	227
1,000	=	454

Index